D1093534

10<u>00</u>

Oswald Garrison Villard

PACIFIST AT WAR

MICHAEL WRESZIN

Oswald Garrison
Villard

PACIFIST AT WAR

INDIANA UNIVERSITY PRESS

BLOOMINGTON

To my Mother
and to the Memory of
my Father

ACKNOWLEDGMENTS

I am grateful for the help given to me by the staffs of the Widener and Houghton Libraries of Harvard University, the John Hay Library of Brown University, the Wayne State University Library and Mrs. William English Walling, for their patient response to particularly grateful to Miss Carolyn E. Jakeman of the Houghton Library and to Wayne State University Archivist, Phillip Mason, for their assistance.

I am also indebted to Oswald Garrison Villard's friends and associates, Roger Baldwin, Senator Ernest Gruening, the late John Haynes Holmes, the late B. W. Huebsch, Freda Kirchwey, Norman Thomas, and Mrs. William English Walling, for their patient response to my questions in interviews or correspondence.

Every researcher is indebted to friends, former teachers, colleagues, and specialists in his field of interest. It would be impossible for me to list everyone who aided me in one way or another to understand Villard and his times. I do want to thank Raymond Miller of Wayne State University and Forrest McDonald of Brown for reading the manuscript at various stages of its preparation and offering invaluable editorial assistance. My greatest debt is to Donald H. Fleming and William G. McLoughlin, Jr., who as professors and friends guided me through the initial stages of this work.

Finally I am obligated to Henry Hilgard Villard, who, while generously offering encouragement, insights, and criticism, maintained an admirable objectivity and in no way interfered with the final judgments, for which I am solely responsible. The debt to my wife, Carol, is immeasurable.

Contents

Contents

Oswald Garrison Villard

PACIFIST AT WAR

CHAPTER ONE

Introduction

In 1877 Henry Villard, returning to America from a business and pleasure trip abroad, moved into the new and fashionable Westmoreland Apartments at the corner of Seventeenth Street and Fifth Avenue just across from Union Square. The building, fitted out with one of the first private elevators in the city, was young Oswald Garrison Villard's home for a half dozen years of his early childhood. In the late twenties the apartments were torn down and the new edifice of the always old Tammany Hall was constructed on the spot. That fate should have placed a new Tammany Hall on the very place of William Lloyd Garrison's death symbolized to Villard the victory of expedient *Realpolitik* over principle.[1] It could serve as a parable of Villard's losing fight over the three preceding decades.

In 1928 Villard, as editor of *The Nation,* was for many a prototype of the American liberal, the friend and staunch supporter of all reform. Ellery Sedgwick of *The Atlantic* announced that *The Nation* was "incomparably the best weekly paper in the country." R. L. Duffus, even at that time a veteran newspaperman, applauded *The Nation* as being "in the best of the liberal tradition." Waldo L. Cook of *The Springfield Republican,* a brother-in-arms through many previous battles, saluted *The Nation* and its editor "as an everlasting moral upheaval that is without rest . . . a sharp prod to our lazy conscience. . . . *The Nation* under its present editor is unsurpassed if not incomparable in the press of America."

The liberal theologian John Haynes Holmes cited Villard as "America's greatest journalist."[2]

Villard was the liberals' liberal. He had a heritage of dedication to ideals. His integrity and devotion to principle was unquestioned even by his opponents. He was, said R. L. Duffus, "All that was humane and good in liberalism." He was also a militant man who "made more acres of public men acutely miserable per unit of circulation than any other editor alive."[3] Villard admitted that his one great failing was that he found it impossible to work happily with men or women who were "incapable of hot indignation at something or other," no matter whether small or big, whether it stirred him personally or not, as long as it was something. "To minimize every evil . . . is to condone it and in time to destroy one's influence."[4] Villard's reputation was that of a maverick, a gadfly who subjected his society to continuous and uncompromising scrutiny. Like his grandfather, William Lloyd Garrison, whom he worshipped, he insisted on being heard and refused to equivocate.

Villard reached the height of his influence and prestige in the late twenties and early thirties. As an outspoken pacifist he weathered the storm of the war years and the wave of reaction that followed. Despite frustrations and disappointments *The Nation*'s circulation continued to grow and it became firmly established as an enduring organ of American liberalism. In view of Villard's patrician background, he displayed remarkable flexibility. He enthusiastically endorsed the major portion of the New Deal program for relief, recovery, and reform and at the age of sixty had repudiated the inhibitions of his nineteenth-century *laissez faire* heritage. Few men of his generation were more receptive to the principle of national planning and to the larger role of the federal government in the economic and social life of the nation.

Above all Villard was a pacifist and his politics was first and foremost the politics of pacifism. His views on the causes of the first World War and his repudiation of America's entrance into the conflict were, for nearly a decade, respected and

4

applauded by a generation of intelligent and informed Americans who were determined that it should never happen again. Many disillusioned liberals, who had supported the war and held out great hopes for the peace, were ready to accept his characterization of the peace as an act of criminal intrigue and deceit and of Woodrow Wilson as the "greatest criminal of all." During the decade 1925-1935 liberalism and pacifism went hand in hand and Villard, after years of abuse, rode the crest of the wave.

Villard always warned that war and liberalism were totally incompatible; and war was to be the nemesis of both his pacifism and his brand of liberalism. Before the onslaught of repeated acts of aggression in the thirties he and men of his persuasion fell back upon old shibboleths and platitudes that summoned up lessons of the past but hardly offered a viable approach to the present danger. Villard even cast doubt upon the sincerity of his pacifism by suggesting that the European democracies were obligated to resist the Fascist and Nazi terror but at the same time denying American obligation. He became more concerned with keeping America out of war than with keeping war out of the world.

Despite his later contradictions Villard was representative of an enduring segment of the humanistic liberal tradition. He was still a man of the enlightenment who firmly believed in the power of reason and justice over force and coercion. There was no place in this liberal vision for the incredible barbarities of the second quarter of the twentieth century. It was not that he was uninformed. Few men were more prompt to recognize the danger of Fascism or more articulate in their condemnation of it. Yet he fought every proposal that could possibly lead to effective American resistance or eventual involvement. For Villard it was an unsolvable dilemma and in the end he made common cause with men and organizations whose principles and values he had spent a lifetime fighting.

To men of Villard's generation the shock of recognition was slow to come and extremely painful. His letters to Norman

Thomas, Dorothy Thompson, Harry Elmer Barnes, Henry Mencken, Albert J. Nock, and other old friends reflect his feeling of being out of touch with the times. He and Charles Beard consoled each other with tales of betrayal and conspiracy in which all that was good and decent had succumbed to treachery and deceit. Writing history, they concluded, was useless since no one ever paid any attention to it.

It is difficult not to become impatient with the rigid, self-righteous moralism of Villard, especially during his later years. His Victorian formality, his humorless and at times almost fanatical dedication to principles, do not always engender sympathy and understanding. His shrill tone and inflexible absolutism seemed on some occasions not only irresponsible but even dangerous. One is tempted to dismiss him as a stubborn old crank who failed to make the transition from the nineteenth to the twentieth century. And yet in the present-day world of garrison states that exist from day to day on the calculated exploitation of fear and anxiety Villard's vision of man's potential and his fears for the future have meaning. After Nagasaki and Hiroshima the argument for war as a means of avoiding a great evil is absurd; Villard's dilemma has horrible significance for our own time.

More important, Villard was a representative figure of his time. His life, as much as that of any other man, illustrates a major hazard of the twentieth century. The ideals to which men like Villard were committed become obsolete as rapidly as the new weapons of destruction. Old signposts seem to lead only to dead ends and those who attempt to hold on to a stable set of beliefs inevitably fall back on a nostalgic longing for an older, less complex age. On the other hand, the alternative— complacent acceptance of a world without principle—provides little hope. Villard's struggle highlights the tragic years which witnessed the loss of American innocence.

6

CHAPTER TWO

A Mixed Heritage

Oswald Garrison Villard, born in 1872, during one of his parents' periodic sojourns abroad, was the product of two great strains in American history: capitalist expansion and humanitarian reform. His material wealth would remain with him throughout his life, as would the rich endowment of New England reform.

Villard's father was Ferdinand Heinrich Gustave Hilgard, the son of a prominent Bavarian judge. He emigrated from Germany after the revolution of 1848 to avoid being forced into the Army by his stern and forbidding father. He arrived in New York in 1853 with only twenty dollars in his pocket, understanding no English and with no friends or relatives nearer than St. Louis. He soon changed his name to Henry Villard to thwart any attempts by his father to trace him.[1]

Henry Villard's career in America was in the tradition of Horatio Alger. He put his education and German-speaking talents to use by obtaining a job with the New York *Staats-Zeitung*. His coverage of the Lincoln-Douglas debates for the German language paper in 1858 launched his career as a news correspondent. He worked at learning the language and soon gained a position with *The Cincinnati Commercial*. He reported the presidential campaign of 1860 for *The Commercial* as well as the St. Louis *Missouri-Democrat* and *The New York Tribune*. He became a famous war correspondent, and a favorite of Abraham Lincoln.[2]

After the war Villard continued as the Washington corre-

7

spondent for *The Chicago Tribune,* and acted briefly as a foreign correspondent for *The New York Herald.* During one of his frequent trips to Germany after reconciliation with his father he met by accident a group of German investors interested in American railroad development. Backed by this group of German bondholders of the Oregon and California Railroad, Villard soon became deeply involved in railway building in the Northwest. He proved to have considerable business ability and imagination. His rise was spectacular. During the seventies he created and became president of the Oregon Railway and Navigation Company, the Oregon Improvement Company, the Oregon Transcontinental Company, and numerous other investment and development corporations.

In 1881, with the aid of eight million dollars loaned to him by fifty "friends," he bought control of the Northern Pacific and during his presidency of the corporation he completed its construction to tidewater at Tacoma. In the decades of the eighties and nineties Villard lost, regained, and lost control of the Northern Pacific. Throughout the years he was engaged in a constant struggle with various financial combinations bent on crushing him and so gaining control of the road, which eventually fell into the hands of James G. Hill. At one point a group of financiers accused Villard of dishonesty and manipulation in selling worthless securities of nonexistent railroads to the Northern Pacific. Although he was vindicated in the courts, he never forgot the treachery of his accusers and passed on his hatred for "the wizards of Wall Street" to his son Oswald, who throughout his life as a journalist never failed to take a crack at Wall Street.[3]

Evidence supports the contention that Henry Villard was sincerely interested in transportation and the development of the Northwest. Although he displayed incredible financial daring he was not merely a financial wizard. The wealthy railroad baron never became a member of "the club" and his closest friendships were not with the great American entrepreneurs of the period. Perhaps this was because his interest and tastes were too cosmopolitan and refined, his talents and accomplishments too varied, and his genuine interest in transportation too embarrassing in contrast to the less constructive energy of many of his competitors. His son Oswald was extremely devoted to his father during his life and to his memory after death. In his own career Villard combined his father's desire to get things done with his grandfather William Lloyd Garrison's crusading idealism.

Henry Villard married Helen Francis Garrison in 1866, while he was still a newspaperman. Fanny was William Lloyd Garrison's favorite among seven children and was named after his mother. Born in 1844 and brought up during the years of the Abolitionist crusade, she was deeply imbued with her father's reformist zeal. She combined an aristocratic dignity with a perfectionist's moral ardor. As mistress of Henry Villard's estate Thorwood in Dobbs Ferry, New York, and in the town house on New York's fashionable East Side, she set an example of restrained Victorian gentility. Her humanitarian and philanthropic activities were well known. Her son referred to her as the "dainty aristocrat" who was also a "saintly sinner" because of her participation in peace parades and her enthusiasm for the cause of women's suffrage.

It is impossible to overestimate the influence Villard's mother had in shaping his personality. Joseph Wood Krutch, the drama critic of *The Nation* in the twenties and thirties, felt that Villard was intimidated by his mother and frightened to death that he might displease her by deviating from her strict moral code. There is, however, no indication that Villard ever looked upon her except as a great inspiration and devoted companion. He maintained the closest contact with her throughout her life and was frequently heard to say that she set the example for the values he admired most in people. At the time of her death in 1928 he wrote that in fifty-six years of comradeship he could not recall a single difference of opinion that amounted to anything.[4] This gentle woman with an almost saintly appearance must be credited with inspiring her son to take up the cause of Negro equality and to dedicate his life to the peace movement. Her strength of purpose, rigid and undeviating, left its mark on Villard. In his autobiography, writing of his mother's character, he stated unconsciously the characteristics for which he himself wanted to be most remembered:

> . . . she was incapable of compromise without being a bigot or narrowly puritanical. . . . She was able, even in her eighties to perceive and to understand the changes in standards and *mores* about her. . . . To few is it given to have an open mind in the fullness of years and the readiness to accept modern ideas and novel policies. To modify any position she took for reasons of expediency was unthinkable; to shift her ground in order to gain personal advantage, or to avoid unpleasantness was as impossible for her as for her father. . . .[5]

Many of Villard's fellow journalists saw the two strains that ran so strongly through Villard's life as incompatible; this, they felt, was the root of his periods of confusion and frustration while editor of *The New York Evening Post* and *The Nation*. Villard maintained that the two were not incompatible but complementary. When one spoke of the obviously different personalities of his father and grandfather he insisted that the two men "could hardly have been closer together."[6] Villard was right in linking the two. Henry Villard was known as a "liberal capitalist." His politics were of the Manchester school of liberalism. He was a man of cosmopolitan tastes who had read widely in the works of Cobden, Bright, Mill, and Bentham; his political ideas were rooted in the liberalism of the nineteenth century. He was a true apostle of *laissez faire*. He fought against the tariff and for good government in the mugwump tradition.[7]

Such views were not far removed from those of William Lloyd Garrison. Along with more compelling reasons Garrison fought slavery because it violated property. To be antislavery was the same thing as to be antitariff. Garrison attacked the government because it "protected" slavery. "Every man has a right to his own body—to the products of his own labor—to the protection of law—and to the common advantage of society."[8]

The brand of liberalism which Garrison espoused, insofar as he had a political philosophy, in no way conflicted with the views of E. L. Godkin, editor of *The Nation* and *The Post* during Henry Villard's ownership. They looked upon economic liberty as freedom from governmental control, in much the same way that Garrison looked upon personal liberty as freedom from chattel slavery. His inability ever to grasp the social and economic implications of his Abolitionist position indicates that much of the driving force behind it was fundamentally alien to the progressives of succeeding generations. Garrison denounced the early labor leaders for attempting to "inflame the minds of our working classes against the more opulent and to persuade them that they are condemned and oppressed by the wealthy aristocracy." He conceded that there was great suffering and want, yet he saw no real solution except "going about doing good."[9] Such views were paraphrased in 1886 when *The Nation* attacked Richard T. Ely's *The Labor Movement in America.* Labor discontent was inevitable. It "is perennial in human nature and is bound to continue no matter what measure we take to cure it."[10] It too suspected labor leaders of "filling the bellies of the poor with the east wind." Oswald was right when he saw no great incompatibility between his grandfather's reformism and his father's liberal capitalism. On some peripheral matters such as prohibition and women's rights they perhaps did not see eye to eye, but there was nothing in the Liberator's position that disturbed the *laissez faire* liberalism of his son-in-law.

By the seventies and eighties the liberalism adhered to by Henry Villard had grown complacent. It tended to seize upon particular reforms as the solution to problems of unsuspected complexity. More often than not it relied on righteous indignation rather than creative analysis. Put the good men in and kick the rascals out and all the flaws in the system will disappear—the good men being the educated men, the respectable men with a sense of *noblesse oblige. The Nation* and *The New York Post,* which Henry Villard purchased in 1881, carried on this formula. Godkin became the spokesman for the respectable class as differentiated from the merely wealthy class. *The Nation,* which was at that time a weekly edition of *The Post,* applied a synthesis of classical economics, moralized Social Darwinism, and Protestant theology to an articulate defense of the status quo. *The Post* and *The Nation* by the 1880's had become the voice of American conservatism.[11]

Oswald Villard was brought up in this tradition. He attended the Rogers Morse Preparatory School in New York City. In 1884 he traveled to Germany with his family and spent two years in German schools including six months in the Kaiserin Augusta Gymnasium in Charlottenburg. The rigid discipline and heavy work load was a sharp contrast to the easygoing finishing school atmosphere of Rogers Morse. These were impressionable years. If they did not turn Villard into a scholar they did contribute to his lifelong respect for the German culture. In 1886 Villard returned to Rogers Morse for a final year in preparation for admission to Harvard.

Villard's grades were mediocre. He was admitted to Harvard with conditions in geometry and algebra. His European travels, however, gave him a sophistication, as did the presence in his home of such family friends as Carl Schurz, Abraham Jacobi, Carl Bitter, and a host of financiers and politicians. He was more at ease in adult company than with people of his own age.[12]

The years Villard spent at Harvard have been called the "Golden Age" of that university. Some of its greatest teachers and scholars were in their prime: William James, George Herbert Palmer, Josiah Royce, and George Santayana in philosophy; Nathaniel Shaler in geology; Albert Bushnell Hart in American history; Goodwin Taussig in economics, and the "king of the Anglo-Saxons," George Lyman Kittredge, in English literature. Nor did the university lack able students:

Norman Hapgood, Frederick Howe, Robert Morss Lovett, Harold Stearns, Herbert Croly, and W. E. Burghardt Du Bois all passed through while Villard was there. They have left accounts of the university community and, in particular, of the heady atmosphere of intellectual awakening they experienced. Villard apparently knew none of these men well while a student and remained quite apart from the intellectual life of the campus.[13]

Villard's letters home were filled with accounts of athletic events, campus gossip, and the burden of maintaining a respectable average. It was not until he was a graduate student that he came into contact with James, Santayana, and Royce, and then only at a faculty dining table. What seemed to impress him most about this awesome trio was their courtliness, their Old World appreciation of quiet grace and leisurely scholarship. Later, like W.E.B. Du Bois, he was to denounce Harvard's apathy and to view the school as the seedbed of sterile conservatism. While there he seemed quite content with the sheltered atmosphere. Du Bois recalls the general reverence for Ricardo, free trade, and the gold standard and a great fear of both trusts and labor organizations as enemies of democracy. Villard accepted these doctrines.[14]

There is no hint in these early years of Villard's transformation into a leading social reformer. Buying a riding habit at Brooks Brothers, taking violin lessons, attending the symphony and social affairs in Boston consumed much of his interest and time. Villard saw it as pretty hard work. His letters to his mother complained of the long hours of grinding at books with no time for pleasure. He was bothered by headaches and stomach trouble.[15]

Although Villard's social calendar seemed full while he was at Harvard, it was almost entirely under the close supervision of his relatives in Roxbury, not because he was being chaperoned but because he did not make friends easily and his relatives were so available. A strong, well-built boy given to mild hypochondria, he was not very good at sports other than

13

riding. He neither drank, smoked, nor played cards. There is only one account of the traditional undergraduate debauch: in the company of his cousins from Roxbury he made a tour of the South Boston and Quincy taverns and dance halls. Villard was shocked by the low life he saw and dutifully reported to his parents that liquor was unquestionably at the root of decadence and poverty.[16] For his age Villard's approach to life was respectably Victorian. It prevented him from establishing many friendships and caused a feeling of alienation. Years later, when he was concerned about the popularity of one of his sons, he recalled his own social difficulties at Harvard. It was a problem he never really solved.[17]

Villard combined the Garrisonian moral conscience with his father's doctrinaire liberalism. An entry in his diary during the year preceding his entrance to Harvard records how he and his friends went downtown to see a streetcar strike on Third Avenue and engaged manfully in the fracas because the strikers were such a "dastardly set." He probably never read Henry George, who awakened the conscience of a generation of progressives, but dutifully denounced his book and "Georgism" and wondered "where it would all end."[18]

At Saunders Hall Villard heard the Senator from Kentucky, C. W. B. Breckenridge, whom he described as a man of magnificent eloquence and beyond reproach except for his heretical faith in free silver. In his mind free silver was a moral question far more than an economic one. To be for free silver or protection meant to be for selfish interests. Villard accepted this without question. During Cleveland's campaign Fanny wrote her son of "Papa's" courage in speaking up at a meeting of conservative businessmen in behalf of free trade.[19]

A moral tone for a sound and considered economic and political position was a continual source of strength for the mugwump, and Oswald learned this early. It never occurred to him that his father's political principles often coincided with his business interests. He firmly believed that the success of his father's interests was compatible with the general welfare. The decade of the nineties was a wonderful time for people of Villard's class. Despite depression and widespread poverty they were truly the "confident years" when ideals and self-interest seemed to coincide and encouraged a comforting ignorance of the stresses of a society in transition.

There is no hint that Villard appreciated the growing protest of either the farmers or labor. He denounced the Debs strike in 1894 and applauded Cleveland's use of troops to quell the disturbance. As a campus correspondent for *The Post*, he recognized the need for a more efficient standing army to curb "the reign of lawlessness" and to "put down Idaho Miners and cattle thieves." He viewed Governor Altgeld of Illinois, who pardoned the Haymarket rioters, as one of the most dangerous men in America.[20]

Although still relying on his secure background, Villard did some writing in college. His first published stories concerned life in the Army. In October 1893 he wrote an article for *The Post* on Army reforms, demanding reorganization and greater efficiency. The first article that the future pacifist editor of *The Nation* wrote for that magazine was a study of Spanish military affairs in Melilla.[21] During his senior year and as a graduate student Villard began to send pieces to *The United States Monthly: A Review of Military and Naval Affairs*. Often they were technical studies of Army administration and the need for reform. By the time he left Harvard he was a military buff and his first regular assignments as a full-time journalist for *The Post* were often coverage of the armed forces.[22]

In September 1895 he joined Company A of the First Regiment of the Massachusetts Infantry. His fellow soldiers were a good hardy lot but they were astonished at the presence of "a gentleman in their ranks." Villard regularly reported his success in the company. His father encouraged his interest in military science and assured him that "Mama has reconciled herself to it."[23] Villard later recalled that he would have liked a military career if he "could have accepted it intellectually."[24]

Villard's enthusiasm for the military life can be explained

only in terms of his later life as a crusader; it constituted a sort of windmill tilting. He was appalled by the inefficiency of the Army and in keeping with his ideas about good government he felt that the practices of patronage and nepotism had made the Army a sanctuary for incompetents. Like the government, it needed upright, dedicated men to make it work for the benefit of the country. In addition his approach to the military was compatible with his conservative political instincts at the time. He stated at one point that it was the increasingly frequent labor disputes that led to his joining the militia.

Despite an undistinguished college career Villard was offered an assistant instructorship in Albert Bushnell Hart's American history course. He later admitted that Hart had chosen him because of his social standing, the fact that he wore nice clothes and was a member of a couple of good clubs. Hart was even more frank in disclosing that he was happy with Villard's acceptance of the position since he was relieved of choosing "a greasy grind of a graduate student." Villard's travels and his cosmopolitan background made him more a man of the world and thus better equipped to train young men.[25]

Villard, who was on a tour of Europe and the Near East when Hart's offer arrived, had given little thought to his future. As it turned out, he did not really like teaching and was somewhat uncomfortable before a class. On the few occasions that he did lecture he had difficulty maintaining discipline.[26] He did, however, develop a keen interest in politics and followed closely Cleveland's second administration. Throughout his life he viewed Cleveland as a man of principle, a rarity among politicians. He often used Cleveland as a standard for judging the moral conduct of other politicians.[27]

In 1894-1895, while Villard was an assistant and pursuing graduate studies, he was drawn closer to the Garrisonianism that still survived the Liberator. His uncle, Frank W. Garrison, encouraged him to take part in the organization of a Cambridge group in behalf of women's suffrage. In an article in *The Nation* he defended the right of women to vote even though *The Nation* had long since abandoned the cause. Villard stalwartly maintained his stand with the support of his mother, who was still one of the leading feminists in the country. In pursuit of this cause he helped organize the Political Equality Association of Cambridge. The first meeting resulted in a serious factional dispute. The bolder spirits demanded that their statement of principle declare openly and without equivocation the right of women to vote. The more cautious felt that such a sensational statement was rash and would frighten potential members away. Villard was among the bold—this was the measure of his radicalism in 1896.[28]

In addition to this foray into the world of reform Villard attended classes in political science and history, graded papers, and lectured once a week on "Topics of the Day" to the students of Miss Ward's school, one of "the most fashionable in Back Bay." He began research on Henry Knox, Washington's Secretary of the Navy, but never completed it. Nevertheless in June he was awarded the master's degree for his research in lieu of a thesis.[29]

Given his family connections and his apparent disinterest in the more fundamental reform movements of the time, one might have expected Villard to take his place after graduation in the business world as a solid, perhaps stolid, citizen with the routine sense of civic responsibility characteristic of his class. There was, however, his writing. While not particularly imaginative, he did show signs of reportorial ability, and he had displayed some interest in journalism. One thing is certain, by 1896 he was bored with the academic community. In the spring of that year, while doing research on his master's thesis, Villard was forced to think seriously of the future. He was offered an instructorship for the coming year in forensics, "Harvard's most unpopular course." Perhaps in grim anticipation of this assignment or perhaps because of his Garrisonian heritage, he decided on the world of journalism. He did come to the conclusion that academic life was too quiet, "like sitting in a club window and watching the world go by." His father was disappointed, for he had hoped that Villard would go on for a Ph.D. He warned his son that journalism was time-consuming, demanded a great deal of effort, and one was too often rewarded with sneers and abuse. Oswald was not deterred, however. Through his father's connections he met Talcott Williams of *The Philadelphia Press* and arranged to serve an apprenticeship under him. He refused an immediate assignment on *The Post* because he did not want to be subject to the onus of being the boss's son; he wanted to "carve out his own career."[30]

Villard lasted six months on *The Press*—from November 1896 until May 1897. He later remarked that it was good training because *The Press* was a perfect example of what a newspaper should *not* be: it truckled to its advertisers and bowed to social pressure; its reporters were apathetic and cynical and its editorial policy was devoted to none of the aims of responsible journalism. The cub reporter did not find the working conditions very glamorous. He complained of the dingy reporters' room, "filthy with animals of all kinds crawling about the walls." Nor did he appreciate the long hours, the low pay, and the calculating attitude of the management. His work was edited to meet the low standards of the paper and when he did develop a story that threatened to be embarrassing to the patrons of the paper, it was rejected.[31]

In the spring of 1897 a "romantic revolution" occurred in the staid offices of *The Post*. Some of the younger and more exuberant spirits on the staff chafed under the tight reins of Godkin. These young men were attracted to the "thriving pulse" of the great city in which they worked and yet their jobs were to report the news precisely as it happened, without embellishment, without interpretation, color, or style; like machines, complained Lincoln Steffens. They wanted more colorful stories, stories about the rich and poor, wicked and good, ugly and beautiful. Norman Hapgood hoped to depict the "moving picture of what was happening in a city full of Italians, Jews, Chinese, Germans, French, rounders, slums and palaces."

To Godkin this was "literature" and not at all appropriate for a serious daily newspaper. After considerable bickering George Seymour, the business manager, and A. J. Wright, the city editor, negotiated the purchase of *The Commercial Advertiser*, one of the oldest papers in New York. Its format, according to Steffens, looked like "a wretched old street-walker or a used up ex-good governor."[32] These men went off to undertake their venture into literary journalism, leaving *The Post* in serious difficulties.

Henry Villard was furious; he could view their enthusiasm only as a betrayal designed to present competition to *The Post*. He called for his son and offered him the vacancy left by Wright. Oswald explained to his father that he was not ready for the job, but he did accept the editorship of the Saturday supplement and assumed the duties of news reporting and writing occasional editorials and special feature articles.[33]

When Villard arrived at *The Post* in May 1897, the paper was engaged in one of its crusades. It opposed the exploitation of the revolutionary situation in Cuba as a means of inaugurating a policy of territorial expansion. *The Post*'s position on foreign policy was compatible with the liberalism of Cobden and Bright, a tradition which was still carried on in America by men like William Graham Sumner and Edwin Godkin. In the lexicon of the Manchester liberals free trade was not merely an economic policy but a method of insuring international peace. Wars were the result of squabbles between nations over commercial discrimination or the conspiratorial tactics of special interest groups hoping to profit by international tension. This was the theoretical basis of *The Post*'s opposition to recognition of the Cuban revolutionaries. The United States, they argued, had no right to interfere; in the tradition of Cobden—"no foreign politics."[34]

Others who had little objection to domestic *laissez faire* or to free trade drew different implications: nations should be viewed as individuals who make up the international community; the struggle for colonies is the same as the struggle for success by individuals within the nation. America, argued the Social Darwinist, must take advantage of her opportunities or lose out in the race for economic and military power. It was, for them, a moral duty which Americans must accept.[35]

Villard was acquainted with the issues. In graduate school he studied the question of America's legal right to interfere in the Cuban controversy. He had lectured to his students at Miss Ward's School on the ignorance of Congressmen who advocated interference. He warned his students that if the tone of belligerency continued, reports of combined European opposition were bound to come true. The older nations "would teach us our place. . . . We are doomed for a great humiliation."[36]

The Post's editorial position bolstered his opinions. On every major incident leading up to the war *The Post* took the side of Spain. *The Post* countered the lurid accounts of Butcher Weyler's cruelty in Cuba by printing stories of the wanton brutality of the Cuban revolutionaries. Godkin, in editorial after editorial, stressed what he considered "the gloomiest part of it all," the destruction of private property by the insurrectionists.

In February 1898 the "Maine" was sunk. *Post* editorials insisted that there was no proof that the ship had been sunk by the Spanish. In any event, they admonished, it was a very unwise decision to send the ship into such troubled waters in the first place. Despite the growing war hysteria *The Post* maintained its position. Villard departed from his concern with strictly military affairs and wrote that the true patriot is not one who plunges the country into war; on the contrary, he seeks every possible alternative. If war is unavoidable, which Villard never accepted, then preparations must be made not in the heat of passion, but with reason and detachment. Only in this manner could needless loss of life be prevented.[37] As a junior member of the staff, however, Villard was not responsible for shaping editorial policy.

Once the war began Villard persistently denounced its conduct. He wrote with slashing sarcasm that, at times, equaled Godkin's. He ridiculed the much maligned Secretary of War, Russell A. Alger, for nepotism in appointments, ignorance of military affairs, and a total lack of judgment. The ludicrous blunders of America's "splendid little war" never left Villard's mind. Years later he charged that "McKinley, in bowing to pressure and undertaking that absolutely needless war, had been one of the greatest murderers in American history."[38]

As the war proceeded Villard became an aggressive opponent of the "larger" policy of Roosevelt, Lodge, and Beveridge, who frankly viewed the war as a means by which the United States might make permanent acquisitions of strategic foreign territory. When it became clear that the annexation of Hawaii was only a beginning and that the administration planned to acquire Puerto Rico and undisclosed islands in the Pacific, Villard was outraged. He recalled that America's heritage rested upon the principle of self-determination and vowed he would vote against McKinley the next time even if he had to vote for free silver.[39]

Villard became an enthusiastic member of the Anti-Imperialist League. Its first important meeting took place in Faneuil Hall in Boston on June 15, 1898. Many of New England's most important citizens joined the crusade, representing a variety of interests: pacifists, free traders, conservatives who feared any new departure, and other irate citizens who held a grudge against the two major parties.[40] Carl Schurz had set the keynote months before when he warned that to turn the war into a victory for conquest and aggrandizement "would be to forfeit America's moral credit with the world." Drawing upon the Declaration of Independence as the precedent, the anti-imperialists saw America's mission as an exemplary rejection of the power-hungry politics of the Old World and the forthright promotion of an idealism that respected the innate dignity of all men and their right of self-government.[41]

By the spring of 1898 Villard had a more important role in shaping the policy of *The Post*. Godkin was seriously ill, and although he occasionally wrote editorials, by the end of July he was no longer on the payroll and Horace White became the editor. White was never the forceful figure Godkin had been and so Rollo Ogden (who became head of the editorial page in 1903) and Villard became the dominant figures on the paper during the great debate of 1898-1900.

Villard considered the terms of the peace protocol outrageous, especially the justifications of the "God-like Mickinley." He was furious over the public's—and even some of his relatives'—general acceptance of the administration's policy.[42] In December 1898 Spain signed the treaty which ceded the Philippines, Guam, and Puerto Rico to the United States and turned Cuba over to America under an indefinite protectorate. Villard insisted that this should be the major issue in the presidential campaign of 1900. He threw all of his energy into the efforts of a small group of anti-imperialists intent on creating a third party. This group met in Indianapolis in the summer of 1900 along with the Anti-Imperialist Congress convention. The anti-imperialists decided that their most effective "means of crushing imperialism" lay in supporting William Jennings Bryan. In Villard's mind Bryan's support of intervention made his anti-annexationist sentiments suspect. He disliked both candidates, and as a leader of the diehard group he pleaded with the convention not to support Bryan or McKinley and to consider "the great moral fortification of standing alone on a righteous platform of a sound gold standard and anti-imperialism." When the advocates of a third party were ignored, they made plans for a meeting in New York in a last ditch effort to find an appealing alternative candidate.

Villard, G. W. Palmer, Moorfield Storey, and George Foster Peabody met on September 5 but failed to find any acceptable man willing to run. Thomas Mott Osborne thought that Cleveland might be persuaded and suggested that Villard, through his paper, make every effort to pull the ex-President out of retirement at Princeton.[43] Nothing came of this. During the campaign *The Post* avoided all responsibility and sat on the fence. Many of the anti-imperialists voted for McKinley. When it became a test between the two evils, free silver or imperialism, they proved to be far more fearful of free silver. Villard, striking a pose that was to become increasingly familiar, refrained from voting and assumed a position of righteous abstention.[44]

Throughout his life Villard would refer to this period as the beginning of his pacifism. The war brought him a profound spiritual experience that forced him to cope with fundamental questions. This mental growth, as he characterized it, carried him far nearer to "Grandpa's teachings" of nonresistance. He discovered the moral satisfaction to be gained in refusing to make concessions to political expediency.[45] Hereafter his support would be given only to candidates who met the qualifications of morality as Villard understood them. He was occasionally to break this rule and succumb to compromise in order to avoid the lesser of two evils, but he did so with reluctance. Although Villard's developing pacifism and his application of moral absolutes were the result of personal experience, the example set by his crusading grandfather grew more attractive to him. Garrison once said that he relished "causes which being right, are unpopular," and also that there was "real exhilaration in struggling in God's name, against wind and tide."[46]

Villard, as a defiant reformer, approached the Christian anarchism of William Lloyd Garrison. "Where the teachings of Jesus and the State conflict," he later proclaimed, "you will invariably find me putting Jesus above the State."[47] But the world had changed since Garrison's time. The Liberator had based his position on a religious faith in individual regeneration and salvation as a cure for social ills. For Villard, as for the clergy leading the liberal wing of the social gospel movement, Christ's teachings were not mythical allegories concerned with personal salvation but practical messages that men could apply to life in this world. For many years he was a close friend and supporter of John Haynes Holmes, who, he felt, applied Christianity to the social as well as the political scene.[48]

His own religion was rational, moral, ethical. He greatly admired Felix Adler, the founder of the Ethical Culture Society. Adler's slogan "not the creed but the deed" was the kind of moral imperative that inspired Villard. It was a high standard, he felt, too high for most churchgoers, "who wish to have their panoplied bishops and cardinals, their chants and incense, their genuflections." "If Christianity means anything," Villard wrote to a Southern clergyman, "it means that all men are free and equal in the light of the Lord . . . those who take a different ground mock religion."[49]

Although Villard had little interest in dogma or theology, his interpretations of "the teachings of Christ" were intensely dogmatic. A recent biographer of Garrison has written: "There was no vacillation in him, no grey in his thinking, only right and wrong, deep black and pure white. There could be no compromises with sin and only Garrison could define sin."[50] This cast of perfectionism, secularized to a great degree, was carried over into Oswald Garrison Villard's approach to controversy. A moral certitude sustained him and provided him with the inspiration necessary to stand upon a righteous platform regardless of immediate consequences. In this sense the Garrisonian tradition lived on, and Villard devoted the greater part of his life to preserving it.

The logic of the anti-imperialist position held by men like Villard provided a substantial part of the justification for the foreign policy pursued by America during and for more than a decade after the first World War. In 1900 these crusaders were leaderless but by 1918 many Americans embraced much of the anti-imperialist program of 1900. The legacy of morality over self-interest did not die with the more pragmatic approach of the new generation of progressives. It was subject to attack and in domestic affairs it was modified to meet changing conditions, but its central vision remained strong.

CHAPTER THREE

Respectable Reform

The progressives have been portrayed by Richard Hofstadter as spiritual sons of the mugwumps who dropped much of the ideological baggage of their parents. This is not true of Villard. At times he supported the causes of progressives, but he was never one of them. He carried a trunkful of mugwump principles with him throughout the progressive era. Villard believed in progress plus the old morality and as an editor and owner of *The Post* and *The Nation* he waged a battle for both.[1]

William Allen White wrote Villard in 1908 applauding him for his management of the papers: "You have done real and definite things in the world, and your papers have inevitably stood for the best things in American life." *The Nation* was read even in the normal schools on the plains of Kansas. Villard modestly credited his success to those who had gone before him: Godkin, White, Schurz, and his father were the true molders of *The Post* and *The Nation*. "Its traditions have so strong a hold that they mold and affect everyone who comes under their influence. . . . If I should die tomorrow, the paper would go on without any change being noticeable . . . it would never abate one jot from its principles."[2]

This may have been true of *The Post*, but it was not true of the times. The first decade of the twentieth century was a period when even McGuffey's Reader suffered a dose of the higher criticism. The old values were not casually discarded; as Elmer Davis has said, the progressive movement was a "carnival of purity." Nevertheless, there was a growing air of self-criticism.

Villard and his newspapers were reluctant to concede the necessity of rethinking old values, and skeptical of the proposed modifications. They continued to look to the past for their ideals. Villard and his papers supported Alton B. Parker in 1904 because Parker told the Democratic Committee that he would not accept the nomination unless there was a solid gold plank in the platform. This was the kind of man Villard felt the country needed. Parker might be the choice of the "Wall Street crowd," but Villard was certain that Parker was not a crass political opportunist like Theodore Roosevelt. In 1908 Villard again refused to support either major candidate. He finally voted for Eugene Chafin, the Prohibition candidate.[3]

Villard's feelings in 1908 outline his political philosophy. He had hoped that Charles Evans Hughes would get the Republican nomination. Hughes was a respectable citizen and had a moderate yet enlightened attitude toward reform. During the pre-convention period Villard solicited Hughes's support for tariff revision. He felt that Hughes could appreciate the "essential immorality of the whole tariff system and the way it was corrupting our public life and youth." The tariff, Villard explained, was a special privilege in disguise which permitted certain favored individuals to avoid making their own way. The government, in effect, gave them a handout; this was political favoritism of the worst kind. Tariff reform should be first on the list of any true reform candidate, as it had been for Cleveland. It would be a direct attack upon political corruption. Villard reiterated the faith of the liberal Republicans of 1872: replace irresponsible and selfish men with altruistic and honest men and all the problems of society will be solved.[4]

In 1912 Villard looked for a candidate who would return the country to "the paths of Grover Cleveland." In 1888 Cleveland had come out for a lowered tariff even though he knew it meant certain defeat. Cleveland's persistence, his dedication to principle, his refusal to compromise were, for Villard, cardinal virtues, far more necessary than creative imagination or a willingness to entertain new ideas and cope with new and pressing problems. Cleveland's failure to understand the dislocation of the farmer and labor during his second administration was of no concern to Villard.[5]

During the early years of the twentieth century Villard became closely associated with middle-class reform. He was an active member of the City Club, "the Tammany Hall of the reformers." His paper kept a watchful eye on affairs in Albany as well as in the city. He was proud of his muckraking role in the exposure of Jonathan Alds, a crooked politician. Villard also belonged to the American Association to Promote Efficiency. His application of morals to politics was a kind of practical idealism.

But the scope of Villard's reform, like Cleveland's, was limited. In 1908 Lillian Wald, founder of the Henry Street Settlement House, who was working for the Child Labor League, asked Villard for his annual contribution. Villard replied that he no longer intended to contribute because "the committee's policy of seeking federal legislation" was in the long run going to do irreparable harm. He was convinced that "this running to Washington for aid sets back local and state progress immeasurably." Villard believed in individual character and responsibility. Federal legislation on such matters would only sap the vitality of the localities. Such legislation was as evil, despite its good intentions, as tariff legislation.[6]

Villard remained unsympathetic to labor organizations. He told his friend Paul Kellogg of *The Survey* (a voice for the social welfare people) that the magazine always took the side of the employees at the expense of the employer. Labor, he charged, consistently resorted to violence and this undermined any legitimate grievances they might have. Villard upheld the right of strike-breakers because "the free right of men to secure their labor must remain inviolate." As manager of his papers, he maintained a nonunion shop. He apparently saw no inconsistency in asking his associate in the fight for Negro rights, Mary White Ovington, if she knew of a "good colored carpenter" he might hire, stipulating that a "non-union man" was desired.[7]

Villard later stated in his autobiography that when *The Post* did recognize the printers' union in 1917 he was quite ready for such a change even though he felt his men were happy and contented. He had, however, been absent at the time of these negotiations and when he was informed of Ogden's surrender, he told his wife, "I would have closed down before yielding." It was a matter of principle for Villard.[8]

Villard has repeatedly been mentioned as one of Woodrow Wilson's earliest supporters. He later claimed that he had been Wilson's ally from the time of his administration at Princeton. It would be more accurate to say that the editorial staff of *The Post* was enthusiastically behind Wilson and that Villard followed along. His correspondence reveals little personal feeling for Wilson in the days preceding his election. He confided to a staunch Wilson man, Thomas Mott Osborne, that he was increasingly less interested in Wilson. He regretted, just a month before the election, that there was not one candidate for whom he could "enthuse unqualifiedly." Villard charged Wilson with playing ball with Tammany Hall. Osborne patiently reminded him of the necessities of politics and explained that it was unrealistic to expect a candidate to speak out on every question and to be totally right on all of them. Wilson stood for most of the things that Villard favored and that ought to be enough. He warned Villard that if he waited for a candidate that met his every specification, he would be doomed to continuous disappointment—a prophetic warning.[9]

Villard did vote for Wilson in 1912, the last time in his life that he voted for a winning candidate. The administration's treatment of the Negro and the policy of segregation and discrimination in federal employment practices soon vindicated, in Villard's mind, his misgivings about Wilson. Wilson's most recent biographer credits Villard with being not only the leading white champion of Negro rights in America in 1912, but also with being Wilson's chief advisor on the race question.[10] In spite of Villard's position of nationwide influence, his experience as advisor to Wilson was bitter and disillusioning. By virtue of his Southern heritage alone, Wilson had only the mildest enthusiasm for Negro equality. During the campaign, however, Wilson did promise Villard and other leaders of the NAACP that, if elected, he would give careful consideration to their demands.[11]

After Wilson's election Villard presented the new President with a proposal for the creation of a National Race Commission composed of responsible citizens from many segments of society. Its function would be to develop a program designed to encourage Negro equality in education and employment. At first Wilson seemed sympathetic, but then he stalled and, finally, told Villard that he could not lend official endorsement to such a commission because it would jeopardize his entire legislative program by antagonizing indispensable Southern support in Congress. Villard was infuriated; he charged Wilson with betraying campaign promises and warned that he should no longer expect support from the Negro community or its friends.[12] When segregation and discrimination in Washington increased, Villard warned the President that he had "better learn that there are some questions that must be decided on the moral issue of right and wrong." Except for this brief and bitter encounter Villard's role during the campaign and the initial years of Wilson's administration was insignificant.[13]

There is little evidence that Villard was aware of or interested in the split in reform doctrine during the campaign of 1912. Roosevelt's "New Nationalism" accepted the concentration of wealth and power in large industrial units as inevitable in the free enterprise system. Roosevelt and his advisors therefore preached abandonment of the trust-busting formula and advocated government control and regulation of monopolies in the interest of the country. Wilson's "New Freedom" saw great concentrations of wealth as inherently dangerous and promised to break up trusts and monopolies and to restore fair competition under careful control. This issue of regulated monopoly versus regulated competition as expressed in the writings of Herbert Croly and Louis Brandeis may have been overemphasized by subsequent historians but at the time the debate was meaningful to thoughtful progressives.[14]

The editors of *The Post* and *The Nation* showed little interest in the more reflective and searching literature of the progressive period. With equal heat they abused Veblen, Lippmann, Beard, and Croly for suggesting that a great many Americans were not economically free and that federal legislation could liberate them. The editors stressed that, on the contrary, American life had been characterized by freedom and opportunity and that progressives, with their emphasis on a more positive role for the state, were threatening this freedom. The editors felt that Wilson would preserve "the ancient freedom and self-dependence of American citizens." To *The Nation* Roosevelt's theories seemed particularly dangerous, not because he tolerated certain monopolies, but because his program of regulation was little different from "full-fledged state socialism."[15]

Villard did not share all these views. In general, however, there is no evidence that the political bias of the editors of *The Post* and *The Nation* differed substantially from his own. Villard hammered away at such things as bossism, high tariffs, special interests, Negro rights, women's suffrage, and peace. These issues were clear to him, and they did not demand an upsetting reappraisal of the changing nature of American society.[16] Villard, like so many of his generation, was prone to oversimplification, but he was often a constructive critic of the status quo. Both women's suffrage and Negro equality had been major crusades of his grandfather. Villard supported these unpopular causes with enthusiasm.

Villard was recruited in February 1909 to write the Lincoln's Birthday call which led to the establishment of the National Association for the Advancement of Colored People. His name, coupled with his energy and organizational ability, did much to build the Association's firm foundation and for the first five years of its existence he was a dominant figure. He served as disbursing treasurer and as chairman of the board. The ridicule he received in the press for his frequent public appearances at biracial dinners and organizing conventions in no way dampened his ardor. Although he later resigned his chairmanship because he found it difficult to share authority with William E. B. Du Bois, editor of *The Crisis*, he remained a prominent member throughout his life.[17] The general failure of progressives to deal with the Negro problem in 1912 presented a glaring gap in their reform ideology and it took a good deal of courage on Villard's part to openly dedicate himself to their cause; the same kind of courage that it took to parade down Fifth Avenue for women's suffrage. Through such concerns as these Villard was brought into contact with a younger generation, which was to exert an important influence on his life.

For many young Americans 1912 was the year of the renaissance. What appealed to them in the New Nationalism and the New Freedom was the word *new*. Young writers, artists, poets, and journalists flocked to Greenwich Village announcing, as one of the new mastheads did, that this was *The Lyric Year*, from Edna St. Vincent Millay's poem. For these younger people the times meant change, challenge, and opportunity. They did not, like Villard, look longingly back to the "paths of Grover Cleveland." The New Freedom for them meant abandonment of the old homilies—a revolt against formalism. H. G. Wells, a new prophet in old England, raised the standard by announcing in *The Atlantic Monthly* that the new generation would leave no stone unturned. He warned that after the onslaught,

> a thousand pretences and ten thousand impostures [would] shrivel in the cold clear air of our elucidations. We are going to write of wasted opportunities and latent beauties, until a thousand new ways of living open to men and women. We are going to appeal to the young and hopeful and the curious against the established, the dignified and the defensive.[18]

31

The renaissance blossomed in many forms. The startling drama of the young playwright Eugene O'Neill was on the horizon and soon Margaret Anderson's *Little Review* would publish bold, new poetry. The new painting in the Armory Show of 1913 shocked the critics, and architecture was already influenced by the genius of Frank Lloyd Wright, who scoffed at the "very rubbish of styles" which Villard loved as being so "classical and so beautiful." Villard's cherished Thorwood, reconstructed and enlarged by McKim, Mead, and White, was considered passé.[19] There was also the new history of James Harvey Robinson and Charles Beard, which, scorning tradition, suggested that the founding fathers had had a few tawdry personal interests. The new woman was emerging and, although Villard supported the extension of the franchise, he could not have appreciated the aggressiveness of Emma Goldman, who announced, in support of birth control, "women need not always keep their mouths shut and their wombs open."[20]

Most of the rebels were socialistically inclined and every week a new little magazine appeared which combined discussions of politics, literature, and the arts in a single manifesto of revolt. Walter Lippmann and Jack Reed, fresh from Harvard, mixed with writers and artists and earnestly discussed the making over of the world. Professionalism and specialization had not yet arrived: poets talked politics and political scientists wrote poetry. Radicals such as Big Bill Haywood and Emma Goldman, avant gardists such as Floyd Dell, Max Eastman, and Hutchins Hapgood traveled in the same circles as Lippmann and Reed. They met at the Brevoort Hotel on lower Fifth Avenue for a drink and wound up in all-night sessions at Mabel Dodge Luhan's apartment at 23 Fifth Avenue. Controversy was the order of the day, but despite deep disagreements, they all welcomed one thing—change. Mrs. Luhan recorded their feelings: "There was a new spirit abroad and it swept us all together . . . the barriers were down and people reached each other who had never been in touch before."[21]

Respectable Reform

The New York Times Literary Supplement was so angered by the constant attacks on its bourgeois mediocrity that it proclaimed:

> Now let us understand each other—you, the mob who are shouting the names of every latest and maddest and most foreign writer, and we who dare to refuse the mob. We are not mediocrities or molly-coddles. We are not servile or supersensitive. We accept Wilde, and Ibsen and Shaw and Von Hoffmansthal, and Strauss, Matisse, Van Gogh.

Floyd Dell added scornfully, "Oh, yes, *The New York Times* accepts everybody." He later recalled how, when he ventured out of the Village into the uptown world, he felt "alien and a little frightened." For the Dells and the Eastmans felt that there were two countries and Oswald Garrison Villard lived in the country north of 14th Street.[22]

In 1912 Villard was forty years old. He had already lived half his life. By conventional standards he was successful: a man of affairs, a pillar of society. He was the president of *The New York Evening Post* Company and managed both the daily and *The Nation*. In addition he owned a small iron mine near West Point and was a director of two insurance companies. Besides these business obligations he was an active member of the Citizens Union and the City Club, as well as being Treasurer of the National Association for the Advancement of Colored People, a Director of the Manassas Industrial School for Negroes, and a trustee of the Kowaliga Colored Industrial League in Alabama. He took an active part in the community life of Dobbs Ferry, where Thorwood was located, and served as president of its Hospital Association, Citizens League, and school board.

Socially Villard was also secure. He belonged to the Harvard, Century, and University clubs in New York and would soon be a member of the Cosmos Club in Washington. He served on the Board of the Philharmonic Society and was later named to the presidency. In 1910 he had published the definitive biography of John Brown. It was reviewed with high praise by professional historians, and he was subsequently named an honorary member of Harvard's chapter of Phi Beta Kappa. He held an honorary degree from Washington and Lee and was soon to receive another from Lafayette.[23]

By 1912 Villard had been married for nine years and had two children, Dorothea Marshall and Henry Hilgard. He met his wife, Julia Breckenridge Sandford, while on a tour of the South in preparation for attending a conference on Southern education. Her father had been a captain in the Confederacy and a prominent banker in Covington, Kentucky. Many years later Villard said that "among the many enduring benefits of this alliance" it had aided him in understanding the Southern point of view on the race question.[24] Alliance is a particularly appropriate term to describe Villard's marriage. When Julia Sandford married him in 1903 Villard was the prominent and relatively conservative publisher of a leading daily. There was nothing to suggest that within fifteen years he would have been widely denounced as a pro-German pacifist or that he would be the editor of a money-losing weekly supporting controversial causes. Julia Villard herself was a woman of independence and integrity—in fact, the Villard children used to debate whether the stubbornness of a Sandford exceeded that of a Garrison or not.[25] As a result she did not always accept her husband's opinions or share his interests, especially his crusade in support of the Negro. Several of Villard's associates recall that on one occasion she publicly embarrassed him by leaving the hall upon discovering that the dinner they were to attend was racially mixed.[26] Henry Hilgard Villard, who does not remember the incident, points out that it could only have been the result of a misunderstanding since Villard was obviously aware of his wife's prejudices on the matter. By the thirties she was able to enjoy accompanying him on an extended trip through Haiti, where they were widely entertained.[27]

Villard was disappointed in his wife's lack of interest in his work; he complained to friends that she did not bother to read his editorials, seldom supported his position, and rarely accompanied him on speaking engagements.[28] The conflict is well illustrated by a story, told with affection by Julia Villard, of her mother-in-law's remark to her after three or four years of marriage: "Well I had thought, Julie, that when we explained to you what was right, you'd come to see the error of your views!" Villard knew better; he wrote in *Fighting Years* that, thirty-six years after he had first surrendered to Southern charm, "the surrender is still complete and my education is still being taken in hand."[29] Julia Villard was, however, firmly convinced that her husband should do his duty as he saw it, regardless of the consequences. Villard could always count on his wife's support in periods of crisis; in a letter to her from England on Christmas day 1918, he wrote: "How could I have come through these long four years of the war without your aid and help and wise counsel."[30] Although she did not provide the uncritical admiration that his mother did, Villard appreciated her detachment; she stood as his "most helpful critic."

Many of Villard's closest associates hardly knew his wife. But Villard himself did not mix socially with the people with whom he worked. An old friend characterized Villard as "Park Avenue all the way"; after work he preferred to return to the quiet dignity of the Century Club or the study of his home in the east Seventies—the home which Julia Villard created and ran with grace and charm.[31]

This dichotomy between Villard's background and his interests did affect his personality. Throughout his life he was sensitive about the luxuriousness of his background, at times even apologetic. On the other hand, no one cherished more his place in the community, nor did anyone have more respect for decorum and tradition. Intellectually Villard might give aid to the young rebels and forthrightly defend freedom of speech and the press, but he was often shocked at the results. Max Eastman, who left the comparative security of an instructorship at Columbia to become the editor of *The Masses*, recalled a visit he made to the hallowed offices of *The Post* on Vesey Street. He remembered Villard's pride in the lack of hustle and bustle usually associated with a newspaper office and his appreciation of the "pleasantly bookish atmosphere." Villard admired young Eastman's enthusiasm, and Eastman looked upon Villard as one of his "refined" friends who could be counted on for support. However, when the first issue of *The Masses* appeared with a vicious lampoon of the Hearst papers and a lurid cartoon of Arthur Brisbane, Villard was offended by the lack of taste. He and his friend, George Foster Peabody, lectured Eastman on the power of refinement and warned the young man that a total abandonment of the social amenities would lead "to careless living, both as to care of body and mind."[32]

Villard held a Jeffersonian belief in the aristocracy of talent and needed to prove that his success was based on his ability and not on the family fortune. This belief in democracy made him abhor the snob and go out of his way to work with people whose backgrounds were quite different from his own. He was delighted when the parade for women's suffrage marched beneath the windows of the University Club and he saw the shocked faces of his clubmates peering out at him. As a member of the Diners Club, a group of "public spirited gentlemen" whose numbers included John D. Rockefeller, Jr., and Henry L. Stimson in addition to some well-known progressives, Villard demanded that they seek out a few real radicals since he felt the club had enough of "high finance." He threatened not to send his boys to Harvard because he felt the place was becoming far too aristocratic, and he was appalled by the "luxuriousness of the establishments along Mt. Auburn Street."[33]

When Villard pictured himself as a crusading editor, he undoubtedly saw the spartan composing room of William Lloyd Garrison. In spite of his deep-rooted desire to emulate his grandfather and do battle for the right he took pleasure in his meetings with the Rockefellers and the Lamonts and was not ready to abandon this role. He was troubled by his double life. To the younger generation he was a stuffy pompous man of the past. They admired his conviction and dedication, but his formality and strict attendance to business, with his apparent lack of humor, put them off. Hutchins Hapgood, who spent a brief apprenticeship on *The Post,* recalled Villard's sincerity in the fight for Negro rights, but he felt that in other matters Villard was a true conservative, "not well disposed to any freedom of expression or sensitive ways of welcoming new developments in art, literature or labor." To Hapgood, Villard represented an "old-maidish dislike of vital impulse and attacked all new directions as crude and verging on the vulgar or sensational."[34]

Half patron, half reformer, Villard led a lonely life in these years. He was not quite accepted by the new world and not enthusiastically supported by the old. He sought refuge in a greater round of civic activities and responsibilities. With no little skill he maintained this rather tenuous balance, confident that he stood for what was right. In 1914, despite his occasional eccentricities, he was an esteemed member of New York society. By the end of the war he had been accused of treason and Bolshevism. War and adversity were to have a profound impact upon his beliefs, and were to be the final molders of his character.

CHAPTER FOUR

Neutrality
1914-1915

When the war broke out in Europe in the summer of 1914, the editors of *The Post* were determined to maintain the traditional judicious tone for which the paper was esteemed. It was apparent to Villard and to his editor, Rollo Ogden, that news of the fighting and partisan feelings in America would tempt the press to sensationalism. Yellow journalism had reached its full flower and the editors questioned whether the paper could compete with rivals who would present much more titillating and lurid accounts.[1]

For Villard the problem had a more personal meaning. He had old family ties with Germany. He belonged to the Germanistic Society and the Carl Schurz Memorial Committee, whose purpose was to promote recognition of German achievements in the arts and sciences and the contributions of German-Americans to America's intellectual development. Moreover, Villard was, by 1914, a pacifist and on his way to the absolute position of nonresistance.[2] In a country whose heritage and temperament would cause the vast majority to be more favorable to the British, Villard, as owner and manager of a large metropolitan daily, was faced with both a business and a personal problem.

The Post, from the beginning, blamed Germany for the start of the war. Villard pointed out that the origins of the war were complex but the German Emperor had made "no real effort to prevent the outburst" when it would have been easy for him to do so. As a frequent editorialist he denounced Germany's violation of the Belgian neutrality treaty and the subsequent invasion of Belgium as the action of "an outlaw nation" which had "lifted its mailed fist against the whole of Western Europe."[3]

Villard drew an important distinction between the German government and the German people. Prompted by letters and appeals from friends and relatives in Germany, Villard stated his position in an editorial on August 8, 1914, entitled "The Real Crime Against Germany." *The Post,* he wrote, had been repeatedly called upon to defend the German position in the face of growing hostility. Villard wanted to make it clear that "the Germany of the Kaiser, the Germany of militarism and the mailed fist is not the Germany that *The Post* has sympathy for." It was another Germany that the editors were "proud to recognize and acclaim—the Germany of high aspirations and noble ideals; the Germany of intellectual freedom; the Germany to whose spiritual energy every nation the world over is deeply indebted."

Villard recalled the contributions of the Germans in science, art, and politics and recounted the glories of Fichte, Kant, Hegel, and Goethe. In defense of his own heritage he reminded his readers of the importance of German-American Forty-eighters who had come to America and made names for themselves. For Villard this was the Germany that had done "more than any other country" for America's university and intellectual life. He concluded with a bitter attack on "the sophism" of the Harvard professor, Hugo Munsterberg, who equated the intellectual and spiritual values of German life with the discipline and nationalistic spirit and purpose of its ambitious militarism.[4] In *Germany Embattled,* written in 1915, Villard developed this point of view at greater length.[5] It was an admirable solution to his immediate emotional dilemma. He could exalt the German past, adhere to his pacifism, support neutrality, and, at the same time, denounce German militarism. Moreover, it anticipated the official policy to be adopted

39

by the Wilson administration. Wilson repeatedly made the distinction between the German people, with whom America had great ties of respect and admiration, and the military regime, which was responsible for acts of terrorism and irresponsibility.

It was the only policy that Villard could have logically and psychologically maintained at the start of the war. From all of the evidence it was honestly held. Written with such conviction, his book impressed many who might have been skeptical. Charles Francis Adams, who conceded that he had lost all objectivity, wrote Villard that his book was an important contribution and hoped that it would be "widely distributed as well as carefully read." It was favorably received even in England, where *The London Illustrated*, *The Morning Post*, and *The Manchester Guardian* praised it for its fair-minded and sensible approach. Villard was pleased by the praise of his former professor, Albert Bushnell Hart, who assured Villard that he had "seized upon essential truths." The ultimate seal of approval came from William Lyon Phelps, who promised to use it as the basis for one of his public lectures.[6]

As the war continued, the British propaganda machine went into high gear, and when the American press discovered the value of German atrocity stories, Villard's position became more difficult. Toleration and detachment were frail reeds before the rising wind of hate manufactured by the belligerents and exploited by the sensationalist press. Villard's editors repeatedly referred to the "anachronistic barbarism" of Germany and with each attack Villard suffered increasing criticism and abuse from relatives and friends of his family in Germany. While it was a matter of principle not to question Rollo Ogden's supervision of the editorial page, he did try on occasion to counteract the more vehement editorials in the paper: "War is never humane," he wrote. "Such atrocities as are reported are an inevitable result of the brutality of war. Such things will be so long as Christianity is unable to banish from the earth that which is the sum of all wickedness."[7]

Villard did ask Ogden to have Fabian Franklin tone down

his editorials. Franklin was a formidable member of *The Post's* staff. A well-known mathematician and economist, he had served as a professor at Johns Hopkins and as a former editor of *The Baltimore News*. He was the husband of the noted psychologist, Christine Ladd Franklin, and a man universally respected and admired. In Villard's eyes all of this counted for little. He saw Franklin as the most intemperate, biased, and pro-British member of the staff. Villard accused him of using the editorial page to release his personal emotions. This, Villard insisted, must be avoided as it only encouraged the general hysteria. "Of course," he admitted, "I am in danger of leaning toward the German side, but I try to be as judicious as possible —I have never gone through such a spiritual crisis as this."[8]

Villard was in a dilemma. As a journalist, editor, and man of affairs he had become increasingly strong in both his convictions and his commitments. He had developed a dislike of the uncommitted man and was most at home when taking a strong position. To his way of thinking detachment and objectivity were not necessarily virtues; on the contrary, they were excuses to avoid controversy. He now found himself calling for an Olympian objectivity from his editors and readers. Villard would have been as scornful as the editor and historian, William Roscoe Thayer, who, upon hearing the President's appeal for neutrality "in thought as well as action," lashed out at the "moral eunuchs" and the "mentally unsexed."[9] Nevertheless his pacifism, his close connection with Germany, and his repugnance for the blatant exploitation of sensationalism and hysteria by the press all compelled him to circumspection and to attempt a tone of impartiality that was quite alien to his own spirit and personality.

Stoddard Dewey, *The Post's* correspondent in Paris, reported to Villard that in France and England *The New York Post* was viewed as "the most pro-German paper in America." Villard replied, "The Germans think we are the most anti-German paper and so there you have it." In a postscript, he told Dewey that the past months had been a period of great "personal distress . . . what with my German associations and relationships." He assured the correspondent that he was "American first" and had always been "a firm believer in Republican idealism and have hated Kaisers, Czars and all they stand for . . . but it is a case where the mind has been willing to oppose the Germans and the heart has been feeble."[10]

The nature of Villard's lifelong emotional ties to Germany is a question that must be faced in any appraisal of him during the period encompassing both the first and the second World War. Ernest Gruening, a longtime friend and editorial associate of Villard's, while never doubting Villard's integrity, has argued that because of his love of Germany Villard was "unwilling to see some of the Teutonic faults."[11] However, this judgment was made after the horrors of the Nazi regime. Villard's private correspondence as well as his published statements indicate that his attachment to Germany as a nation was based upon his romantic conception of the German liberalism of 1848. His associations in Germany were largely with the people of that tradition. To Villard the Forty-eighters remained the heroic figures of modern Germany. He connected their history with the growth of democracy in America. He had learned about them through his father and through family friendships in America. As a youth he saw much of Carl Schurz and Abraham Jacobi, a former Forty-eighter and well-known specialist in children's diseases. Carl Bitter, the sculptor whose bas-relief adorns the facade of New York's Metropolitan Museum and who became president of the National Sculptor Society, was a frequent visitor to the Villard home. Militarism as symbolized by the Junkers was, at all times, scorned by Villard.[12]

There is some evidence in Villard's correspondence of a spirited antagonism toward the British, which implied a kind of indirect pro-Germanism. During his first fifteen years on *The Post* he often acted as the editor in charge of military matters and carried on a corespondence with a number of American military men. One correspondent in particular,

Admiral F. E. Chadwick, was pro-German and argued in 1914 and 1915 that Britain and not Germany was responsible for the war and that the whole world would benefit from a German victory. He wrote Villard that Germany had a good chance of winning the war and that he hoped *The Post* would be sympathetic to the German side in its accounts of international news.[13]

Villard replied that he was "much interested" in the Admiral's opinion that Germany might be victorious. In *The Post,* with the detachment of an expert, Villard praised the competence of Germany's military machine. The sinking of three British cruisers in twenty minutes was one of "the greatest feats in naval history" and ought to put an end to Churchill's scoffing dismissal of the submarine as a tactical weapon.[14] At least part of Villard's respect for Germany's military strategy can be attributed to his long-time interest in military affairs. Villard never countenanced, however, Chadwick's thesis that Germany was fighting for a righteous cause, although he readily conceded a growing antagonism toward the British.

What enraged Villard was British censorship, which seemed to him a repudiation of the renowned "British sense of fair play." To Roy Martin of the Associated Press he claimed that of all the abominable things about the war the British censor was one of the worst—"It almost makes me pro-German." To Sir John Barran Villard wrote that he was beginning to feel that the moment that the Allies conquered Germany the "ideals of the Bernhardies and Treitschkes will have conquered England. I am still as much opposed to German militarism as ever but I have no enthusiasm left for the British."[15]

Villard's mail became increasingly poisonous as the war lengthened. Most of the criticism was anonymous but occasionally he heard from old family friends. James Loeb, the German financier, who had been a close associate of Henry Villard, was disgusted with Oswald's position. That Villard, "the son of a good German father," should have allowed himself to become so misinformed as to "the real causes that led to the conflict" seemed unintelligible to him.[16] *The Gaelic American,* in line with its vigorous anti-British policy, carried a letter to the editor charging Villard with having inherited a good deal of money which had been obtained through the help of the Deutsche Bank; hence he was using German money against German interests .The correspondent reported that Villard's relatives in Germany had "cast him off." Villard admitted to Rollo Ogden that there was unanimity of opinion in letters from relatives abroad. They upset him, since they repudiated his own belief that the German people did not really support the actions of the German government.[17]

Villard responded to criticism by professing deep love for the German people but disapproval of their government's international policy. Dearly as he loved Germany and proud as he was of his German background, he could not support German militarism. He denounced those German professors who had issued "An Appeal to the Civilized World" supporting the German cause and claimed that such a betrayal of the integrity of the intellectual community of the world would do irreparable harm to Germany and its cause in America.[18]

Villard never became associated with the various German-American organizations in the United States that supported the German cause. He ridiculed them as "professional pro-Germans who are doing more harm to Germany than any other segment of society." In a speech during a patriotic celebration at Stockbridge, Massachusetts, in 1915 he asked rhetorically what Carl Schurz would have thought if he returned to find that German-Americans' affection for their native land had interfered with the proper loyalty toward the land of their adoption: "He would have been dismayed to find that some among them had been seduced into using their power in American politics for foreign ends."

While he did not join the bandwagon of those advocating further restriction of immigration, he did agree that the "swearing in of hordes of immigrants for political reasons" had been injurious to America's best interests. He rejected the possibility of any double allegiance: "One cannot be a conscientious adherent to a monarchy and a republic at the same time." In an outburst of patriotism Villard demanded that German-Americans place their chief pride in the words, "Americanus sum—hold fast to what is good in the past, but when you give yourselves to us, give yourselves without restraint to our Republic."[19] For this outburst, which was widely publicized, Villard was attacked by Americans for protesting too much and by German-Americans for a narrow provincialism. Professor Munsterberg, in *The New York Times,* ridiculed Villard, "born of a German father in Germany, who knew so little about German government that he wrangled like 'a freshman debater'."[20]

Villard's alienation from German-Americans and relatives abroad extended to his staff on *The Post* as well. Technically, his position still conformed to the official position of the administration. His neutrality was absolute. Gradually, the editors of *The Post* came to reject such neutrality as a moral impossibility, but Villard remained adamant. He personally continued to denounce both German militarism and British violations of American neutrality rights.

Villard remained uneasy over the question of neutrality, but his increasing commitment to pacifism enabled him to avoid the question of national guilt. His pacifist sentiments, which had been aroused by the Spanish-American war, were strengthened by the spectacle of a world conflagration. As America drifted toward involvement in the war, pacifism was no longer an abstraction but a well-defined position on which Villard could take a rigid stand.

His reputation as a leading pacifist was so well known by 1908 that Charles Evans Hughes as Governor of New York wanted to appoint Villard as a representative from New York to the National Peace Conference in that year. By 1915 *The New York Times,* reporting a speech of Villard's, referred to him as "one of the leading pacifists in the country."[21] His pacifism had become extreme in its militancy. When the preparedness debate occupied American politics in 1915 and 1916, Villard brooked no compromise in his outright rejection of military preparation. Norman Angell, the British journalist and future Nobel Prize winner, considered Villard as typical of the most extreme wing of the movement. Villard, he wrote, was to the left of even the Quakers, who, "in regard to international policy are usually moderate, realistic, middle of the road . . . able to reconcile inflexible principle with practical cooperation in halfway measures." For Villard the term, "halfway measures" had no place in a truly pacifistic position.[22]

In 1910 Villard refused an appointment as a director of the New York Peace Society, charging that some of the leaders gave only lip service to the movement. In 1915 he resigned from the New York chapter. He quoted his friend, John Jay Chapman, who referred to it as a "somnolent and inactive reform association." It had a fine name and "an aroma of original benevolence," but was really the kind of organization "that attracts respectable, rich, lazy, and conservative people."[23]

When the advocates of military preparedness became more aggressive, Villard made every attempt to whip American pacifists into more organized opposition. He attacked the activities of Roosevelt, Lodge, Augustus P. Gardiner, and all who aided in the propaganda for an expansion of America's armed forces. He claimed that the peace movement was a moral movement which would not thrive in "an atmosphere of half-heartedness." He ridiculed the timidity of some members of the peace organizations. The Carnegie Endowment for International Peace was, he thought, the prime example of "moral cowardice." By its very prestige, it was subverting the whole peace movement. "Its work has no moral inspiration. It may give banquets for foreigners, make studies of international law, but it has no fire." He didn't think this was surprising. When Carnegie entrusted the foundation to such men as Elihu Root, Joseph H. Choate, Robert Bacon, and Charles

W. Eliot "he largely destined it to ineffectiveness." These men, Villard charged, were "not the stuff of which reformers are made." He advocated driving from the peace movement all but those who held to the extreme position. Villard recalled the glories of his grandfather and Wendell Phillips: "They tasted deep of the unexampled spiritual happiness that comes only when men burn all their bridges behind them." "It is only the extremist and fanatic who make a cause successful."[24]

Villard's pacifism offers an interesting paradox given his long interest in the military. He was a large and vigorous man, a fine horseman, who took delight in recalling how in the summer of 1898 he had been mistaken for Theodore Roosevelt.[25] He denied the charge of cowardice that his pacifism encouraged, and after the war, while in Germany during the revolution of 1919, he subjected himself to tests of personal courage in order to prove that he was not a coward, that he did not shrink from war out of fear but only out of conviction. Years later, in describing these experiences, he told with boyish pride of how he had looked down the barrel of a threatening pistol and had felt no fear. He candidly admitted that he "wouldn't have missed it for the world."[26]

Villard's pacifism did not contain the sense of human tragedy and the introspection that is often characteristic of the religious pacifist. It was one-dimensional. His belief was buttressed by his faith in practical Christianity. Acceptance of the absolute Christian ethic protected him from the moral anxiety of such reflective thinkers as Reinhold Niebuhr, also of the same tradition, and a staunch pacifist until the 1930's. Niebuhr finally came to the conclusion that a policy of pacifist nonresistance involved a decision that might, under certain circumstances, be as injurious and irresponsible in its consequences as taking up the sword. For Villard no such ambiguities existed. "Resist not evil," the biblical basis for pacifist nonresistance, was an immutable law which the church violated every day but the true Christian lived up to. Between war and peace, between force and nonresistance, there was no alternative.

47

War was never justified under any circumstances. Such was his strait-laced brand of Garrisonianism.[27]

As a practical journalist, Villard did not dwell upon the moral certainties of his position. Instead he used his knowledge of military affairs to prove that war was anachronistic, that all history showed that military men were unreliable and that war was ineffective in obtaining the goals it sought. The only concession he ever made to armament was his support, when all negotiations had failed, of an effective small standing army for defense purposes only. He maintained that a little efficiency in administration and organization, rather than expansion, was all that America ever needed to defend its own shores.[28]

The peace movement in America from the outbreak of the war in 1914 until America's entrance in 1917 was engaged primarily in a holding action. It fought preparedness until America's actual involvement and thereafter devoted itself to preparation for an "enlightened peace which would do away once and for all with the conditions that caused war in the first place." The basic philosophical arguments of the movement rested on a profound faith in man's ultimate perfectibility and the idea of progress through reason. War was viewed as an anachronistic barbarity, "a frightful indictment of Christianity." No one, not even Roosevelt or Bernhardi (Villard often equated the two) with all their "twaddle about the necessity to preserve the manhood of nations, . . . could defend this war without damage to their reputations for humanity or intelligence."[29]

War, the peace advocates argued, was caused by the men in civilized communities who would resort to anything for power or riches. The militant wing of the peace movement always pointed to the arms manufacturers and corrupt statesmen as the primary sources of war. Villard openly asserted that it was the gun-makers and the "masters of privilege" who supported the preparedness movement in America and that this was true of all the belligerents. Furthermore, these men sought war as a check on domestic reform. When a nation turned to war, it surrendered its civil liberties and resorted to police state methods and the power of central authority. Villard always maintained that war and liberalism were incompatible.[30]

In the closing months of 1914 Villard and *The Post* were secure in their position. Villard had solved, with some anguish, the German-American problem and taken up with vigor the administration's policy of neutrality. His articles and editorials were enthusiastic in praise of Wilson's "nonpartisan attitude toward the belligerent nations."[31] The President applauded Villard's work and thanked him personally for the "flood of light" he had thrown upon public affairs as well as the "generous spirit" with which he treated the administration's policy.[32]

Villard helped establish the League to Limit Armaments to counteract the barrage of propaganda being spread abroad by the newly founded National Security League.[33] This preparedness organization was led by A. P. Gardiner and George Haven Putnam, the wealthy New York publisher, and endorsed by General Leonard Wood. It gained the support of a great number of wealthy citizens, who contributed amply to its campaign funds. When Villard sent out the call to support his antipreparedness league, he was optimistic. The President had referred to the preparedness advocates as needlessly "nervous and excited."[34] Villard also received a pledge of $10,000 from Bishop Greer of the Anglican Diocese of New York. He wrote his uncle, Francis J. Garrison, that when "the bishop of the richest and most fashionable diocese in America" not only raises money for the cause but "publicly announces from his pulpit that he believes in non-resistance," this showed that there was great potential strength needing only to be tapped.[35]

During 1915 Villard was occupied almost entirely with America's neutrality and the question of preparedness for war. The preparedness advocates claimed that only a prepared nation could possibly remain neutral. America must, they felt, back up its neutral rights with potential power. Villard, on the other hand, argued that to proclaim a peace-loving neutrality

49

and at the same time increase armaments would be to subvert the former.[36] He reiterated the superiority of moral force over brute force. It was the munitions makers who employed the "lobbyists, diplomatic agents and bribers who in turn promoted war," and the war itself should provide a lesson in the "folly of worshipping brute force." Villard pointed to the message of the man in the White House, who had stated that "Europe turns to us because this country loves justice, seeks the true path of progress and has a passionate regard for the rights of humanity."[37]

The sinking of the "Lusitania" on May 7, 1915, brought Villard to Washington as a correspondent for *The Post*. He denounced the sinking as "not only a breach of international law but a violation of the fundamental decencies of civilization." While partisan Americans demanded a more aggressive policy on the part of the administration, Villard assured his readers that Wilson would take a far-sighted view and would consider the consequences of any rash action. Roosevelt fumed and fretted over Wilson's policy of immorality and described the "Lusitania" tragedy as an act of piracy "on a vaster scale of murder than any old-time pirate ever practiced." Villard replied scornfully that he never doubted Roosevelt's qualifications as an authority on piracy.[38] For Villard, Wilson could now do no wrong. Even his playing golf on the day following the emergency was interpreted as a deliberate gesture to create calmness and stem the tide of hysteria. Almost as though the President were taking notes from Villard's daily utterances in *The Post*, on May 10 in Philadelphia he gave immortality to a phrase coined by Villard, "too proud to fight."[39] "Peace," said Wilson, "is a healing and elevating influence . . . strife is not. There is such a thing as a man being too proud to fight . . . such a thing as a nation being so right that it does not need to convince others by force that it is right."[40]

Roosevelt denounced this as immoral twaddle and accused "Professor Wilson" of taking his cue from "Flubdubs, mollycoddles and flap-doodle pacifists."[41] Villard, on the other hand, felt that Wilson spoke not only for American rights but for civilization and humanity. The President was not to be stampeded by militarists like Roosevelt. Such men throughout the world were "blind to the moral side of the matter and never stopped to think beyond the blood letting." Roosevelt for his part detested the likes of Villard. He wrote a friend: "It is sometimes necessary to skin skunks; but it is necessary to choose the skunk! . . . Really I do not think Oswald Villard ought to be honored with an attack. To change the metaphor, he is the kind of crawling thing we step on, provided the resulting crunch won't leave too large a stain on the floor. . . ."[42]

Villard supported the "diplomacy by note" carried on by Wilson after the "Lusitania" sinking. He did insist that in order to make effective the President's demands that Germany abandon submarine warfare, America must also demand that the British cease their violations of America's neutral rights. He wrote to Secretary Lansing after the third Wilson note that many of his German friends in America had "been stunned by the severity of Wilson's demands" and felt that a truly successful and permanent conclusion to the negotiations would rest upon "the force and energy" that America put into a note to the British demanding recognition of American rights.[43]

Villard constantly repeated a conversation he had with Secretary Lansing in which the Secretary had said that when one is dealing with a murderer and a thief one must concentrate on the murderer. Germany was violating human rights by using the submarine, while England was only violating property rights which could be settled following the war. Villard remarked that this might be so but he saw no excuse for allowing the thief to escape. He also was inclined to think that the effects of England's blockade were as brutal as those of the submarine and justified retaliation.[44]

Although he criticized the administration's lack of vigor toward Britain, Villard continued to applaud the "trained and devoted servant in the White House." Wilson had revived "the spirit of the whole nation and had set a new standard of dealing with foreign nations." The President, he assured his readers, "will try with all his powers to solve the problem of German negotiations in accordance with the wishes of the people." To Villard this meant "punishment without war . . . if he cannot find a way out who could?"[45] He wrote the President praising his resistance to the demand for large armaments: "That you may achieve what I believe to be your purpose—the demonstration to the world that we can achieve our rights by firm insistence upon the justice and humanity of our contentions—without resort to war—is my profoundest wish." Wilson replied that he read very carefully all of Villard's work in *The Post* and that he wanted Villard to know how sincerely he valued his support and approval.[46]

When Ambassador Bernstorff handed the cable to Secretary Lansing on September 2, 1915, in which the Germans declared they would no longer pursue submarine warfare without warning noncombatants, Villard took this as a vindication of his position. In an editorial entitled "The Great Triumph," he wrote an ecstatic appreciation of Wilson:

> Without mobilizing a regiment or assembling a fleet, but by sheer dogged, unswerving persistence in advocating right he had compelled the surrender of the proudest, the most arrogant, the best armed of nations, and he has done it in . . . the fullest and most patriotic devotion to American ideals . . . The greatest lesson of all is the unconquerable power of moral ideals. . . . We, of *The Evening Post,* acknowledge to him today the colossal debt that this country and humanity owe him. No one can overestimate it; no one can even see how far reaching its effects may be. It may result in the ending of the war of the nations . . . Americans may be proud of their country as that which, more than any other, is an example of a guiding star to all mankind.[47]

Villard, in a final and magnificent gesture, broke a precedent of 114 years by running on *The Post*'s front page a picture of the President—"The man who, without rattling a sword, won for civilization."[48]

No incident better illustrates the devotion of Oswald Garrison Villard to the causes for which he fought. Also evident is his tendency toward hero-worship and his persistent faith in the power of individual men to shape the course of history, which was later to cause him extreme anguish and disappointment. Like so many of his generation, Villard was a true child of the enlightenment. He believed that reason and justice would triumph over the forces of evil and darkness. His attitudes toward peace and neutrality, his slant on the rights of the Negro, women's suffrage, and civil liberties reflected a reform tradition that preceded the Civil War. He drew sustenance from the martyrdom of John Brown and the nonresistance of Garrison combined with the romantic, rebellious liberalism of the Forty-eighters. Villard had tremendous faith in the defiant man of reason who would risk martyrdom to turn back the tide of hysteria. Villard saw himself in this light and there is no doubt that he wished the President to play this classic role.

If Villard's enthusiasm occasionally clouded his judgment, he was more aware than many of his younger progressive contemporaries that war and progressivism were not compatible, that the reform impulse of the age would wither and die if the nation armed and went to war. He understood that mobilization for war would increase the power of the state. This new power, he feared, would not be in the interest of the individual citizens who made up the state. At the center of his political belief was faith in the individual and in his right to political and economic self-expression.

Villard predicted that history would proclaim Wilson's policy one of the triumphs of diplomacy. This has not been the case. Many historians have, in fact, charged Wilson with allowing Germany to assume indirect control of American policy by leaving the initiative to the German strategists. Subsequent experience should not blind us to the depths of conviction of men like Villard who sincerely felt that reasonable, intelligent statesmen could live by an international code of ethics and morality and could, through discussion and negotiation, come to equitable agreement. In the fall of 1915 this belief was shared with equal conviction by Woodrow Wilson.

The significance of Villard's actual role in the negotiations that took place in August and September of 1915 is hard to ascertain. He was at one point the intermediary between the German Ambassador Bernstorff and the State Department. He also kept Secretary Lansing informed on German-American opinion, although in Lansing's correspondence with Villard there is a tone of suspicion and skepticism. Lansing tended to suspect all pacifists of being sympathetic to Germany.[49] Nevertheless, it is apparent that many journalists concluded from Villard's frequent associations with Bernstorff and a number of prophetic news scoops during this period that he was a semi-official spokesman for the administration. *The New York Herald* reported in August that "official Washington has suddenly come to realize that a new figure of great importance has sprung up . . . that Mr. Villard's views carried great weight with the President has been known for some time . . . but that Villard was powerful enough to shape Administration policy was not known." *The New York Times* reported a rumor that Villard was to replace Colonel House. It is certain that much of this was sarcasm and deliberately designed to embarrass Villard and the administration by associating Wilson with a pacifist and a German-American.[50] In retrospect Villard perhaps saw himself as closer to the sources of power and influence than he actually was. In his autobiography he claimed credit for arranging a meeting between Bernstorff and the President which contributed to the successful conclusion of the negotiations. At the time, however, he admitted to John Palmer Gavit that this was merely another rumor, but that it had helped him journalistically by getting him admitted to important offices in the capital.[51]

As long as the President continued his policy of moderation

Villard's relationship with the administration was cordial. The subsequent change in the President's attitude toward preparedness put a quick stop to speculations about Villard's influence in governmental circles. In a few months Villard's attitude toward Wilson underwent a transformation. Doors that had been open to him were closed and friendships that had been warm and relaxed grew strained. The demands of politics forced the President to abandon his pacifistic inclinations, and Villard's early anticipation of a breach with Wilson was confirmed.

CHAPTER FIVE

The Maelstrom of Militarism
1915-1916

As far back as April 1915 Villard was reading newspaper reports that the President would be sympathetic toward legislation for increased expenditures and manpower for the armed services. He had been assured earlier by Joseph Tumulty, the President's secretary, that the President would not weaken, but now Villard wrote him again for reassurance.[1] There is no recorded answer in Villard's file. He soon realized that Secretary of War Lindley M. Garrison (no relation) had gone over to the militarists' side, but his faith in Wilson was still strong. He assured *Post* readers that he "doubted very much" that Wilson would succumb to the propaganda of the National Security League.[2]

By the summer of 1915 it was apparent that the President was not only going to support bills designed to increase armaments but was going to take charge of the movement. Villard tried frantically to have representatives of the League to Limit Armaments see the President and to get an interview himself. He was rebuffed. Tumulty told him that the President was sorry that his engagements were such that he could not "grant interviews of this sort at the present."[3] Villard wrote Wilson that he hoped "with all his heart" that he would set his face "against any surrender to the advocates of militarism," and that he would at least not make any decision until all the facts were set before him, promising to present these facts in a series of articles. The President replied curtly that he would "value highly" the forthcoming articles.[4]

Villard was tormented by this situation. It was galling no longer to have free access to the President or even to Tumulty. He felt that his influence had been jeopardized by the rumors that he was to replace House. In spite of a letter to his wife in which he stated, "It shows in this matter of preparedness that [Wilson] is not willing to hear both sides—not even from a man who has labored as hard for the administration as I have,"[5] he claimed to have no personal feelings in the matter, only a feeling of pity.

Villard's letters at this time are in marked contrast to his wild enthusiasm of only a month earlier. Where he had praised the President as "intensely human," he now agreed with those who saw a "bloodless and calculating man." He was afraid that Wilson, in changing his stand on preparedness, was no longer leading but being led by political expediency.[6]

Villard's accusation of perfidy was one of his characteristic failings. He was unable to believe that the opposition could be motivated by beliefs as sincere as his own. Throughout his life he turned on friend and foe and accused them of a betrayal of principle motivated by self-interest. John Palmer Gavit once told Villard that this was the greatest defect in his liberalism, and reminded Villard of his own suffering from snap judgments: "You will never be a real liberal until you rid yourself of this habit, personally and in your capacity as an editor."[7] But Villard continued to maintain that tolerance can have a palsying effect upon righteous conviction.

Wilson came out for a five-year Army expansion plan on October 15, 1915. Villard was shocked. "The militarists have taken the country by storm," he wrote his English friends, Joseph and Sophia Sturge. Wilson's capitulation was all the more tragic because it came simultaneously with his demonstration of the efficacy of moral power over brute force in subduing the Germans.[8]

To Villard, acceptance of preparedness meant the end of genuine neutrality. He accused the President of "tying the hands of the United States Government and depriving it of its unexcelled moral position." Certainly, Villard demanded, his former supporters were entitled to some "cogent, far reaching, compelling reason for the President's turnabout to force."[9] On October 30 he wrote the President expressing his disappointment and "profound regret" that Wilson had abandoned his slogan "Humanity First." He reminded Wilson that his greatest hold on the people had invariably come when he had chosen "the highest moral ground . . ." and warned him that his new course would draw the nation into "the maelstrom of militarism and raise up a military and naval caste dangerous to the democratic way of life."[10]

Villard's letter undoubtedly upset the President. Villard was the spokesman for a substantial body of sentiment in the country, as demonstrated by the vigorous debate then going on in Congress. Wilson wrote Villard that he had not arrived at his decision without "prolonged and serious consideration of the many sides of the question." "It always adds to my hesitation," he continued, "to make a decision on such a serious issue" when he found himself in opposition to such men as Villard "whose character and judgment" he valued so highly. "These things search the heart and judgment."[11]

Here is the traditional confrontation between the crusading dissenter and the dedicated, practicing statesman. Wilson was under pressure on many fronts. Some were political. By supporting preparedness he would undoubtedly weaken the opposition of belligerent partisans who denounced his caution and patience as weakness and vacillation. But it is an oversimplification to attribute his actions to nothing but political motives. He was unquestionably distressed by his decision, but at the same time he felt that America was not militarily prepared for every emergency. Villard never seriously entertained the fear that a German victory would present the slightest threat to the national interest. Some of Wilson's closest advisors, however, disagreed. Wilson scoffed at those who spoke of potential invasion, but he feared future German aggression in the Western Hemisphere should Germany succeed in dominating Europe.[12] Villard failed to appreciate the fact that Wilson was doing everything in his power to maintain the principles that Villard stood for. He was more pacifistic than anyone in his cabinet and he had a horror of war and militarism equal to Villard's.

Villard, as an editor of a journal of opinion, felt he had a duty to present informed criticism, to exert pressure, and to judge the President according to his knowledge of affairs and his own convictions. An amiable solution to such a confrontation is unlikely. Despite recent tendencies to exalt "realism" and "practical politics" it is as naive to expect the dissenter to shoulder the burdens of popular leadership as it is to expect the popular leader to abandon his responsibilities to the entire electorate by adopting rigid absolutism. Both kinds of man play a vital role in the working processes of democratic government.

When Wilson made public his intention to take the issue of preparedness to the people, Villard became fearful. He had great respect for the President's powers of persuasion. He wrote the Sturges that the President would risk his political career in supporting the measures, and in the end the forces of peace would be defeated.[13] Villard described the President's speeches on his Western tour as demagoguery. He was trying to "scare people into his brand of preparedness with veiled hints of serious complications in the background."[14]

Villard fought the issue until he collapsed from exhaustion. The tone of his letters, speeches, and articles is one of resignation. He felt that America was about to take "a homeopathic dose of poison." Villard, as well as most of the peace advocates, turned more and more toward the hope of a negotiated peace as the only way of saving the country from becoming involved in the war.[15]

It was known that Wilson had been attempting to persuade the belligerents to agree to accept the good offices of the United States. Colonel House had been sent to make arrangements for mediation. The peace advocates had long cherished the idea of a "Conference of Neutral Nations,"[16] i.e., a conference held in open session by neutrals in Europe, who, with American support and aid, would continually call on the belligerents to proclaim their war aims and arrange terms for a settlement. American pacifists worked to get official American support for the conference which had met as part of the International Women's Congress in May 1915 at The Hague. Delegates visited fourteen countries and according to Jane Addams were treated with courtesy and respect.[17]

When these pacifists approached the American State Department, they found most important officials unsympathetic. Emily Balch, the close friend and associate of Jane Addams and future recipient of the Nobel Peace Prize, wrote Villard that a meeting with Secretary Lansing had been disheartening to say the least. Lansing's attitude had been completely "amoral and cynical and on an unspeakably lower level than the ideas of European statesmen" she had interviewed.[18]

The diaries and letters of House and Lansing indicate that they viewed the pacifists with some amusement but at no time very seriously. Lansing told Villard that Miss Addams had been hoodwinked by the European diplomats. Neither Lansing nor House favored any support for a negotiated peace in the spring of 1916 because they felt there was no chance of success. America, by becoming a part of the plan, would lose its influence when the time did come to act.[19]

The critical point in the whole plan for a negotiated peace in 1915 was seldom grasped by the pacifists. The belligerents' interest in negotiation depended on the military situation at any given moment. When the Germans had an advantage, they would not consider any reasonable suggestions; and when the situation was reversed, the Allies looked askance at proposals for a compromise settlement.[20]

During the spring and summer of 1916 the interest of Americans turned toward the coming presidential election. Villard, realizing that his estrangement from the administration had jeopardized his effectiveness as chief Washington correspondent for *The Post*, returned to New York. The choice of Democratic and very pro-Wilson David Lawrence to replace him indicates the degree to which Villard was falling out with his own staff. In February he had written his mother discussing the possible sale of *The Post*.[21]

The year 1916 was one of great despair for Villard. He liked to be in the center of things. In the winter of 1915-1916, however, he had lost much of his prestige.[22] The most important contributing factor was Villard's fortuitous association with Henry Ford's Peace Ship. At a press conference in November, which Villard attended, Ford introduced the idea to an astonished press corps, promising that "the boys will be out of the trenches by Christmas." Villard never approved of the venture, which he thought naive and disorganized. He was particularly critical of Ford's reckless promise to end hostilities, which could only bring disappointment. On November 25 *The New York Herald* printed a story which was picked up by the country's newspapers stating that the Ford Peace Ship would sail on December 4 to "end the war." The same article went on to say that Henry Ford was so opposed to war and armaments that he had given Oswald Garrison Villard a check for $20,000 to establish a bureau in Washington to protest the President's preparedness program.[23] Villard's supposed connection with the Peace Ship, soon to be ridiculed by the press, unjustifiably linked him with the lunatic fringe of the peace element. He denied the connection and explained that although the money had been pledged he had never received a check from Ford, but to no avail.[24] In addition, two famous news scoops by Villard proved to be false. This led many who once believed him to be in touch with the prevailing powers to view him now as a cast-off.[25]

These circumstances helped foster Villard's disappointment with Wilson and the administration. His editorials became more critical in their attacks on the President's personal motives. He wrote to Henry Morgenthau, who was chairman of the finance committee of the Democratic National Committee, in April 1916 that Wilson had been the greatest disappointment in his entire life, and that his misunderstanding of Wilson had shattered his faith in the value of his own political judgment. To George Foster Peabody he vowed that he would never again let his enthusiasm for any public man run away with him. To William Lyon Phelps he bitterly exclaimed, "I believed in him and worked for him as I have done for no other man in the twenty years of my active career . . . he has done me a great personal harm." Villard exaggerated the personal equation. His relationship and support of Wilson had run hot and cold as far back as the presidential campaign of 1912. But Villard had a need for warm personal commitments even if his personality often frustrated such attachments. Though Villard had never really been close to Wilson, he believed he had been, and therefore he felt Wilson's change of attitude was betrayal of friendship and trust. To David Lawrence, not a sympathetic listener, Villard accused Wilson of "undergoing . . . a grave moral deterioration." He was "beginning to despise the man."[26]

Following Wilson's renomination Villard reported hopefully that the President would have a difficult time overcoming the disillusionment of his former supporters.[27] This was wishful thinking. Some were suspicious but an overwhelming number of important leaders, teachers, social workers, and even prominent members of the peace movement turned to Wilson in 1916. Those committed to a program of social reform, who had supported Roosevelt in 1912, went over to the Democratic candidate. Some of Villard's closest associates in the peace movement such as Jane Addams, Lillian Wald, Amos Pinchot, George Foster Peabody, John Dewey, and Max Eastman threw their support behind Wilson.[28] This did not persuade Villard. Since he had little enthusiasm for Hughes he announced that *"The Post* might not be able to espouse anybody's cause."[29]

Villard, standing on principle, refused to support either candidate, but *The Post* came out in September for Wilson.

Villard stood alone. He did refrain from publicly repudiating the President but he told his friends that he would never vote for him. The man "has not a principle on earth that he would not bargain away. If the Socialist ticket had anybody on it but Benson, I think I would vote for it. As it is, I must seek refuge with the Prohibitionists."[30]

There is something curiously inept about Villard's stand. As editor and owner of a respected and influential newspaper, he avoided the responsibility of leadership. When so many issues of national importance faced the electorate, he rationalized himself into voting Prohibitionist. It is difficult to grasp Villard's rejection of one of the most pacifistic Presidents ever to occupy the White House. It illustrates the degree to which Villard allowed his personal involvement to dictate his political judgment. But more than that, Villard's unbending position reflected the lukewarm character of his connection to the reform movements of the progressive era. Wilson's adoption of much of the New Nationalism in his legislative program for 1916 provided little incentive for Villard. If anything, it only bolstered his intransigence.

But Villard, an incurable optimist, quickly forgot his vow to resist political enthusiasm. With the temptations of the campaign over, he wrote Tumulty, it might even be possible for Wilson to direct "the greatest administration the country has ever seen." He assured him that if the President would make known his willingness to abandon "a policy of pure expedience" it would do much to "rekindle the faith of friends like myself in whom it is dead or dormant."[31] Villard longed to make the rounds again as the Washington correspondent and to regain the influence he had in the summer of 1915.

With the decline in tensions following the Sussex Pledge by the Germans, Wilson had adopted a much sterner attitude toward British violations of American neutrality. In May the State Department sent a sharp note to Spring-Rice, the British Ambassador, protesting the British examination of American mails. Lansing warned that the government would "no longer tolerate the wrongs which citizens of the United States have suffered."[32] Villard, who had always insisted on a sharper policy toward Great Britain, was delighted over this change in tone.

By November 1916 Anglo-American relations were at their lowest ebb. With the election over, Wilson was more receptive to pressure for an all-out attempt to force a negotiated peace. He finally decided to act independently of the Allies. He even lost some of his respect for House. The famous House-Grey memorandum, which had come close to an outright commitment to support the Allies against Germany, if the latter refused to negotiate on terms agreeable to the Allies, had been a failure. Since the British had been reluctant to submit to negotiation, Wilson decided to act with genuine impartiality. House and Lansing pointed out the risk of Germany's agreement, which would then make it appear as though America were cooperating with her as opposed to the Allies. Wilson was aware of the risk but remained adamant, replying that if Germany proposed an armistice looking toward peace he would gladly support it regardless of the British position.[33]

Nevertheless Wilson procrastinated. The German deportation of Belgian civilians was his official explanation for delay. The Germans, flushed by a recent victory in Rumania, sent out an independent offer of negotiation to be relayed by Wilson to the Allied powers. While taking the initiative they made it perfectly clear that if their proposal was rejected, they would be forced to resume unrestricted submarine warfare.[34] It is doubtful if Villard had knowledge of the complexities behind these events. His contact with German policy was Ambassador Bernstorff and Wilson had told Villard in February that Bernstorff was "out of touch with Berlin."[35]

When news of the German offer was released Villard chided Tumulty with the President's loss of the initiative. Nevertheless there was still opportunity "to achieve immortality." The President, Villard pleaded, could take the lead toward general disarmament and the establishment of a "peace league of nations." Villard demanded to know if the administration intended to seize this chance or continue to be "ruled by 'Madame Expediency' and let the Germans have this final honor also." Villard complained that "neither Wilson nor House ever ask what is right for humanity but are always blocked by the latest technicality—a letter from Lord Bryce— the opinion of some war correspondent." "Why in God's name," he asked, could they not try "just once going ahead and letting the rest go hang." Villard quoted Wendell Phillips: when told that "the south would be a hell if the slaves were freed," Phillips replied, "I entrench myself on principles of human liberty and leave the working out of details to almighty God!" "Isn't there one principle on which the White House can entrench at any cost?"[36] Editorially he asked if Wilson would once again "parrot the indecision of Macbeth 'letting I dare not wait upon I would.' Is there to be any action without the never ending weighing of the consequences and wonder if this is the right time to do a noble deed?"[37]

In retrospect Villard's position might be interpreted as innocent. He ignored the potential blow to Wilson's prestige should all the belligerents reject his offer of mediation. He was not concerned with the possibility that Germany but not the Allies might accept the offer to negotiate.[38] But Villard could say with justification that his demands were in complete harmony with Wilson's ostensible policy. If there were risks involved, they would be undertaken in the cause of peace instead of war.

Villard still took the premise of genuine impartiality and desire for peace seriously. He would have been appalled had he known of the duplicity involved in the House-Grey memorandum and particularly of the commitments made by House to the Allies. Wilson had been uneasy over the apparent willingness of House to guarantee America's participation on the side of the Allies if Germany proved recalcitrant, so much so that he insisted on qualifying those guarantees.[39] Villard had long believed what Wilson in November 1916 had begun to conclude: there was no real distinction between the war aims of the combatants. If this were the case, and there was evidence for this assumption, then there was no reason for an offer of mediation to be dependent upon the preferred military position of the Allies and subject to their prior approval.

Despite the disapproval of House, Lansing, and other pro-Ally advisors, Wilson finally insisted that the note he had drafted weeks before be sent to all the belligerents as equals.[40] But the note was considerably weakened. House and Lansing persuaded Wilson to omit those parts which they felt certain would be unduly offensive to the Allies. Instead of the original threat that the "United States might have to throw her weight" on the side that indicated a sincere desire for mediation, he merely requested a statement of war aims. But Wilson did express in unequivocal terms the impartiality that Villard and peace advocates had long considered indispensable. He stated his belief that "the objects which the statesmen of the belligerents on both sides have in mind in this war are virtually the same, as stated in general terms to their own people and to the world."[41] Although Wilson repeated the lofty ideals expressed in the published war aims of both sides there was by implication a recognition of the insincerity of these published statements, and this confirmed to the letter Villard's own estimate.

The British and their sympathizers in America were shocked by Wilson's equation of their cause with that of the Germans. Lord Bryce sent a personal note of protest to Wilson, and Sir William Wiseman, the head of the British Secret Service in America, immediately called on House to protest the language of Wilson's note. General Wood, at a rally in Carnegie Hall to denounce the Belgian deportations, deplored the lack of leadership in Washington.[42] Naturally Villard was ecstatic. Any presidential action which repudiated the interventionists was cause for jubilation. Even though the note did not go as far as he would have liked, its candid appraisal of the belligerents did rip aside the veil of hypocrisy which had for so long made any genuine approach to mediation and peace impossible. Referring to the President's well-publicized admission that he had a one-track mind, Villard quickly wired Tumulty: "The railroad stock is now quoted at $1000. No finer act done in my memory."[43]

Once again Villard's elation was premature. Complications over terms made the peace offer unacceptable and the German official reply was nearly as unenthusiastic as the British. With this rather anticlimactic episode Wilson decided to present his case before the world. On January 22, 1917, he made his famous "Peace Without Victory" speech to Congress. Wilson attempted to lay the foundation for a new diplomacy acceptable to liberal opinion. He called for a peace of equality with no victors and no vanquished, an honorable settlement to pave the way for a lasting peace. Even after this speech Villard remained suspicious of the President,[44] who, in these last days before American entry, was daily speaking and acting in direct accord with the desires of the noninterventionists. House reported in January that some of Wilson's advisors considered him a "peace at any price" man.[45] For all his pains the control of policy in Germany was captured by the militaristic naval clique and even while he was presenting his "Peace Without Victory" message the German supreme command decided to renew unrestricted submarine warfare on February 1.

When news of the German note reached the press, Villard, along with the peace advocates in general, demanded that the administration once again remain calm. Villard denounced the German position as "outrageous and utterly indefensible," but he felt that no rash action should be undertaken without careful consideration. If America should enter the war the last bright hope of mediation would disappear and "every forward movement would be checked, every reform postponed, censorship . . . the loss of civil liberties." Then he warned of the most devastating possibility of all: "The progress of socialism would certainly be great if the war continued for any length of time."[46]

This last threat contradicted one of Villard's major arguments that war would inevitably lead to reaction. In any case it points up the difference between Villard and many progressives who were turning to the war as a way of bringing on a kind of national planning. This was especially true of *The New Republic,* which in a complete about-face came to see America's participation in the war as a means of achieving the "progressive nationalism" the magazine had promoted from its inception in the fall of 1914.

In some matters Villard's opinion was not far from Wilson's. When Wilson went before Congress to sever diplomatic relations with Germany on February 3, 1917, he stressed that his purpose was not a declaration of war and that America had no quarrel with the German people. This was the line of the pacifists. Villard repeatedly argued that it was the diplomats who favored war. He was accused of slander when he said publicly that he had "too much proof of people who give large checks to preparedness and the universal service movement" whose motive is the suppression of the coming social revolution to "doubt that money was one of the main factors behind the forces of intervention."[47] Wilson himself feared this as he received sudden support from men who had fought his domestic program. At one point he wrote to House that "the Junkerthum is trying to creep under the cover of the patriotic feeling of the moment."[48]

After the publication of the Zimmerman note to Mexico it was apparent that Germany had finally decided to risk war with the United States. Villard's letters and editorials are filled with grave misgivings. He conceded the stupidity of the German government, but he assured his readers that it did not represent the German people: "Redemption of Germany can only come with the arrival of peace, but this should not be a harsh, forced punishment." Germany, Villard claimed, had received her punishment already "in the court of morals, in the court of world opinion Germany has been adjudged guilty and it is a terrible punishment which confronts her—the loss of the favorable opinion of the world." Americans must keep in mind, he warned, "that war will injure America far more than it will Germany."[49]

68

The Maelstrom of Militarism

When Wilson in March managed to subvert the efforts of those who had filibustered to defeat the arming of American merchant ships, the war was, in fact, under way even though there had not been a formal declaration. By the twenty-third of March, after the sinking of three American merchant ships, Villard knew the end had come. But along with the rest of the pacifists he continued to make speeches appealing for peace and denouncing militarism.

In his correspondence he reviewed the events that had led up to the war. To James Oppenheim, the editor of *The Seven Arts,* he wrote that America was going to war because the President and his cabinet had refused to hold the scales of neutrality in balance. He recalled how he had appealed to Bryan, then Lansing, and others in the State Department as well as to the President to make neutrality truly effective by acting with impartiality toward both belligerents. Villard held Wilson primarily responsible. Britain had treated America abominably ever since the war began, as everyone in the State Department knew from Lansing on down. "There is not a breach of international law that she has overlooked, interference with the mails, preventing American newspapers from receiving German periodicals, partisan and lying censorship. She has violated Holland's fishing rights, crushed Greece." Such action, Villard said, would turn any man of justice against the British ruling class. He conceded that this did not mitigate German ruthlessness or violation of law, but that England had justified her actions under the same plea as Germany—the necessity of war. America should have "from the start spoken out as emphatically against England as against Germany."[50]

With the collapse of neutrality Villard came out publicly for nonresistance. When baited by Henry Wise Wood of the National Security League, Villard returned a categorical no to the question of whether he would resist the invasion of the United States. Villard cited the young Detroit pastor Reinhold Niebuhr, who, in an article in *The Atlantic Monthly,* referred to the war as "The Nation's Crime Against the Individual" and suggested that the patriots were "duped by pretexts that hide the real issues." Villard too stressed the encroachment of the state on the individual's conscience and spoke of the "serenity of spirit, the exaltation of mind, the universal peace that comes when men have cast the die and gone the whole length . . . ." Villard's remarks brought a shower of abuse from the press and important public figures.[51] Threats from various groups and business organizations to wage a boycott against *The Post* led him to regret somewhat his public statements for nonresistance. He was now alienated from the staff of his own newspaper. He wrote his mother that their faces instantly reflected how obnoxious his views were to them. He reassured her, in a typical reply, that he felt that the Garrisonian blood in him demanded steadfastness to principle.[52]

The President was undergoing much the same anguish as Villard. On the evening before his declaration of war, he stated in precise terms just what the war would mean to Americans. His feelings, as recorded by Frank Cobb of *The World,* in effect rephrased Villard's continual warning that war and individual freedom were incompatible. War, he said, would destroy America's power to bring about a quick and just peace. Liberalism in America would disappear because "America can't fight Germany and maintain the ideals of government that all thinking men share." Wilson predicted with uncanny perspective that "brutality would enter into the fibre of our national life. This brutality would affect Congress, the courts, the policeman on the beat, the Constitution cannot survive another war." To Cobb he questioned anxiously, "if there is any alternative, for God's sake let's take it."[53] Wilson believed that to enter the war would be to sacrifice the power and prestige of a disinterested moral position. He was dismayed at the ironic situation that would make him depend on the support and enthusiasm of his political enemies, those with a vested interest in the war.

This tormented man was the man Villard indicted for the rest of his life as the betrayer "who had put us into the war." With so much in common Villard, on the day following the

President's war message, began his campaign to place Woodrow Wilson in the camp of the militarists and those who argued that war is a realistic and legitimate means of settling international disputes. On April 4, 1917, he wrote that the President had become the pawn of the leaders of the old-fashioned diplomacy of intrigue and deceit. He traced Wilson's position from antipreparedness in the winter of 1915 to the declaration of war and interpreted it as the history of backsliding and failure to stand on principle. He quoted from Wilson's speeches, "America must not become an armed camp," and then pointed to the deliberate effort of Wilson to create " the greatest navy in the world." Wilson, he recalled, had been elected on a campaign slogan, "He kept us out of war" and now "he is winning the acclaim of the very business interests that opposed his reelection."

To Villard the issue was a simple one, the clash of two fundamental philosophies:

> The one the belief that the terrible menace of German militarism is best extirpated by force . . . the other that to involve all the American people in this war is to intensify the very evils which are attacked. The one thinks that good can and does come out of wholesale slaughter, provided that the objects are unselfish and the ideals pure. The other holds that by going into the war the United States loses its wonderful opportunity to set a noble example to the world and of finding some better way out of the crisis than by war.[54]

Villard never accepted America's entrance. He was numbered among that small group of purists who remained steadfast to the doctrine of nonresistance. Only when Wilson began to articulate the plans for peace did he again throw his support behind the administration.

A generation of historians, disillusioned by later events, have seen Villard and men of his persuasion as victims of a misguided idealism; as products of a legalistic-moralistic tradition that blinded them to the realities of world politics; as men in a kind of fairyland that needed constant protection from reality, from "exposure to the violence and prejudice and lust that lay within the environment it was presumed to replace."[55] One study of the period portrayed Villard as a man driven by an "obsessive zeal for the right" who "made a virtue out of ignoring expediency." The fatal flaw in this position, it is charged, is that it confused moral and ethical questions with what were in fact questions of national security and the role of power in international relations.[56] In contrast to Villard the editors of *The New Republic*—Herbert Croly, Walter Lippmann, and Walter Weyl—are credited with a far more rational approach to foreign policy. The magazine's self-appraisal of its policy as one of "stern realism" and skepticism of the "moonstruck morals" of pacifism can justifiably be seen as a precedent for the politics of the 1940's and 1950's. *The New Republic* prevailed upon its readers in the fall of 1914 not to let "irrelevant moral judgments or blind patriotism befuddle a cool disinterested appraisal of the national interest." Their editorials during these years have been described as "distinguished by their objectivity, deliberate calmness and sense of balance."[57]

Such a judgment mistakes opportunism for realism, and indecision for flexibility.[58] *The New Republic*'s editorials often veered from one position to another. They ultimately rationalized America's participation in the war as the most forceful means of promoting social progress. They supported their changing positions with such glib journalistic phrases as "differential neutrality," "aggressive pacifism," "constructive patriotism," and "a new kind of war." It is difficult to describe Croly's exhortation that the "American nation needs the tonic of a serious moral adventure" as an example of calm detachment and stern realism.[59] If Villard's intransigence revealed a man who demanded nothing short of a brave new world, *The New Republic*'s optimism over American participation indicated an incredible ability to idealize the real. Woodrow Wilson, after the breakdown of his peace without victory campaign, sadly wondered why his request for a declaration of war should be received with such jubilation. The editors of *The New Republic* provided an answer remarkably remote from his uncertainty: "The cause of the allies is unmistakably the cause of liberalism and the hope of an enduring peace . . . it is now as certain as anything human can be that the war will dissolve into democratic revolution the world over."[60]

Like Villard, the editors of *The New Republic* sought heroes with enthusiasm. While he was never satisfied, they were too easily accommodated. They thought that Wilson had come to their way of thinking, to a kind of softened Rooseveltian nationalism. It would be more accurate to say that they had merely adjusted themselves to the forces which had been beyond Wilson's power to control. Randolph Bourne, a frequent but disillusioned contributor to *The New Republic*, put the case succinctly: "If your ideal is to be adjustment to your situation in radiant cooperation with reality, then your success is likely to be just that and no more. . . . if your policy as a publicist reformer is to take what you can get, you are likely to find that you get something less than you should be willing to take."[61]

Immediately after the declaration of war Villard stood defiant. He received a jocular note from David Lawrence reporting that Joseph Tumulty was preparing a special concentration camp just for Villard.[62] Sarcastically Villard offered Tumulty his sympathy for having to watch the beloved chief congratulated by Henry Cabot Lodge, and enthusiastically endorsed and called upon by Theodore Roosevelt. He noted bitterly that Wilson was being "acclaimed with joy by every munitions maker and every agent of big business and all the forces of evil combined," and reminded Tumulty that he had predicted that Wilson would succumb to pressure and repudiate his peace position: "My reputation as a prophet has been enhanced," he boasted. Villard closed with a passage from Wilson's "Peace Without Victory" speech:

It must be a peace without victory, victory would mean peace forced upon the loser, a victor's terms imposed upon the vanquished. It would be accepted in humiliation, under duress, at an intolerable sacrifice and would leave a sting, a resentment, a bitter memory upon which terms of peace would rest, not permanently but only as upon quicksand.

"As for myself," he said, "I am having these beautiful sentiments printed on a large card as a sort of loyalty pledge to the President."[63] He did. Over the years those words printed on yellowed pasteboard remained with him as mementoes of war.

CHAPTER SIX

The New Diplomacy
1916-1917

In May 1919 Hutchins Hapgood wrote Villard welcoming him into the ranks of dissenters. Hapgood was prompted to do this because of the "remarkable change" that took place in Villard's political and personal position during the war. Villard's editorial direction had made *The Nation* one of "the most fearless and sound and forward looking journals in the country."[1]

Villard, in a revealing reply, gave his interpretation of the change:

> Of course there has been a great change in me. I do not see how anyone could have stood still during the last four years. One must have either moved to the left or to the right, and I have gone to the left; not so far as you I fancy. I cannot embrace either the socialist or communist doctrine . . . but one must be either for or against the present political order.

> I do not want my children to live in a world managed politically as the present world has been. I realize fully the danger of my position so far as *The Nation* is concerned. It is that I shall fall between the two stools through unwillingness to go to the extreme left, but that I cannot help. Perhaps I am too well off and too happily situated in life—perhaps I haven't been close enough to the working people. Yet I have had my suffering too during these last four years, and I am still under heavy social pressure of all kinds, but my suffering has not been quite due to that; it is due to the sense of spiritual out-

rage at the injustice and wickedness that we are seeing . . . the difficulty is that I do not see a way out which militates against any leadership on my part.[2]

In April 1917 a vast number of Americans did not want war, but for most of them reluctance disappeared with the final declaration. Woodrow Wilson, who had desired a "peace without victory," looked with little favor on a "war without victory." The President, under fire from more partisan Americans, found himself calling for an unconditional surrender and warning, "woe be to the man or group of men that seeks to stand in our way."[3]

Those who had supported American preparedness were the most outspoken in their demand for 100 per cent support of the American government and its associates. Both the National Security League and the League for National Unity were largely supported by the conservative well-to-do classes in America, who viewed the war as a defense of nineteenth-century tradition. Even George Creel, the head of the Committee on Public Information, conceded that the National Security League and the American Defense Society were obnoxious in their extreme insistence on chauvinistic conformity. It was only logical, he wrote Wilson, that progressive-minded people would oppose the war effort and be skeptical of America's aims.[4] Many reformers feared that the war would bring the end of domestic reform. The socialistic groups asserted that America's entrance "was instigated by the predatory capitalists" and that the motive was protection of loans to the Allied powers. The war was neither in the interest of the working man nor was it a war to save democracy.[5]

Villard's participation in the anti-preparedness campaign, his publicly defiant pacifism, and his German-American background made him the perfect target for professional patriots. He was accused of being a friend of socialists and anarchists, a veritable agent provocateur in touch with the Kaiser.[6] America's ambassador to Berlin, James W. Gerard, told reporters that *The Post* invariably represented the German point of view. Villard was personally harassed, his children were jeered at in school, his dachshund pup stoned, and he was referred to as "the Kaiser" by his neighbors.[7]

Villard bore the accusations of the sensationalist press good-naturedly but the subtler repudiation by members of his own class left lasting scars. In March 1917 he was asked to resign his presidency of the Philharmonic Society. Old Harvard classmates and members of his club were ostracizing him or were painfully embarrassed at chance meetings.[8] The banishment from the world of respectability deeply disturbed him. Despite some eccentric political positions, he had never cut himself off from his class and its standards of culture and morality. Now his friends, who felt the war was defending the American way of life, related him to the IWW, the anarchists, and all the other subversive elements of the time.[9] In the face of this, Villard maintained his pacifist convictions and in the long run gained stature and respect as an independent critic and journalist. But in 1917-1918 he felt abandoned by the very class whose values had motivated his actions in the past.

Villard felt alienated from American society in general. He shared Randolph Bourne's despair at "the cry of hate and vengeance so strident, the chorus so mighty that to be out of it was at first disreputable and, finally, almost obscene."[10] It was, Villard said, like standing on the bank "watching the tremendously reinforced tide of national life go by."[11] Every day Villard saw some of his former associates in the peace movement capitulate. Men like Nicholas Murray Butler and Rabbi Benjamin Wise, who had been among the charter members of the League to Limit Armaments, now came out with statements in support of the war and charged those who continued to oppose it with contributing to the German cause. Prominent American Socialists such as William English Walling, J. G. Phelps Stokes, Robert Hunter, and Charles Edward Russell abandoned the party because of its opposition.[12]

Because Villard's pacifism was an ethical position rather

than a religious one, he was not prone to a quiet withdrawal from affairs. He was, for some time, affiliated with the Fellowship of Reconciliation, which was largely devoted to a religious exposition of the pacifist cause and was a haven of comfort to less militant souls.[13] After American intervention the Fellowship, under the guidance of Villard, Norman Thomas, and other aggressive leaders, took a more positive position, stating that they were not merely against war but "a Fellowship devoted to the establishment of a worthy peace."[14]

Villard advocated a hard-hitting liberal journal to present the Fellowship's position and program, one that dealt with specific issues and defended pacifism, free speech, and other civil liberties in a realistic vein.[15] He feared a whining, self-pitying tone and felt that only an active and militant program could save the pacifists from ridicule and ineffectiveness.[16]

Villard's position, adopted shortly after American involvement in the hostilities, contained two major objectives—liberty at home and peace abroad. He favored immediate and specific statements of war aims by all belligerents and continued efforts to achieve a negotiated peace. He also hoped for a "scientific" peace that would be impartial and insure a lasting settlement, rather than sow the seeds for future wars.

Villard threw himself into the battle for the first aim immediately. When a pacifist rally in Philadelphia was broken up by the police on April 5, the editor of *The Philadelphia Public Ledger* wired Villard to ask him whether his position on opposition to the war had changed. Villard replied for publication: "I believe the American constitutional right of free speech should never be abridged. It is the cornerstone of our liberty and of democratic self-control. The right to criticize the Government is never more vital than in war time."[17]

To David Lawrence, a staunch supporter of laws to suppress subversive utterances, Villard wrote that *The Post* had a duty to fight unremittingly for freedom of speech and the press. Refusal to go along with the "mob spirit of the present moment would mean financial loss," but "it is pleasant," he said, "to serve one's country even when one's country temporarily doesn't appreciate it."[18] Suppression of the liberal press was more dangerous than the "socializing of the state." "Vigilance is the true price of liberty," he proclaimed in *The Post*. "Prussianizing is coming not only by statute but also by a change in point of view. Those who preach the complete subordination of the individual to the state are the real Prussians and are more to be feared than a careless editor or any commander of a Prussian U Boat."[19] Freedom of the press was seriously challenged during the war, and Villard vigorously protested the rider, attached to the Trading With the Enemy Act, which would give the Postmaster General power to crack down on the liberal journals at his discretion. Such permission would do "more than anything else to create sedition and disloyalty and anarchy than anything that has taken place."

At this time Victor Berger's socialist *Milwaukee Leader* was being suppressed as seditious. Villard warned Tumulty that such tyranny was outrageous: "His political doctrines are not yours as they are not mine, but he is surely legitimately engaged in presenting the news of the world from the point of view of socialism. Is it not possible," he pleaded, "to make Postmaster Burleson and his underlings understand that the Socialist doctrine is now supreme in a half dozen European countries" and that "it is a perfectly legitimate political propaganda for a mode of living that most of us would be for because of its essential democracy if we could believe in its economic basis?" Villard's repeated attempts to arrange an interview with Wilson met with equally persistent refusals.[20]

Villard and Roger Baldwin, a director of the American Union Against Militarism and future president of the newly-formed Civil Liberties Union, presented a plan to Wilson for the protection and sympathetic treatment of conscientious objectors. Tumulty assured them that it would be given careful consideration. When the mistreatment continued, Villard wrote Tumulty criticizing the administration's laxity and noted, "How much less generous America's laws are than the

British."[21] He reported all infractions of the law respecting the rights of conscientious objectors and defended stoutly public statements that justified the right of men to refuse to take arms.[22]

Liberty at home, however, was inextricably connected with the "peace abroad" plank of his program. The hysteria and hate generated by the war would make the pacifists' objectives for the peace far more difficult. Wilson had repeatedly asserted that when German militarism was defeated America would treat the Germans with respect and comradeship, and this principle was reaffirmed by all those in favor of a new diplomacy of enlightened benevolence.

Villard's ideas on peace and international relations reflect a general body of thought expressed by liberals in England, France, Germany, and Russia, in opposition to the "old diplomacy" of division of the spoils and intrigue. A new age had dawned when nations could conduct their relations on a more reasoned plane. The balance of power theory was repudiated. Villard was still confident that free trade and anti-imperialism would lessen the possibility of future war.

As early as December 1914 Villard called for a comprehensive plan for disarmament and a world federation. On April 25, 1915, he wrote a glowing tribute to Wilson for a speech the President had made before the Associated Press calling for a new international order and a greater voice for the people in the conduct of diplomacy.[23] Villard was giving voice to demands for the "new diplomacy" eventually pursued by Wilson.

The "realist" school of historians have interpreted Wilson's diplomacy as uniquely American, a reflection of America's traditional sense of mission. This nation was immature and had little appreciation of the intricacies and importance of the European balance of power. Wilson was leading an evangelical crusade for peace and ignoring the realities of the world situation. These critics firmly maintained that such a naively idealistic course was American in origin and development.[24] In fact, this approach reflected the aspirations of liberal thought throughout western Europe and to some degree in Russia. The principles of disarmament, open diplomacy, a more democratic control of foreign policy, and a world federation formed the basis of the program of such British liberals and independent socialists as E. D. Morel, J. A. Hobson, and Norman Angell more than a decade before Wilson's public acceptance of them.[25] Liberal editors in London reported England's participation in a war for "the spiritual governance of the world." The cheerful phrase, "the war to end wars," so often attributed to American innocence, has been credited to H. G. Wells and had been used as far back as the Crimean conflict.[26]

The liberals and radicals in England who remained steadfast in their opposition to the war established, in the fall of 1914, the Union for Democratic Control, which attracted such distinguished statesmen and journalists as Charles Trevelyan, G. Lowes Dickinson, Arthur Ponsonby, E. D. Morel, Norman Angell, Noel and Charles Buxton, Ramsay MacDonald, Philip Snowden, George Lansbury, and H. N. Brailsford. Its statement of objectives anticipated all of the major ideas later contained in Wilson's Fourteen Points. G. Lowes Dickinson is credited with the phrase, "league of nations."[27] Lawrence Martin has written that "at the outbreak of the war the United States had a President who not merely developed a foreign policy explicitly based on liberal principles but consciously relied for inspiration on the example of English writers and statesmen."[28]

Villard, like Wilson, was in touch with many members of the British movement in the period 1914-1920. He heard from C. P. Scott of *The Manchester Guardian;* H. W. Massingham of the London *Nation;* Francis W. Hirst of *The Economist* and later founder of the journal *Common Sense;* and Lady Barlow and Caroline Cummings of the Union for Democratic Control. J. A. Hobson later became a London correspondent for *The Nation.* Sophia Sturge, who had first notified Villard of the formation of the U.D.C., introduced him to E. D. Morel through correspondence. Villard agreed wholeheartedly with the organization and praised Wilson for presenting a program "which the U.D.C. and other British dissidents have already insisted upon."[29] British and American censors hampered Villard's communication with British liberals, but he continued to write the Sturges by way of the West Indies and kept up with the activities of the U.D.C. and the British liberal dissent in general.[30]

A lack of democratic control, Villard wrote his British correspondents, was at the bottom of the European struggle and America suffered from the same problem. He favored a constitutional amendment that would require a national referendum for a declaration of war.[31] The British, in early August of 1914, debated this issue and opposition forces protested that Lord Grey had secretly committed the British to an alliance with France without properly consulting the people's representatives.[32]

Some historians have interpreted this demand for more democratic participation in foreign policy as reflecting the old progressive maxim that the best cure for the evils of democracy is more democracy. The powers of mass persuasion in more recent years do not suggest that referendums would effectively prevent war. However, this, like other aspects of the new diplomacy, was not peculiar to American progressives.

Liberals were split over the degree to which they accepted the war and felt that a complete victory over Germany was necessary to achieve a sound peace. Once war began, many liberal statesmen claimed that only a decisive victory would insure their liberal peace policy. In England all discussion of a negotiated peace had been throttled by the government. Wilson's apparent abandonment of the "peace without victory" formula was complete by the fall of 1917. When David Lawrence interpreted Wilson's appointment of Colonel House to the Inter-Allied Conference in October 1917 as a sign that America planned to urge the Allies into a statement of war aims as a means of bringing about a negotiated peace, Wilson wrote him a stern letter:

My whole feeling is this: I think you newspapermen have no conception of what fire you are playing with when you discuss peace now at all in any phase or connection. The Germans who have, in effect, realized their program of Hapsburg to Bagdad could afford to negotiate as to all the territorial fringes, and if they could bring about a discussion of peace now would insist upon discussing it upon terms which would leave them in possession of all that they ever expect to get. It is, therefore, very indiscreet in my judgment and altogether against the national interest to discuss peace from any point of view.

Villard viewed this message as "the most disheartening thing to come out of Washington."[33] He shared the fears of the liberals and radicals in England and France. Ramsay Mac-Donald in England, noting the change in the tone of Wilson's speeches, remarked that "whilst you can have a peace without victory, history shows that as a rule nations have had victory without peace."[34]

Wilson was aware of the growing disillusionment among the liberals and radicals in the Allied countries, and with some justification he accused them of underestimating the complexities of America's diplomacy. In a speech in Buffalo he said: "What I am opposed to is not the feeling of the pacifists, but their stupidity. My heart is with them but my mind has contempt for them. I want peace but I know how to get it, and they do not." He denounced Germany for causing the war; House was not on a peace mission but would discuss "how the war [is] to be won, and he knows as I know, that that is the way to get peace, if you want it for more than a few minutes." Villard never forgot this sword-rattling belligerence and sneering ridicule of the pacifists. It confirmed his suspicions that Wilson was not a man to be trusted. Others were shocked by the President's tone; George Foster Peabody, who had previously criticized Villard for not supporting Wilson in the presidential campaign, wrote the President protesting his deplorable attack on men of good will.[35]

Wilson's policy of unconditional surrender was drastically

affected by the revolutionary upheaval taking place in Russia. From the very beginning, his foreign policy had been influenced by the rise of the Bolsheviks to power and particularly by their intensive peace campaign. The Petrograd Peace Formulae of May 1917, echoing Wilson's "peace without victory," had called for a peace without annexations or indemnities based on self-determination. On November 8 they issued a decree of peace and followed this with the publication of the notorious secret treaties, which exposed to the world some of the more nefarious aspects of the old diplomacy. By this aggressive policy they seriously challenged Wilson's leadership of the liberal peace movement and, as one historian has estimated, "contributed as much as Woodrow Wilson to the onslaught on the old diplomacy."[36]

This peace offensive ultimately forced Wilson to abandon his goal of unconditional surrender and to reconsider efforts to agree on war aims. The European nations were war weary and the Russians suggested that peace was within reach. British journals seized upon the release of the secret treaties to step up their crusade for peace.[37]

Villard did more than anyone else to see that the secret treaties received wide circulation in America. He later claimed that he had received them from a Russian sailor who had smuggled them past American censors under his shirt. *The Post*, against the desires of its editors, published the documents on January 25, 26, and 28, 1918. Villard believed that their publication might force the Allied governments to abandon the old diplomacy; if this failed it would at least prevent America from negotiating further secret agreements. He had the treaties printed in pamphlet form and sent to every member of Congress. Copies were offered to all the leading newspapers in the country.[38] Although he was praised by some liberals and radicals, the State Department paid little attention to the treaties and the nine papers that did accept Villard's offer merely published short excerpts.[39] The pro-Ally *New York Times* denounced their release by the Bolsheviks as "beyond the pale

. . . an act of dishonor." "[A] nation that gleefully publishes secret treaties and confidential correspondence would not stop at a little thing like repudiating debts, public or private, or confiscating all property of nationals and foreigners alike." *The Times* was sure that it was "Socialism—German Socialism— that had brought Russia to ruin."[40]

Villard would always claim that Wilson's ignorance of the treaties led in large part to his failure to achieve the goals of a liberal and impartial peace at Versailles: "Having undertaken the greatest brief in the history of mankind those advocates [Wilson and his advisors] failed to prepare themselves by reading material widely circulated in public print in their own country."[41] Although in the summer of 1919, before the Senate Committee on Foreign Relations, Wilson denied knowledge of the treaties, it has been established that he was aware of them as early as April of 1917. While he may not have known all of the specific agreements, he recognized that they hardly represented the disinterested aims and objectives that supposedly justified America's participation in the war.[42] Wilson clearly ignored them in order to mitigate the differences between the Allies and the United States. By the end of the war, he hoped, America's position of power could force repudiation of any previous agreements that were incompatible with his views.[43] Wilson was also fearful that the diplomacy he had advocated since 1916 was being exploited by the Bolsheviks for revolutionary ends completely incompatible with the kind of world order he envisioned. These suspicions contributed to Wilson's reluctance to draw attention to the secret treaties and thereby become too closely aligned with the Bolshevik peace offensive.[44] The wisdom of Wilson's decision is debatable, but one cannot overlook the failure of the press to maintain its primary objective of keeping the public informed. Villard's publication of the treaties, given growing anti-Bolshevik hysteria in America, was an act of courage and public service. The refusal to make Allied war aims clear contributed in part to the "blissful illusion of America fighting on the side of simon-pure angels against pitch black devils," which encouraged the subsequent disillusionment and abandonment of a commitment to world unity after the war.[45]

Walter Weyl of *The New Republic* was profoundly disturbed by the refusal of his fellow editors, Croly and Lippmann, to join Villard in publishing the treaties. This and other examples of the magazine's accommodation to administration policy undoubtedly prompted Weyl to write a critical essay "Tired Radicals," which the editors refused to publish. When independent journalists become part and parcel of the establishment, he wrote, they abandon their indispensable function in democratic society. In 1919 Weyl praised Villard's reorganized *Nation*, which, he felt, encouraged independent criticism.[46]

Villard's insistence on front-page coverage of the secret treaties completed his estrangement from the editors of both *The Post* and *The Nation*. The editorials of *The Nation*, largely *Post* reprints, severely criticized Russia for releasing the treaties in the first place.[47] The editors viewed Villard's indiscretion in this matter, in addition to his pronouncements on pacifism and a negotiated peace, as evidence of his desire to weaken the war effort. Although he had several disagreements with John Palmer Gavit, Villard's disputes with Rollo Ogden were the most rancorous. The tall, spare editor, formerly a Presbyterian minister, had worked as hard as Villard to maintain a judiciously neutral editorial policy before American entry, but he could no longer accept Villard's stance and regarded Villard's apparent enthusiasm for Russia's peace proposals as dangerously close to treason. Villard, in turn, considered Ogden an insipid backtracker. Although Ogden was a shy and retiring man, he was driven by a pious moral intensity and a courage equal to Villard's. An open break in their relationship became just a matter of time.[48] It had always been the official policy of the Villard ownership to refrain from interfering with the chief of the editorial page, but this was becoming very difficult for Villard.

By the end of the year Villard had stopped writing for the paper altogether.[49] In order to have a medium for his own opinions he took over *The Nation* in January 1918, and with the resignation of Howard de Wolf Fuller, Villard became *The Nation*'s editor-in-chief.

At the time of this decision, Villard was planning an extensive speaking tour on the duty of the press in wartime, to be climaxed by an address at the fiftieth anniversary of the University of California. *The Post's* favorable reaction to Wilson's Fourteen Point speech had encouraged him for the moment, and he left in February on his Western trip.[50] In Villard's absence, however, *The Post*, prompted by the harsh terms of the Brest-Litovsk treaty, grew extreme in its belligerency. Villard was both astonished and angered by the tone of the editorial page. He wrote his cousin, Billy Garrison, that he was now "completely out of sympathy" with Ogden and was considering selling *The Post* and concentrating on *The Nation*. He notified Ogden that if he did want to keep *The Post* he would, out of conscience, have to dismiss the editor.[51] When Villard returned from California, he called Ogden into his office. Villard later recalled Ogden's offer to resign as "the most contemptible bit of groveling abasement and whining" he had ever listened to.[52] This does not jibe with what others knew of Ogden, but Villard's tone does illustrate the intensity of his feelings and his lifelong need to settle old scores. Ogden agreed to remain until Villard had reached a decision as to his own plans. Shortly after Villard began serious negotiations for the sale of the newspaper. On July 6 a formal announcement was made of the separation of *The Nation* and *The Post* and on July 31 Villard offered his associates on *The Post* an option to buy the paper. Two days later these men turned the option over to Thomas Lamont, who bought the paper on August 2, 1918.[53]

The sale ended Villard's career as a daily newspaperman. It was, for him, a very painful decision.[54] He had been a good deal more suited to the impulsive demands of fast news-gathering and snap decisions than to the considered and deliberate judgments required of weekly journalism.[55] Moreover, the indirect sale of *The Post* to Thomas Lamont, a member of the House of Morgan, caused him considerable criticism and embarrassment.

He had repeatedly vowed to his Leftist associates that the paper would not be sold to Wall Street, thereby contributing one more daily to the capitalist-controlled press.[56] Many liberals, who had begun to take an interest in Villard's *Nation*, felt that the sale had been a betrayal. Villard wrote years later to Lamont that no single act had subjected him to such bitter attacks. "I was denounced as a fake liberal, a fraud, a man who had sold out to the forces he opposed." Villard, at the time, claimed that he had not known that the option was to be given to Lamont, and that his staff members had treacherously turned over the option. Villard's extreme bitterness at the time of the sale contributed to a final and permanent break with Ogden.[57]

In looking back over his ownership of *The Post,* Villard had nothing to be ashamed of. The newspaper had maintained a remarkable share of its old influence and prestige through perilous times. His influence on editorial matters is subject to some controversy. Allan Nevins, the historian of *The Post* during this period, has asserted that many people erroneously supposed Villard to be the active head of *The Post*: "Actually Ogden decided all positions, wrote nearly all the main political editorials and exerted himself firmly in office management." However, Nevins, himself a former employee of Villard's, wrote Villard in 1922, not long after the sale, that "you and Mr. Ogden were preeminently the makers of *The Post* and that you shaped it on more sides than Mr. Ogden."[58]

It is true that *The Post* was often far more enthusiastic in support of the war than its owner. On the other hand, the restrained and judicial tone of the newspaper in comparison with its competitors was due in part to Villard's insistence. Villard maintained, when questioned about his role as director of policy, that he had hired every editor and mapped out every policy and position in conjunction with Ogden—"until the war came."[59]

Villard, with mixed feelings, threw himself into the work of transforming *The Nation* from a staid literary magazine into a crusading liberal journal. Over the years Villard had shown little sympathy with *The Nation*'s primary interest in literature and the arts. The editors did not pursue the kind of vigorous interest in contemporary affairs that he expected of a journal of opinion, and he could not appreciate their academic literary scholarship and concern for style. He recognized their ability in matters which were of no immediate concern to him, but he looked upon their genteel inclinations as smug and all too often reactionary. Villard considered Howard de Wolf Fuller, who had become the editor upon Paul Elmer More's retirement in 1914, a "very dull person . . . stubbornly narrow [and] utterly unyielding in his prejudices."[60] This feeling of antipathy was shared by the editors. Villard appeared to be a vulgar crusader with philistine tastes. More, upon hearing of Villard's decision to take over the editorship, wrote his fellow custodian of culture, Stuart Sherman, that it was tragic to see *The Nation* fall into the "dirty hands of Villard." Villard would make the magazine his own personal organ, and More predicted that it would disintegrate into a "riot of isms and a feast for all ists."[61]

Villard did not take over active direction of the magazine until the separation of the weekly from *The Post* on July 6, 1918. During this six-month interval his managing editor, Henry Raymond Mussey, ran the magazine. Mussey was a pacifist who had only recently left the faculty of Columbia University under pressure.[62] Villard did write some important editorials during this period, which indicated the direction the magazine was going to take. He also began to recruit a staff of young editors and reporters who were sympathetic to Villard's position toward the war and the peace. For the most part, however, Villard was preoccupied with straightening out financial problems concerned with the liquidation of *The Post* properties. Finally, in late summer of 1918, he was able to settle down to work in earnest on *The Nation*. Under Villard's leadership the entire character and editorial tone of *The Nation* was transformed.[63] In a very short time it became one of the most influential liberal weeklies in the country and a serious rival of *The New Republic*. Its point of view became a rallying point for a number of brilliant young writers who were to be prominent in the field of journalism and letters for years to come. Villard was free at last from the restraining protocol and decorum of *The Post*. No longer was he forced to sit by grimly while antagonistic editors daily repudiated his convictions. He developed a new initiative and fighting spirit which established him as one of America's foremost liberal journalists. Villard continued his discussion of the peace aims in the editorials of *The Nation* and soon brought his magazine into the limelight as one of the most representative and important factions in the great debate over the treaty and the League of Nations.

CHAPTER SEVEN

The New "Nation"
1918

"We are getting down to the fundamental issues . . . I am optimistic enough to believe that the world is going to be a better, cleaner place when the fire dies out," Arthur Draper (London correspondent for *The New York Tribune*) wrote Villard in November 1917.[1] Villard was just as optimistic. The Pope's peace message on August 1, 1917, contributed to the growing pressure from powerful sources for negotiation by the belligerents.[2] Then the Lansdowne letter was published in the London *Daily Telegraph* on November 29, 1917. Lansdowne, the architect of the Entente and a staunch Conservative, had abandoned the theory of the "knock out blow" and called for negotiation. Although Lansdowne's motive was to save the traditional institutions from the growing revolutionary movement in Europe, radicals and liberals were willing to accept support from any quarter and Lansdowne's letter did much to encourage demands for a statement of peace aims in England.[3]

Villard suggested that David Lawrence should become more aware of what was going on in Europe and report the growing demand for peace. Washington, he asserted, was either ignorant or unconscious of the fact that the Lansdowne letter was merely one sign of a more widespread revolt against the continuation of the war. He directed Lawrence to the London *Nation* and *The Manchester Guardian*, periodicals which reflected the movements under the surface in England.[4]

Villard wanted nothing more than to create an American

counterpart of *The Manchester Guardian* or the London *Nation*.[5] Even before selling *The Post,* he began to build a program for *The Nation.* On January 3—just five days before the Fourteen Points speech to Congress and a few weeks before he assumed the editorship of *The Nation*—Villard wrote an article entitled "Some Reconstruction Proposals," which presented the fundamental principles that he believed necessary for a lasting peace. The article was filled with allusions to a new world in the making. He also praised those "amazing men, Lenin and Trotsky," whose peace offensive might pave the way for a serious exchange of views on the part of all belligerents.

Since, to Villard, peace was almost a reality, he demanded that thinking men consider how the world must be reconstructed. They must agree on some broad general principles. The definition of these principles must be based upon a solid moral foundation. Villard did not minimize the immensity of the task but insisted that only by beginning in advance of peace could those who demanded a punitive settlement be thwarted.

Villard then listed the minimum requirements. First must come disarmament, total and immediate, including the end of conscription. Secondly, in keeping with his faith in Manchester liberalism, he called for free trade and concomitant freedom of the seas. Quoting Lincoln's dictum that "no man is good enough to govern any other man without that man's consent," Villard endorsed self-determination as "the guiding principle for the adjustment of national, international and racial relationships." Finally, Villard urged the establishment of an international parliament and an international court to consider all issues between nations, including those affecting national honor.

Villard anticipated the charge of unrealistic idealism. He had discussed these four basic principles with many men, he said, and had found few who did not agree that "if any one of them fails of universal acceptance, then by that much will the millions that have fallen in this war have died in vain." The amazing events of the past three years—the overnight downfall of Czardom, for example—entitled some men "to hitch their wagons to stars as never before."[6]

Villard's speeches on his Western tour in the spring of 1918 were solidly in support of the President's Fourteen Points. It almost seemed as though the personal breach between them had healed. At Berkeley, California, he applauded Wilson's abandonment of the old isolationism and provincialism. He demanded that the nation's press become more attuned to international events and cast off the chauvinism that had characterized their support of the war. The press, said Villard, had a deep responsibility to "crystallize public sentiment in favor of the position that Woodrow Wilson stands for now and after the war." Wilson had realized the futility of war and rightly demanded that it cease. There were no issues between individuals that could not be adjudicated in a proper tribunal, and "none between nations which will not similarly lend themselves to settlement by international judges sitting in an international court." He said he was proud that he had dedicated himself "to the ideals toward which President Wilson now leads the world."[7]

Villard, like many other liberals interested in a negotiated peace, momentarily misunderstood the President's intentions. Although Wilson's Fourteen Points speech demanded a statement of war aims and envisioned a peace with magnanimity and justice, it was much more critical of the German government than of the Allies. The terms he presented could only have been accepted by a defeated Germany. Perhaps Villard was encouraged by Wilson's implicit denial of all prior territorial agreements, but it soon became obvious to him that Wilson's Fourteen Points and subsequent speeches were in no way compatible with his peace without victory position.

In Baltimore, on April 6, the President announced that since the Germans had ignored his peace proposals and insulted him by their demands on Russia at Brest-Litovsk, America would resort to "Force, Force to the utmost, Force without stint or limit, the righteous and triumphant Force which shall make Right the law of the world, and cast every selfish dominion down in the dust." The press took this to be the cue for increased bellicosity, and the "bitter enders," as Villard referred to them, demanded a march on Berlin.[8]

Villard, preoccupied with management details of *The Nation,* refrained from commenting. But William MacDonald, an historian whom Villard had recently recruited, became a particularly severe critic of Wilson. He was quick to point out inconsistencies in the President's speeches. He applauded Wilson's statement of American war aims but was deeply disturbed that "destruction or reduction to virtual impotence of every arbitrary power everywhere" should still be a primary aim. This implicit demand for a democratic Germany would hardly serve to shorten the war. There was also the matter of United States recognition of the Soviet government. In spite of solicitous gestures toward Russia and the peace offensive, Wilson refused to commit America to resumption of full diplomatic relations with Russia.[9]

Villard was deeply concerned about Wilson's continued lack of interest in freedom at home. As early as February he warned Colonel House: "The President will be completely unable to put through his peace program in America unless he can rally behind him the liberal and radical opinion of the country." Instead, "the Administration has been antagonizing, by the stupidity of Burleson and Gregory in their prosecutions of newspapers and periodicals, the very liberals who will be so important to him." Villard wanted Wilson to call in some of the liberal editors of the country, who were "very dubious, not to say bitter about him." He suggested the editors of *The New Republic, The Independent,* and the managing editor of *The Nation,* tactfully excluding himself, as a start.[10]

Villard had struck upon a weakness of the President that was to have drastic consequences. By 1918 much of the restlessness among Wilson's earlier supporters was due to his neglect of civil liberties. Villard felt a serious reciprocal discussion dealing forthrightly with the problems of civil liberties would add needed support to Wilson's peace program and educate the public for this kind of peace. But Wilson, who seldom took men into his confidence, was not likely to invite a meeting with a group of such independent and critical persons. Villard must have felt some sense of vindication as some of the President's most ardent supporters began to accept his earlier predictions that the war would bring intolerance, bigotry, and a general decline in progressivism. John Dewey, who stoutly defended Wilson in the spring of 1917, was now severely critical of the "coercion of opinion." Some of the editors of the rival *New Republic* were becoming disillusioned with their "new kind of war," although their editorials remained hopeful of a "glorious victory." Walter Weyl confided to his diary that Wilson was allowing "liberalism to go by default," and lamented the "timidity of liberals who do nothing to embarrass him."[11] This was obviously a criticism of his colleagues, Croly and Lippmann. In private, however, even Herbert Croly was becoming pessimistic about the outcome of the war and the chances for a democratic revolution. Only Lippmann retained the faith. Croly remained silent and refused to let his own or Weyl's pessimism invade the editorial pages. Their relationship with the administration made criticism seem out of the question.[12] Ironically, it was the "moonstruck moralist," Villard, and not the "stern realist" who understood the dire consequences of Wilson's neglect of civil liberties. Amos Pinchot caustically commented, when the espionage acts were being carried out with unusual rigor, that the President "puts his enemies in office and his friends in jail."[13]

Colonel House promised to bring the matter to the President's attention. On one occasion House called in Lincoln Steffens and admitted that the administration had overdone the propaganda for war and that it was now necessary to begin a campaign of propaganda for peace. He made up a list of speakers to tour the country, with Jane Addams heading the list. He wanted Steffens to make a dry run to see how much peace talk would be received because, according to Steffens, he feared that "in the present state of the popular mind" the milder pacifists "might be lynched."[14] But Wilson did nothing.

Villard did not cease to expose every violation of civil liberties that he and his reporters could uncover. Despite Wilson's Fourteen Points, Villard charged, civil liberties were "trampled on at home by the very champions of carrying democracy to Berlin. A ringing declaration along this line and a Republican promise to undo the wrongs committed is surely a vote getting issue."[15]

The Nation was one of the first liberal journals to oppose America's Russian policy. To many American liberals and almost all radicals, the Russian revolution, even after the fall of Kerensky and the rise of the Bolsheviks, was a symbol of the advance of freedom throughout the world. Villard had written a spirited defense of socialism as a legitimate form of government as early as 1917. When it was rumored that Wilson might succumb to Allied pressure for intervention, William Mac-Donald demanded to know the reason for this change in policy. America had hardly lived up to its protestations about helping Russia and had treated "as an outcast among the nations the only organized government that Russia knows."[16]

Wilson's announcement of America's participation in the Allied intervention in Siberia in July 1918 increased liberal and radical skepticism on both sides of the Atlantic. Wilson had expressed extreme reluctance over the move, which he said was the only way to prevent the transference of German troops to the Western front; many felt, however, that intervention was not a purely anti-German tactic.[17] Villard and Albert Jay Nock (the brilliant and somewhat eccentric journalist who had just joined *The Nation*) wrote bitterly, "The President has assured us that it is only to be a little intervention, and we are to forgive it or approve of it on the grounds of its littleness." The entire venture was a prime example of the secret diplomacy that the President had so recently repudiated.[18]

Tolerance toward Russia was a consistent characteristic of *The Nation* over the next twenty-five years. Villard, who rejected socialism and the violence of the Bolsheviks, adamantly opposed the blind fear and hate that grew up in America. In opposing the more extreme reactionaries, he usually took the side of the radicals, who viewed the Russian revolution as the dawn of a new day. *The Nation* criticized Wilson for not being in touch with the socialist forces. His choice of Elihu Root to lead a mission to Russia immediately following the March revolution indicated a serious lack of communication with the socialists.[19]

When Samuel Gompers was appointed American delegate to the Inter-Allied Conference of Labor and Socialist Parties that met in London in September 1918. *The Nation* severely criticized Wilson's "use" of Gompers to represent labor. Gompers was inextricably attached to the administration and refused to speak to socialists from any country fighting the Allies. British labor leaders like Ramsay MacDonald felt that the A.F. of L. was hopelessly out of date.[20] Villard and Nock joined in a double-barreled attack on the administration in the September thirteenth issue of *The Nation*. Villard criticized the Department of Justice for its massive raid on "slackers" in the metropolitan area. Nock labeled Gompers a drummer employed to "sell this country's idea of victory to the pacifist elements . . . in England."[21]

When this issue was ready for circulation, Villard was notified by the Postmaster General's solicitor that *The Nation's* mailing rights had been revoked. Villard rose to characteristic heights of indignation, but was secretly delighted at this public proof of his charge that freedom of the press was dead in America. He later feigned innocence when he wrote in his autobiography that he and his editors had not the slightest notion what could be labeled unmailable in the issue; just two days before the incident he had written Billy Garrison that he and his staff were "worried about the forthcoming issue of *The Nation*" and that they would be "relieved" when it had passed the censor.[22] He may have privately hoped that his denunciation of the Department of Justice caused the suspension but his close personal friend, Franklin Lane, the Secretary of the Interior, told him it was definitely Nock's criticism of Gompers.[23]

The whole affair was cleared up in a few days. Villard, through the intervention of House, Lane, and Tumulty, persuaded Wilson to rescind the suspension personally. But in those few days *The Nation* was catapulted into national prominence. The incident received wide press coverage and many Americans who had probably never heard of Villard or *The Nation* wanted to get a look at this subversive sheet. *The New York Herald,* a paragon of public virtue and patriotic belligerence, had reported that *The Nation* was the favorite reading matter of enemy aliens. George Harvey was furious over this free publicity and attacked officials for even bothering with a "pacifist jellyfish like Villard."[24]

Villard wrote a letter of thanks to Judge Lamar, solicitor for the Post Office Department, for "the splendid advertisement." He doubted whether $100,000 could have bought such publicity.[25] Villard delighted liberals by relating that the responsible agent in the department had reportedly said that he knew exactly what he was after—"pro-Germanism, pacifism and highbrowism."[26] Certainly no incident however humorous could have better served Villard's personal campaign against infringements upon civil liberties, nor could any incident have brought *The Nation* more effectively to public attention.

While Villard was crusading for freedom on the home front, the tide of the war in Europe turned. The German summer offensive bogged down in July and by August some men in the German high command were conceding that the end was in sight. At the same time Wilson received news that the liberal elements in Europe were losing faith in him. Forces in England that were completely out of sympathy with his peace plans were becoming more and more insistent on a punitive peace. Wilson, even though he had paid no attention to Villard's proposals, was well aware that the belligerent mood in his own country was not conducive to a just and reasonable peace.

Urged on by Colonel House and Walter Lippmann, Wilson took the occasion of a Liberty Loan rally in New York on September 27, 1918, to allay the fears of the liberal elements in England and America. A few months earlier Wilson had heard from the Assistant Secretary of the Treasury, Oscar T. Crosby, who had just returned from Europe, that the Allied leaders did not place much stock in Wilson's league of nations plan. At that time Wilson replied: "I know that Europe is still governed by the same reactionary forces which controlled this country until a few years ago," but that, if necessary, he could "reach the people over the heads of their rulers."[27] His speech in New York was designed to do just that. He spoke eloquently of how, without design or deliberation, the war had become a people's war. He insisted that America enter into no special agreements. It would stand only for "impartial justice in every item . . . no matter whose interest is crossed." He felt it necessary to speak out forcibly and to clear the air of "all the irresponsible talk about peace intrigues and weakening morale and doubtful purpose. . . ." In closing, Wilson again stressed the role of the plain people: "The counsels of plain people have become on all hands more simple and straightforward, and more unified than the counsels of sophisticated men of affairs, who still retain the impression that they are playing a game of power and playing for high stakes."[28]

Villard applauded the speech and especially the President's direct challenge to the Allies that the "peace must involve no discrimination against those to whom we wish to be just and those to whom we do not wish to be just." But Villard could never accept Wilson's premise that the war had been a "people's war," and in an accompanying editorial he charged Wilson with secret diplomacy in connection with the Russian intervention. Villard conceded only that the words of the President about the peace were those of a true statesman; the performance had yet to live up to the rhetoric.[29]

99

During the historic month of October 1918, while Wilson was engaged in intricate negotiations with Germany, the belligerent tone in America reached fever pitch. With victory imminent the desire for revenge vented itself. Lodge and Roosevelt, perhaps sincere in their belief that Wilson might be tricked by the German diplomats, were the most vociferous in their demands for an unconditional surrender. There was no German government, Lodge said, with which he would discuss anything. On the other hand, the partisan tone of their statements indicated their interest in the political advantage of maligning the President and implying a lack of red-blooded Americanism in his willingness to deal with the enemy.[30]

Roosevelt in particular took this tack. His hatred of Wilson had become so obsessive that it usurped his judgment. In a letter to Senators Lodge, Poindexter, and Hiram Johnson, he insisted that America "dictate peace by the hammering of guns and not chat about peace to the clicking accompaniment of typewriters." As for the Fourteen Points as a basis of peace, they were hypocritical and evasive and satisfied none but the "pro-German and Pacifist and Socialist and anti-American internationalists." He called for a Senate resolution repudiating anything but an unconditional surrender. In general the press was equally belligerent, and many Americans looked eagerly toward a march on Berlin.[31]

When Germany capitulated on November 2, Villard shared most Americans' feeling of joyous relief that the senseless bloodshed had come to an end. However, reflection and the relaxation of tension brought forth mixed feelings. Were the terms of the Armistice too harsh? Would they encourage the forces of reaction to attempt a complete annihilation of Germany at the peace conference? Villard, pondering these questions, chose this time to launch his most vigorous criticism of Wilson since the preparedness struggle and America's entrance into the war.

Villard had remained steadfast in his belief in the wisdom of a peace without victory. He now feared that the fact that Ger-

many and Austria had been humbled would make the task of
all liberals and men of good will more difficult.

> The more is the pity that Wilson has made the great blunder
> of allowing his dull and narrow Postmaster General, his nar-
> row Attorney General, and all the other agencies under his
> control to suppress adequate discussion of the peace aims. A
> blind subordination to the patriotic mania that we should
> stand by the President and trust all to him is likely to cost us
> dear. At the very moment of his extremest trial our liberal
> forces are by his own act, scattered, silenced, disorganized, some
> in prison. If he loses his great fight for humanity, it will be
> because he was deliberately silent when freedom of speech
> and the right of conscience were struck down in America.

Villard implored liberals to overlook the President's failings
and to rally behind the man in his fight against the reactionary
forces in the world.[32]

Despite this ominous warning Villard and his editors seemed
to flirt with the very forces they feared. William MacDonald
voiced another criticism of Wilson in an article which appeared alongside Villard's. In view of Wilson's frequent appeals that politics be adjourned, he was appalled that Wilson
should call upon the people to return a Democratic Congress in
the coming election so that he might carry out his peace program more effectively. The President, he charged, had erroneously equated patriotism with membership in the Democratic
party. Although there were obvious political motives, the Republican opposition was "one of the most hopeful signs of
political health." While conceding that the editors were somewhat suspicious of the Republican program, he nevertheless
felt encouraged that the party did not "plan to knuckle under,"
or allow itself to be "branded as a party of obstruction without
vigorous rejoinder." MacDonald repeated Roosevelt's charge
that Wilson had really been evasive as to the kind of peace he
hoped to secure. He warned that if Wilson was "to retain his
leadership in ideas . . . he must drop his discredited role of

autocrat, abandon the secrecy and aloofness that has been his bane, take Congress and the public into his confidence, and play the game of world statesmanship in the open. If he will do this his mistakes as a politician will be forgotten."[33]

Villard and his chief editor were treading on dangerous ground. Their criticism of Wilson stemmed from hopes that were in no way compatible with Republican opposition. To slyly encourage Republican obstruction would hardly serve their interests, but the animosity and distrust that had fermented in Villard's mind over the years now came to the surface. From the fall of 1918 until the absolute rejection of the treaty and the League in 1920, the editorial page seemed almost to hope that Wilson might fail. Villard's letters reflect his distrust. He had a heated exchange with David Lawrence, who deplored both Villard's and MacDonald's editorials and was especially irked by the charge that the President had not made his peace program clear. Villard wrote that although he had not written that article he was in complete agreement with every word. Wilson, he argued, had already abandoned six of his Fourteen Points: "When," he asked, "has Wilson ever taken a position from which he will not recede? You know that I think he is intellectually insecure, without stability and without any principles on which he will stand at any cost." He and his editors "have about as much confidence in Wilson's devotion to the things he says as our soldiers have of a German soldier crying Kamerad with one hand behind his back."[34]

The Nation became Villard's instrument of public revenge for the personal wrongs he felt he had suffered. In the first issue of *The Nation* following the armistice, he wrote two articles occupying a double page. The first announced that the Kaiser's abdication symbolized the decline and fall of despotism throughout the world. The editors of *The Nation* hoped that the "spirit of revolution abroad will not die until the makers of secret treaties are cast out along with the armament makers, the worst enemies of mankind." Villard longed for "no end of democratic ferment in Europe until the professional diplomats of the past have been ground flat." The Kaiser, he argued, was but the "vilest flower of a system." It was "the system as well as the spirit which has to go." If the war had proved anything to Villard it was that "the spirit of Prussianism exists everywhere . . . in Paris, in London, in Rome—and in Washington. Only in Moscow is it wholly crushed to earth."[35]

Villard then turned to the President. Wilson had only himself to blame for the recent election of a Republican Congress, because he had made the election a partisan affair. He was certain that if the peace negotiations were prolonged until the following spring, it would be within the power of the Republicans to block any treaty which did not "conform to their reactionary views."

Wilson faced the greatest challenge of his career. "Today more than ever he must choose between liberalism and reaction. As to his success Villard had his doubts. "Of late the President has seemed so infirm of purpose." He yielded to the "inexcusable blundering invasion of Russia." He yielded to a revision of the freedom of the seas and now, with the armistice, he yielded on his stand against punitive peace by accepting the principle of reparations. Villard asked, "Is the President to rank merely as the maker of skillful phrases and the enunciator of a wonderful platform of principles for a new world, only to retreat when pressure is exerted? There never has been a time since he left Princeton that he would put his back to the wall and say, 'Here I stand. I cannot do otherwise'."[36]

Villard seems to have already made up his mind that the peace and treaty would be a failure before the conferences even began. Wilson had just fought off the reactionaries in his own country as well as Europe. With great difficulty he had forced the Allies to accept his Fourteen Points. Wilson was closer to the ideals and principles held by Villard than any other major figure, yet Villard seemed bent upon undermining the President's power. The personal animosity and old grudges that colored his judgments at this crucial moment in history are most apparent in his closing paragraph:

Mr. Wilson once taunted the pacifists by saying he had contempt for them because they did not know how to get what
they wanted and he knew what he wanted and how to get it.
It was a false taunt; but it may soon be thrown back at him by
others besides pacifists if he does not first show the world that
he knows what he wants and second that knowing he will
stick to it and insist on having it at any cost; that he will go
down to complete defeat rather than yield another inch.[37]

Although many American historians have stated that rumors
of Wilson's compromises and concessions at the conference at
Versailles in the spring of 1919 led to the liberals' bewilderment and subsequent abandonment of their former leader,[38]
Villard's tone and dire prediction is representative of a general
criticism that was growing more apparent each day in liberal
and radical journals in England and America. Versailles was
not a breaking point for those who led the fight against the
treaty and the League. The criticism began when the war
began. Failure to meet liberal goals was anticipated throughout the armistice period and the entire dissenting brief was
well prepared and articulated before the treaty was signed.[39]

The picture of American idealism crushed by the shortcomings of Versailles and reduced to a tragic disillusionment
needs some revision. The London *Nation* and *The Manchester
Guardian* in England expressed more confidence in Woodrow
Wilson than Villard, but they too prepared a careful critique
against the conference and repeatedly predicted its failure.
To assume that the defection and disillusionment that followed was a result of American isolation from Europe, or
American idealism betrayed, is questionable.

As for Villard, personal motives partly influenced his course.
He sincerely favored a peace based on the Fourteen Points.
Nevertheless, convinced of Wilson's weakness, he obviously
derived a certain satisfaction at the thought of the President's
probable defeat. He prepared well in advance to take his place
beside those "pacifists and others" who would throw the taunt
back at Wilson.

CHAPTER EIGHT

Victory Without Peace
1918-1919

On November 18, 1918, Woodrow Wilson shocked the country by announcing that he would head the American delegation to Paris. The editors of *The Nation* privately questioned the wisdom of the move,[1] but publicly said little except that the delegation should be representative of all America and not any special interests, and that it should be thoroughly endowed with a high-principled world view.[2] For himself, Villard decided that as chief executive of *The Nation* he would attend the conference.[3]

Despite his background, Villard was remarkably sympathetic toward the forces of revolution in Germany as well as in Russia, principally as a reaction against the growing anti-Red crusade in the Allied countries and in America. *The New York Tribune* announced that "Bolshevist Russia is the only armed enemy in the field. The allies are still at war with her. She must be crushed as Germany has been crushed." Such hysteria, Villard believed, jeopardized the possibility of a liberal peace conference and provided ammunition for the forces of reaction. Accordingly, he and his editors made a deliberate effort to present the Bolsheviks and the German socialists in a favorable light, and stressed the principles of self-determination and self-government as the bedrock of the administration's peace proposals.[4]

When David Lawrence, still writing for *The Post,* insisted that America must deal only with a German government that met all the requirements of American democratic principles, Villard sent off a vigorous protest. While he was delighted that the Kaiser and his government had been ousted, he feared that American requirements might not be nearly progressive enough and therefore he denounced any interference. He saw in Lawrence's suggestion a loophole for the return of "reactionary imperialism." He reminded Lawrence that America had already "touched bottom in this kind of interference with Russia," and that a similar policy for Germany would "make a mockery of our whole pretense that we stand for democracy, self-government, and the right of people to develop along their own lines, whether they spell bolshevism or not. A people's right of revolution is one of the most sacred there is and no outsiders have a right to interfere with it."[5] A few days later, in response to rumors of a more ambitious invasion of Russia, Villard repeated his position in the columns of *The Nation*. He tried to maintain a tone of disinterested detachment and objective neutrality by insisting that *The Nation* was not pro-Bolshevist:

> It never has and never will approve of reform by violence. But the right of revolution is sacred to a people and the very principle of self-determination forbids us to interfere with political developments in either Germany or Russia. What would we Americans have thought of any foreign nation which should have dared to police us in the days of our chaos and of our infirm government, during the trying and unhappy years of 1781-1789.[6]

Villard was not, like later isolationists, indifferent to the kind of political developments that took place in Russia or Germany. He was not encouraging America's withdrawal from European affairs. But he saw in the various revolutionary forces in Europe, and particularly in the socialist parties in Germany, the only source of liberal ideals that could help check the reactionary forces at the peace conference. He believed that the Bolshevik government would ultimately pass through the initial stages of chaos, violence, and suppression, to order, stability, and a democratic socialism. He looked with enthusiasm on the rise of a pacifist socialist like Kurt Eisner in Bavaria, who repudiated German militarism and promised to build a democratic government. For these reasons he was suspicious of demands for intervention under the guise of democratic rhetoric. He recognized the need for fundamental change in Europe and his hope lay with the forces of movement.

Villard arrived in England on December 13 and was immediately introduced into the circle of British liberals whose letters had comforted him during the war. He was the guest of C. P. Scott of *The Manchester Guardian;* he spent considerable time with H. W. Massingham of the London *Nation.* His own London correspondent, Herbert Horwill, introduced him to Fowell Buxton, a descendent of Thomas Fowell Buxton, the great English abolitionist and friend of Garrison. Fowell Buxton edited the radical *Cambridge Magazine.* Ramsay MacDonald, who was an almost legendary figure to Villard, more than fulfilled his expectations. MacDonald was a true pacifist "who has not been willing to abate one jot from his convictions and, therefore, has been the best hated man in England," a position that perhaps Villard, remembering Garrison, aspired to in America.[7]

Villard's letters were full of enthusiasm for his new friends. He later recalled that he did not believe that Tories or Rotarians or imperialists could possibly experience the satisfaction with a reunion of their kind that he did with the British liberals:

> For one thing there is the joy of being instantly on the footing of an old comrade or friend; we can take many things for granted at once. To be opposed to war; to hold no hate for any peoples; to be determined to champion a better world; to believe in the equality of all men and women; and to be opposed to all tyrants and all suppression of liberty and conscience and beliefs—when one stands on this platform, one has a ready key to priceless friendships.[8]

Villard hoped to make the new position of *The Nation* clear to his new found friends. They were obviously more familiar with *The New Republic,* which had carried articles by such famous leaders of the British Left as H. N. Brailsford, Alfred Zimmern, H. G. Wells, Graham Wallas, S. K. Ratcliffe, and Bernard Shaw.[9] It was not long before *The Nation* did rival *The New Republic*'s reputation among British liberals. Its greatest appeal, however, was to those who had never supported the war.

The week before Christmas Villard gave a talk before the Radical Club at which Pethwick-Lawrence, H. W. Massingham, Robert Dell, Ramsay MacDonald, and the Snowdens were present. At this time Villard wrote that the liberals pinned all their hopes on Wilson and "cannot bear to think that my lack of faith in him has any foundation . . . their only hope is Wilson—they hate Lloyd George with a deadly hatred, feeling about his lack of principles as I do about Wilson's, only a hundredfold more."[10] There was "little to do but back Wilson up against all the rest of the land grabbers."[11] It was the French, Villard observed, who hated the Germans most and were intent on evening the score for what Germany had done to them in 1871.[12]

The hardship and austerity in Britain convinced Villard that whether the "war was fought in vain or not depends wholly on the peace conference." In a rare moment of sympathy for Woodrow Wilson he said, "Never in the history of the world did so much rest on the shoulders of one man."[13]

Seeing the streets of London filled with maimed soldiers, Villard was even more certain of the validity of his pacifist position. He wrote his children, Dorothea and Hilgard:

> When you grow up you will probably meet some people who will try to make you believe that there are worse things in the world than war. But don't you ever believe them. There can be nothing worse and you must say to them that your Daddy told you differently and he knew what he meant.[14]

To his eight-year-old son he wrote of seeing the famous conscientious objector, Hubert Peet, in the Pentonville prison: "I hope that you will never be willing to do anything else than this man has done if you are asked to kill anybody."[15] The kind of men who would lock up a soul like Peet because he held to his conscience "deserve Bolshevism and much worse, and I believe they will get it."[16]

Like most Americans in Europe at the time, whether conservative or liberal, Villard believed that revolution was on the march. He still felt that only a liberal position at the peace conference would temper the revolutionary upsurge and direct it toward democratic goals; an illiberal treaty would certainly incite more violence and destruction. By January 1, two weeks before the first session, Villard in his private correspondence was predicting that the conference would achieve nothing: "What I feel is that we shall get a nominal League of Nations, enough for Wilson to boast about, which will not be worth the paper it is described on."[17] He complained that the American press was giving an entirely false picture of events. David Lawrence was "far too cocksure." More reliable, Villard thought, was Robert Dell, who had been expelled as *The Manchester Guardian*'s Paris correspondent for writing that the Allies were constantly withholding information from Wilson and concealing their designs to scuttle the League and demand a punitive peace.[18]

When Villard prepared to leave for Paris he had trouble obtaining an entrance visa because of the growing reputation of *The Nation* as a liberal pacifist journal. Before he sailed he had enlisted the aid of Ambassador Jusserand. In England, however, the visa was not forthcoming. Finally, through the work of Jusserand and Melville Stone, the head of the Associated Press, Villard was granted permission to enter France. He later heard that Clemenceau had personally agreed only after he was assured that Villard had abandoned his "furious pacifism" and other radical beliefs.[19] "You can imagine how I have complied," Villard reported. He was obviously delighted to think that heads of state considered his influence so powerful as to be dangerous.[20]

The first week in Paris only increased Villard's skepticism. He wrote that the "public now knows what it has all along suspected, namely that despite Wilson's optimism the battle for a clean peace is far from won," although there were some forces fighting for a just peace, most notably the British Labor party. Also, the increasing demand for intervention in Russia loomed large: "Ideas cannot be fought with bayonets," Villard wrote. "Fighting battles against a state of mind is one of the poorest games rulers can play and yet that game is in full swing against Russia."[21] *The New York Times* reported in January that the Paris peace conference had "set aside the question of peace and resolved itself into a discussion of ways and means to check the spread of Bolshevism."[22] Theodore Roosevelt, only three days before his death, insisted that Americans could respect only one flag, the American flag. This excluded the Red flag, which "symbolizes all wars against liberty."[23] Hearing of the Colonel's death on January 7, Villard commented that it was "a divine mercy for the country and another piece of Woodrow Wilson's extraordinary luck."[24]

Despite Villard's pessimistic attitude toward the treaty, he wrote William MacDonald that the danger of a full-scale invasion of Russia seemed over. The Bolsheviks had consolidated their power, contrary to reports in the reactionary press. He added that if MacDonald were there he would be convinced "of the wisdom of the President in coming. If we get anything at all worthwhile the credit will be his." Wilson, he conceded, had steadily "grown stronger since he came over."[25] Villard wrote his wife that he had talked with General Smuts about the General's comprehensive plan for a League of Nations that was receiving careful consideration by Wilson and his staff.[26] Villard, at this time, gained the exclusive permission to print Smuts's plan, which appeared on February 8 in the newly established *International Relations Supplement* of *The Nation.*

Villard was caught up in the excitement of Paris during the conference. His letters and diary describe endless dinners, dashing to and from public offices tracking down rumors, and nights at the theatre.[27] Yet Villard's accounts are mixed with depression and indignation over the ostentatiousness of wealthy Americans and Europeans wallowing in luxuries from profits "made out of the blood and suffering of their country-men. . . ." The upper class in Paris were "gorging themselves while the people starve."[28] Villard stayed at the Hotel Vouille-mont across the Boissy-d'Anglas from the Crillon, where he spent much time in heated discussion with other correspon-dents at the hotel such as Ray Stannard Baker, William Allen White, Ida Tarbell, Norman Angell, and Frank Simonds.[29]

On January 18, 1919, Villard attended the first public session of the conference. *The Brooklyn Eagle* reported that "O. G. Villard Slept Sweetly as Peace Conference Opened." William Allen White, in his syndicated column, gleefully described the scene: "No better commentary could be made on the spec-tacular ineffectiveness of the opening session of the 'Supreme Conference in the History of Mankind' than the simple fact that Oswald Garrison Villard . . . protagonist of peace went sound asleep watching it . . . his head rose and fell with his breathing like that of a deacon with a clear conscience lulled to sleep by a soothing sermon."[30] Villard indignantly denied the story. His eyes were closed, yes, but: "I was trying to think what to write, how to describe what was going on, how artificial and even repellent the whole scene was to me. . . ."[31] In his diary he wrote that the session was "rather solemn and depressing"; that Wilson had "received no applause"; that "there was not one laugh." To his wife he reported that "the hypocrisies voiced were enough to last me a long time. I shall not see any more sessions unless many more seats are assigned to Americans, but shall not care as it was such a dull affair."[32]

Villard quickly lost his indifference when it was announced that newsmen would be barred from future sessions of the Supreme Council. In a letter to Mussey he referred to the "humbug author" of "open covenants openly arrived at," and agreed with William Allen White that "the conference will be nothing more than the good old-fashioned dividing up of the spoils. Clemenceau, George, and Sonnino having gotten rid of the secrecy rule will proceed to remove from Woodrow Wilson every stitch of clothing and turn him adrift naked into a disillusioned world."[33]

Villard maintained a glimmer of hope however; it was rumored that Woodrow Wilson "has a very good League of Nations scheme and even if we can get only a beginning of a proper league it will be something." This was the closest Villard ever came to accepting the half-a-loaf argument of many of the Wilson supporters. He immediately qualified his enthusiasm: "It is proposed to leave to that league the settlement of an infinite number of problems which are before the conference." If this were done, Villard predicted that "in view of the return to secret diplomacy among the heads of state, the world will be worse off than ever, for the world will then continue to be controlled by four men. That is in itself the most dangerous situation the world has confronted since Napoleon was crowned."[34]

Villard's cabled messages to *The Nation* were remarkably mild during the last weeks of January and the first week of February. His feelings fluctuated daily, but because Wilson, in his intentions, was head and shoulders above the other heads of state, Villard felt obliged to temper his criticism and even express sympathy for the overwhelming responsibility Wilson carried. Despite his own reservations he was sure that the liberal opinion of the world was still behind the man, and he agreed that Wilson was their only hope "that the outcome will be anything else than a disastrous defeat for liberalism everywhere."[35]

Villard tried to keep some esprit, but like so many of the correspondents, he was becoming restless. The daily news conferences conducted by Lansing and Bliss were a "farce." He felt that his articles to *The Nation* were unnewsworthy largely because reliable news was so difficult to obtain.[36] Paris was flooded with rumors. Captain Walter Lippmann, a member of the President's Inquiry, who spent some time with Villard, wrote of the atmosphere of the conference days: "Newspaper correspondents, struggling with this illusive and all pervading chaos, were squeezed between the appetite of their readers for news and the desire of the men with whom the decisions rested not to throw unconcluded negotiations into the cyclone of disorder."[37] Villard, discouraged with the secretive atmosphere, wanted to get out of Paris and into Germany. He managed to get there, in spite of the President's travel restrictions, by way of the conference of the Socialist Second International meeting at Berne.[38]

A. J. P. Taylor has said that the Second International was planned by European labor radicals as a kind of anti-conference of their own, whereby they would lay down the terms of a peoples' peace regardless of what the official statesmen were doing. The implication is that European radicals had made up their minds before the treaty was written that it would not be acceptable to the workers of the world.[39] This helps to explain Villard's own early skepticism. His approach to the treaty and the League was couched in the rhetoric of European radical dissent; his emphasis on a "peoples' peace" took the official line of the European socialist groups. His letters and dispatches from the Berne Conference reflect his agreement with the general point of view expressed there. He advocated "taking the whole matter of peace out of governmental hands and placing it in the hands of a democratic gathering of democratic people, the real representatives of those who have fought and bled and died for their countries."[40] Villard thrilled at the intensity of Kurt Eisner, the Bavarian Socialist, who bitterly attacked German militarism and repudiated the Majority Socialists who supported the war. In a ringing appeal for open diplomacy, Eisner warned the world that a war could not be terminated by lies nor a revolution be organized by lies. The Socialist's brave fight against reaction, his unflinching courage and open defiance were the virtues that Villard had earnestly looked for in Paris.[41]

Villard's position was that of the Union for Democratic Control and of Wilson when he had deliberately encouraged the revolt of the masses in Germany against their rulers. Now with victory won, but with Bolshevism gaining more and more strength, the expedient wartime measure of flirting with revolutions was no longer popular. For Villard to pursue such a tack was hardly an aid to Woodrow Wilson. On the contrary it encouraged the growing Leftist critique of the treaty. Despite the failure of the revolutions and the perversion of their objectives Villard never repudiated his support of the delegates at Berne.[42]

On February 17 Villard prepared to leave Switzerland. He crammed his luggage with coffee, soap, chocolate, and various other scarce items for his relatives in Munich and Berlin. The customs officials berated him publicly and told him he could never return to Switzerland, but they allowed him to leave, neglecting to search his person, which was equally padded with contraband. From Lindau he entrained for Munich, where he was to stay at a hostel, the Beselerhof, which was diagonally across the street from the Bavarian Landtag. Munich was in a state of chaos. Eisner, who led the revolt against the former government in November, had established the first German Republic, and had been chosen President. Though not an extreme radical, he had opposed the new German government led by the Majority Socialist Friedrich Ebert, who was trying to unite moderate factions in order to draft a democratic constitution creating the Weimar Republic.[43]

Villard found himself in the center of the warring factions and was threatened at the point of a pistol when he attempted to interfere with officers who were beating up some veterans. Two days later (February 21, 1919), he was present in the Landtag when Eisner's secretary rushed into the chamber waving the President's gold-rimmed glasses and shouting that Eisner had just been assassinated. Villard rushed across the street to cancel an engagement. In his absence an assassin burst into the chamber and fired at one of the moderate Socialist ministers, whereupon guns from the galleries were turned wildly upon the press box, forcing the correspondents to crawl out of the chamber on their hands and knees. Villard was deeply disappointed at missing the show.[44]

That night Villard watched the fighting in the street from his hotel window between the vengeful radicals and the moderate and Right-wing extremist groups. A few days later Villard attended a meeting of the Council's Congress, composed of delegates from the Soldiers', Workmen's, and Peasants' Councils and largely dominated by the extreme Left-wing Spartacists. The session was interrupted by a group of uniformed, armed men who insisted that everyone in the Landtag chamber raise their hands over their heads. When Villard demurred, he was singled out and forced to comply. The men dragged out the two Communists, Dr. Max Levien and Kurt Muchsam, and proceeded to pistol whip them before they could be rescued.[45]

For the next weeks Villard traveled through the darkened, curfewed streets of Munich. He visited Levien, whom he later described as an extraordinary personality. His bandaged head made him resemble a pirate chief surrounded by a band of ruffians. Villard admired Levien's forcefulness but regretted that Bavaria should be so devoid of leadership after Eisner's death that an extremist should assume control. While he had no sympathy for Communism and was far from committed to Socialism, he was sympathetic to substantial improvements in the lot of the working class. He later wrote that the brutal assassinations of Karl Liebknecht and Rosa Luxemburg, the popular moderate leaders of the Spartacist movement, was a "short sighted crime" because these two "extremely fine spirits, whatever their political views, would have exercised an ameliorating power had they but survived."[46]

Villard left Munich for Weimar, which he found teeming with old, reactionary men who gave only lip service to the ideas of the Republic. From there he went to Berlin—it was Munich all over again. The city was in the throes of a general strike. Shootings in the streets occurred daily as the Spartacists bitterly fought the Majority Socialists. The people seemed strangely divorced from the partisan battle raging about them and took little notice when a soldier or even a civilian was shot down in broad daylight. One day when an insurgent leaned out of a window directly over Villard's head and shot a sentry, Villard scanned the roofs for snipers. He was informed by his companion that such consternation was considered bad form.[47]

Considering Villard's background and the relatively bland atmosphere of American politics, his apparent coolheadedness and objective analysis of what was occurring in Germany does him great credit. He was excited and pleased to be one of the few American newsmen in Germany and was enraptured by his position as a foreign correspondent. In his letters and later published accounts he compared the conditions in Germany to those of the French Revolution.[48]

A visit with his Aunt Emma in Munich gave Villard an insight into the plight of those in the middle class, who were terrified by the violence around them. He felt compassion for her despair and bewilderment: "She has had to sell her jewels to keep going and she has not bought a dress since the war began. Her loneliness is pitiful and her fright at what is happening is well warranted. She kept asking me why, why, why, had the Kaiser fled and the King fled? The very ground seemed sinking beneath her."[49]

Villard's sympathy for his wealthy aunt did not blind him to the dangerous reactionary forces that remained in the country. He had little respect for the compromising Majority Socialists, who through their brutal Minister of War, Gustav Noske, employed members of the reactionary officer class to put down the Spartacist uprisings. More discouraging was the lack of genuine leadership among the Left-wing Socialists, whose lofty aims far surpassed their political ability. Villard felt at the time and continued to believe that the Majority Socialist government was too timid and cautious. They had been too soft on the old reactionary elements, and although he repudiated violence, he felt their revolution had not been drastic or thorough enough. Their obedience to old forms and institutions made the creation of a genuine democratic socialist state impossible.[50]

Villard was certain that the havoc and chaos would provoke a Bolshevik blood bath. He felt the only way to bring some sense of order and sanity to the situation was for the Allies to provide the German people with food at once. Villard insisted that the blockade, still in effect, was encouraging the Bolsheviks.[51] Villard wired Colonel House and Hoover from Germany describing the terrible conditions and pleading with them to do all they could to urge the British to lift the blockade. House and Hoover were apparently impressed, since they gave Villard's descriptive wires to the Associated Press and his pleas were published throughout the world. The blockade was lifted soon after.[52]

When Villard returned to Paris on March 18, he was a celebrity. The government's intimidation of newsmen traveling in Germany had allowed him to cover the situation virtually without competition. He wrote proudly to his wife of his reception and his lengthy interviews with Lansing, Lloyd George, Tasker Bliss, and the American journalists: "All the newspapermen think I have had the most interesting experience of anybody. I would not have missed it for the world."[53] Villard wrote Herbert Horwill, "You would be amused at my sudden return to respectability; from being the despised pacifist I was, I am suddenly respected again and a person of influence." He reported that "even the Army . . . is now apologizing in the person of Pershing himself and placing a motor at my disposal. . . . Thus do the wicked flourish."[54]

Villard told Lloyd George that he doubted whether Germany would accept the kind of treaty that was in the making. Lloyd George replied that "in that case we will slap the blockade on again." Villard told him that the moral sentiment in England and France would not allow a renewal of the extreme blockade. Only garrisoned troops in Germany would compel their submission and popular sentiment was opposed to this. Undoubtedly Villard overestimated the forces of resistance, for he continued to believe that Germany might refuse to sign the treaty and while in Germany he had encouraged officials to do so if it was not in accord with the Fourteen Points.[55]

After this conversation, Villard was convinced that Wilson and the American delegation did not really know what was going on. Villard attempted to see the President but Wilson was not interested. When he asked House to arrange a meeting, House told him that the President had said he knew all that Villard knew "and a good deal more besides."[56] Nothing could have angered Villard more. Although Villard was rebuffed by Wilson, he had long talks with Secretary Lansing and Lord Robert Cecil. Lansing, he reported, was dismayed over events and agreed wholeheartedly with Villard's analysis of Germany. He told Villard that "what Europe was facing was so menacing" that he could no longer take any interest in the League of Nations.[57]

The atmosphere in Paris had changed while Villard was away. His absence roughly coincided with Wilson's trip home to present the plan of the League to the Senate. The disheartening reception in America had encouraged his adversaries in Europe to demand more concessions.[58] There were rumors that, in view of the Senate opposition, plans were afoot to scuttle the League at Paris.

Wilson was remarkably successful during the first phase of the conference from January 15 to February 15. He did center world attention on the League of Nations. He forced the reluctant Allies to accept the Covenant as an integral part of the treaty. He thwarted an early attempt to parcel out the colonial spoils by demanding a League-controlled mandate system. On his return to Paris on March 15, he had, in his opinion, foiled an attempt to sidetrack the League by agreeing to a "preliminary treaty of peace" and settlement of the League question later.[59] But Wilson's optimism was premature. The French, under the guidance of Clemenceau and supported at critical moments by Lloyd George, now demanded guaranteed security against future German aggression, by rendering Germany economically as well as militarily impotent. This new French belligerence, encouraged by Wilson's loss of prestige at home, was largely responsible for the pessimism that had grown up over the future of the treaty and the League. Ray Stannard Baker has referred to this period as the "dark days of the conference," and Villard's letters support Baker's description.[60]

He wrote Herbert Horwill in London on March 20 that Frank Simonds, *The New York Times* correspondent, had told him that the conference was utterly wrecked. Simonds had been fired because *The Times,* resisting the truth, would not tolerate his pessimistic reports. Melville Stone told Villard that he had canceled his boat home because he expected the conference to break up within a week. There were rumors that a number of younger men on the American delegation planned to resign because the Fourteen Points were now being abandoned one by one.[61]

The final degradation of the short-lived experiment in new diplomacy was the reduction of the Council of Ten to the Council of Four on March 15. John Dos Passos' description of Clemenceau, Lloyd George, and Wilson as "three old men shuffling the pack, dealing out the cards" gave classic expression to this resentment.[62] Villard wrote his friends that his lack of faith had been justified. The note of personal vindication, characteristic of his earlier letters, reappeared in an almost buoyant satisfaction over the imminent failure: "If the conference should go down it would be the most remarkable moral happening in history, for it was conceived in hypocrisy and falseness and carried on in a spirit at variance with the pretended objects of the war. *It would prove that war cannot be ended by war and many other admirable things.*" Almost as an afterthought he added, "When one thinks of the misery and disillusionment that will come if it fails, one hopes for its success."[63]

Villard continued his pleas for aid to the German people. His harping on their sufferings irked some of his journalist colleagues. William Allen White wrote his wife that over luncheon Villard was so full of sympathy for the poor Germans that "I wanted to choke him . . . once a Dutchman, always a Dutchman. He wants Germany let off from any penalty for the war—and I had to pay for his food while he talked away."[64] In fact, Villard had based his argument primarily on the grounds of checking the spread of revolutionary violence. He had written to his wife that the Germans could never make up to the world the misery that they had wrought.[65] White later conceded that Frank Simonds and Oswald Garrison Villard were the wisest journalists at the conference.[66]

Villard's last cables did not deal with the intricacies of the conference itself, largely because he did not have the facts. The all-absorbing subject for speculation was the Russian revolution; he discussed the probabilities of world-wide revolution and possibilities of Allied withdrawal of forces from Russian soil. He was aware of the clandestine efforts of the American delegation to reach agreement with the Bolshevik government, but his hopes fell when he learned that the Prinkipo conference had failed to reach a cease-fire agreement between the Bolshevik armies and the counter-revolutionary forces, and that the quasi-official mission of William C. Bullitt and Lincoln Steffens to Moscow did not produce any fruitful results because of the reluctance of the Allies to give de facto recognition to the Bolshevik government.[67]

On March 20, immediately before his departure, Villard wrote his wife of the breakdown of negotiations with the Russians: "Never was there such a bankruptcy of statesmanship, chiefly because of Wilson's cowardice and insincerity. It can be written down now that whatever happens it will be such a miserable compromise as to avail nothing for the security of the world."

Villard, in a moment of self dramatization, assured his wife that he could understand the gravity of the crisis because he had looked revolution in the face. He suggested that she buy a secluded farm in the country. "I could," he wrote, "go to Russia in a responsible position and do a whole lot of things. But it's home for me. I have had all I want of Europe for some time."[68]

This last sentence was prophetic of the mood of many Americans in the spring of 1919. Villard always claimed that his position was a truly internationalist one, but when he returned home he soon joined his editors in giving aid and comfort and eventual victory to the isolationist band who also had had all they wanted of Europe for some time.

CHAPTER NINE

The Little Band of People Who Saved the Country

1919-1920

When Villard rejoined his staff in April 1919, *The Nation* had already begun its mission to undermine the treaty and the League. As early as February, Albert J. Nock denounced the whole conference in Paris for "consistently ignoring the spirit and principles of liberalism."[1] By March 22, no longer content with predictions of failure, Nock took a position of outright opposition to the treaty and the League. This, the most savage attack yet printed, hinted at what was to come. Wilson's insistence that the League be an inseparable part of the treaty was little more than the cheap political trick of a "rider." Sensitive to fighting alongside such traditional enemies as Senator Henry Cabot Lodge of Massachusetts and Senator Philander C. Knox of Pennsylvania, he argued that *The Nation* was opposed to the outcome of the conference because it had not lived up to liberal commitments or aspirations.[2]

Villard's first important article after his return appeared in the April 26 issue. By that time Wilson had passed through the real power struggle in Paris and concessions concerning the Saar Basin, the Rhineland occupation, German reparations, economic rights on the Shantung peninsula, and various other liberal aims had leaked to the press. Villard indignantly announced that the peace conference was no conference; it was a "palpable fraud upon the world." As far as Villard was concerned the League was "only another Holy Alliance."[3]

Villard was astonished at Wilson's audacity in agreeing to a security pact with England to protect France against future aggressions. Given his pacifism as well as his disrespect for the Allied leaders, he could not possibly appreciate the concept of a collective security maintained by such bankrupt statesmen. This threat of force to police a world which so few had any part in making "dealt the coup de grace to [Wilson's] own creation." Villard warned ominously that the proposed League gave the possibility of a "world dictatorship so odious as to make a revolution in Russian style seem almost tolerable." Despite "the slogans and the confident belief that it was to be a war to end war and to make the world safe for democracy, the war thus far has made the world less safe for democracy than it has been in any previous period in modern times. . . ." He harped on his early opposition to American intervention while liberals who supported the war flocked to his standard.

After final agreement and the presentation of the treaty to the Germans on May 7, Villard again expressed hope that Germany might refuse to sign the document. He was certain, in any case, that she faced a disastrous future, which was evidence of the lack of any statesmanship at the peace conference. It was "neither wisdom nor common sense nor humanity nor diplomatic strategy to put any country, whatever her sins of the past, into such a position. For when the crash comes it will not be Germany alone that will suffer."[4]

Villard shared the duties of criticism with William Mac-Donald, who produced one of the most scathing repudiations of the treaty, the League, and Woodrow Wilson made from the extreme Right to the extreme Left. The language of Mac-Donald's piece ("The Madness at Versailles") surpassed even the previous harshness of Theodore Roosevelt.[5] MacDonald made it clear to newcomers to the ranks that some men of vision had foreseen the outcome all along. Twenty years later Villard still saw MacDonald's article as one of the most "powerful and prophetic editorials ever to appear in *The Nation* or perhaps any other journal."[6] At the time it received nationwide attention.

News leaks and rumors had prepared the world for "a vigorous peace," but not, MacDonald stated, for one of "undisguised vengeance," which "would openly flout the plainest dictates of reason and humanity," and repudiate every generous word that Mr. Wilson ever uttered. "In the whole history of diplomacy" he could think of no treaty that more properly "deserves to be regarded as an international crime." Wilson had repeatedly asserted that America had no quarrel with the German people. The President had warned that a harsh peace would be worse than useless. But now, MacDonald said, "Germany and the German people are virtually destroyed": her territory diminished, her economy ruined by the burden of fantastic reparations, her defenses dismantled while her enemies surround her fully armed.

MacDonald charged that none of the participants were without blame, but "the verdict of history will cast the larger blame on Woodrow Wilson." He had been the hope of democracy and "the fear of his enemies was the confidence of his friends." All the world now knew how Wilson had repaid this confidence:

> The one time idol of democracy stands today discredited and condemned. His rhetorical phrases, torn and faded tinsel of a thought which men now doubt if he himself ever really believed, will never again fall on the ears of eager multitudes.

Then MacDonald, again indirectly, implied that *The Nation*'s editors had known it all along: "The camouflage of ethical precept and political philosophizing which for long blinded the eyes of all but the most observing, has been stripped away and the peoples of the world see revealed not a friend faithful to the last but an arrogant and a compromising politician."

MacDonald declared that the forces supporting the treaty and League were the "staunch supporters of power and privilege, the controllers of great wealth and dictators of social favor, the voluble champions of established order against every form of revolution, the preachers of hate, prejudice and the timid and dependent whose souls are not their own." MacDonald turned the issue into a battle between the "radicals and reactionaries," thus making clear *The Nation*'s Leftist orientation. The overthrow of Czardom in Russia, the constitutional struggle in Germany, the establishment of a soviet government in Hungary, were all examples of a widespread revolt against tyranny in Europe and *The Nation* and other "friends of freedom must now rally" to the support of the great revolution to come.[7]

Villard was delighted with the reaction to the editorial. He sent MacDonald, who was en route to Europe, a batch of press clippings which roundly denounced the magazine. Villard also reported that a member of the Harvard Liberal Club in Boston had publicly announced that it was the greatest editorial to appear in the last hundred years. The Collector of Customs in New York added his bouquet by demanding that the government not allow such "rot" to be published. Villard wrote that Senators Hiram Johnson, Robert LaFollette, and Joseph I. France of Maryland had praised the editorial and added that "the *Evening Post* crowd" was referring to him as "Comrade Villard."[8]

Villard was confident that *The Nation* had struck a vein of liberal thought that would do great things for the journal's reputation and circulation. In the eyes of many liberals *The Nation* had overtaken its most important competitor. Herbert Croly's editorial entitled "This is Not Peace" indicated to Villard and others that *The New Republic* had at last come over "to our side."[9] *The Nation* had never supported the war. It had expressed suspicion of the conference at Versailles long before the treaty was published. Mussey, as early as March, noted that *The Nation*, unlike other liberal journals, was pulling ahead, and assured Villard that if they stuck to their guns the magazine could become the "most influential organ in the United States as far as the interpretation of events and the guidance of serious and responsible thought is concerned." He spoke of circulation figures in the neighborhood of 100,000.[10] Villard laughed this off, but he wrote his wife that he felt he might actually make some money out of the magazine or that it might at least pay for itself, which would be unique for a journal of its kind.[11] From August 1918 to July 1919 *The Nation*'s circulation rose from 8,756 to 29,450. By September it had surpassed the circulation of *The New Republic*.[12]

It is not true that *The Nation* was pursuing a "new tack" because it was "paying dividends."[13] Villard's emotions were mixed when he attacked Wilson, the treaty, and the League, but there is no evidence that he ever pursued any policy because of its financial advantage. To suggest this is to misunderstand Villard and to underrate him. He was happiest when he was representing minority opinion. No man enjoyed political conflict more than he did. Even though the circulation was rising, Villard lost out of his own personal funds from July 1, 1918, to June 20, 1919, over $90,000. *The Nation* did not pay for itself until 1927–1928.[14] On the other hand Villard was correct in assuming that *The Nation*'s stand had struck a responsive chord among American liberals. Letters poured in from admirers. "The Garrison blood seems to be coming into its own," one supporter wrote. "It is a very spectacular thing to watch."[15] Villard's personal reputation among American liberals had grown along with *The Nation*'s ascendency. He was no longer considered a stuffy old-timer but a fighting editor ready to give any voice a hearing and to do battle on all fronts.

The public accusation, made before Senate and State investigating committees, that Villard was one of the foremost propagandists and supporters of Bolshevism in the country contributed to Villard's new image. The charge was false but it brought him to public attention. In December 1918, while Villard was still in England, A. B. Bielaski, an investigator for the Justice Department, presented a list to the Senate Judiciary

Committee, which included Villard among the most prominent pacifists and pro-Germans in America.[16] Because the list
named so many Americans of unquestionable loyalty, nothing
came of the charges, but the conservative press made a good
deal of the incident. In January and February of 1919, during
the sessions of the Overman Committee investigating German
and Bolshevik propaganda (which conservatives saw as the
same thing), Villard's name was again mentioned.[17]

Archibald E. Stevenson, a zealous protector of American
institutions, testified before the Overman Committee on all
forms of radical activities. Stevenson, promising not to name
innocent parties, submitted the names of 62 persons engaged
in subversive activity including those of Villard, Roger Baldwin of the Civil Liberties Bureau, Max Eastman of *The
Masses,* Norman Thomas, and the Reverend John Haynes
Holmes. Stevenson charged that all were pacifists before American entry, pro-German during the war, and now active supporters of Bolshevism. They had access to the universities through
the American Union Against Militarism, and he agreed with
Senator William H. King of Utah that the universities "were
a festering mass of pure atheism." Stevenson indicted *The
World Tomorrow,* the organ of the Fellowship of Reconciliation, as "an extremely radical sheet . . . opposed to militarism,
conscription" and even war. What was worse, this magazine
was "now taking up the economic questions of the day along
similar lines." When Stevenson told the Senate committee that
the groups were made up of "intelligentsia and anarchists,
radical socialists and . . .," he was interrupted by a committee
member who asked for a definition of "intelligentsia." Senator
Knute Nelson of Minnesota clarified the meaning for his
colleagues: "Intelligentsia means those anarchists who confine
their operations to brain storms and not physical force."[18]

These charges only added to the prestige of the accused in
the eyes of liberals and radicals. Villard feigned indignation
but undoubtedly relished the personal notoriety and appreciated the free publicity. The press boosted Villard's radical

reputation further by its coverage of a series of speeches made immediately after his return from Paris, in which he discussed the revolutionary upheaval in Europe. He invariably demanded that Americans look at the Soviet "experiment" from a "scientific" point of view, stating frankly his belief that the "Soviet form of government has come to stay in Europe." Americans would gain a good deal if they studied it instead of blindly attacking it; they might even benefit by adopting some of the aspects of the Soviet system. "There is something attractive in group representation which is what the Soviet is." Villard prodded provincial Americans: "No one who has studied recent events abroad can rest assured that America will remain apart from the imponderable world currents and keep unchanged the old America so many of us liked so well, loved so profoundly."[19] Contrary to frequent press reports, Villard did not support Bolshevism or advocate the introduction of Communism in America. He insisted on making a distinction between the theoretical system of Soviet government and the violence of the Bolshevik regime.[20]

Villard's emphasis on the difference between the Soviets and the Bolshevik party and his sanguine assumption that the former might become the bridge to a democratic socialism seems naive. Since the exact intent of various factions during the revolution is still being debated, however, it is unreasonable to expect that observers in the West contemporary with the revolution should have had a firm grasp on the situation. To hold out hope for the victory of some form of Russian democracy over minority dictatorship was not unreasonable in 1919, and Villard believed that the Soviets contained the potential for a vigorous form of native Russian democracy.[21] What is more important, Americans, in their dialogue on the Russian revolution and other radical upheavals, were really debating domestic politics. Regardless of their political persuasions they saw in the revolutionary movements the fulfillment or failure of their own hopes and fears about the future of American society. Villard could not accept the measuring of all revolutionary movements abroad with a yardstick marked off with indigenous American values, and his conservative critics interpreted his tolerance as leading to violence and anarchy, and to the inevitable destruction of American values and institutions.

No one had greater attachment for the "old America" than Oswald Garrison Villard, but his experiences in Germany and Paris had profoundly impressed him with the belief that ideas could not be controlled by bayonets.[22] Certain that the Western world had entered a period of drastic and inexorable transition, Villard feared that America would suffer a revolution like that in Russia "unless a radical program of reform, giving to the laboring classes a different position in the life of the nation, was speedily put through."[23]

After his appearance before the liberally oriented New York State Reconstruction Commission, *The New York Tribune* announced in banner headlines that Villard advocated soviet rule in the United States.[24] Villard wrote many letters protesting this distortion of his words. He had actually said: "There is nothing sacrosanct about our existing form of Government. It must be modified from time to time as conditions change. Thus it is recognized abroad that the Soviet form of organization has come to stay until it has been tried out . . . if it proves its value abroad in solving these terrible problems of human government . . . it will undoubtedly have to be adopted here." If not, "it will be discarded abroad and will not be used here."[25]

Such influential editors as Frank Cobb of *The World* judged *The Nation* as "distinctly Bolshevistic . . . and the most intelligent interpreter of Bolshevism in the United States."[26] Cobb's judgment of the magazine was justified but did not accurately portray Villard's personal position. Villard had come a long way in his political beliefs during the war. But he never found it easy to dismiss the more unsavory aspects of Bolshevik terror, as did the younger generation of liberals who joined the staff during these years. They became increasingly impatient with his commitment to such "bourgeois values" as civil liberties, freedom of the press, and parliamentary democracy. It is doubtful that Villard accepted Henry Raymond Mussey's flight of fancy when he described "the dictatorship of the proletariat" as "a reasonable and peaceful readjustment of institutions and relationships so as to make possible, for the first time in the world's history, the reasonable satisfaction of the reasonable wants of the common man." Nor did he look with much pleasure on an editorial by MacDonald with the leader, "Take Every Empty House," demanding that metropolitan mansions left vacant during the summer be confiscated and turned over to the poor who were crowded into sweltering tenements.[27]

R. L. Duffus, a frequent contributor to *The Nation*, later recalled that Villard once told him that whenever he left the office for a few days "the staff goes Bolshevist." Duffus agreed that "in a way it did." He also noted that Villard "purposefully chose men who were more radical than he was."[28] Villard understood that his reputed radicalism was not deep political conviction but merely a reaction to the fear and prejudice that gripped the country. He wrote Emily Balch that the political climate was so disgusting that it "tends to make every liberal more and more a revolutionist as time goes on . . . it is the universal opinion that anyone who differs with the prevailing point of view should be shot."[29] He went along with his rambunctious editors, whose common interest in defeat of the treaty and the League sustained his courage and gave to the office a sense of purpose and new esprit de corps.

Villard's superficial alliance with the radicals broke down over the issue of economic and social reform. Despite his sympathy for the revolutionary upheavals in Europe and his endorsement of the Second International at Berne, Villard showed no deep understanding of the economic implications of the radical critique of the treaty and the League. The anti-imperialists and Manchester liberals, like Villard, believed that tariff barriers and spheres of influence caused wars. Government's role was to protect private property and preserve law and order so that each individual could pursue his own self-interest in the market place. This philosophy naturally benefited the "have" nations and justifies E. H. Carr's charge that the League of Nations would create a "paradise of the economically strong who wanted to enjoy the fruits of [their] strength without let or hindrance. . . ."[30]

But Villard should not be singled out for his blindness to the basic cause of the upheavals in Europe. His acceptance of Wilsonianism is consistent with his Manchester faith. What is surprising is that many American progressives accepted the same international policy while maintaining that it was inadequate for domestic problems. The debate over the League and the treaty centered on political issues—world government, international parliaments, self-determination. Petitions to the conference concerning racial discrimination or unequal economic opportunity within a state were pushed aside as domestic issues. Supporters of Wilsonianism could thus applaud the overthrow of the Czar because his regime had been undemocratic, but to accept a new radical government that called for national planning was to undermine the major premises of their ideology.

In 1919 only a few progressives had begun to see the inconsistency here. Walter Lippmann, a disillusioned member of the Inquiry, summed up the failures of Wilsonianism in its repudiation of New Nationalism and return to the New Freedom of 1912—a mixture of Jeffersonian democracy and British Cobdenism. "It does not stress planning, organization, technique, but conscience and morality."[31] Villard would not agree; it was the moral shortcomings of the treaty he was most concerned about. Lippmann's criticism, therefore, could be applied directly to Villard. Villard, and most of his contemporaries, believed that, given political freedom and self-expression, economic opportunity and equality would follow. It is to Villard's credit, however, that he was one of the few who denounced the conference leaders' refusal to accept the Japanese demand for a statement supporting racial equality.[32]

131

By and large, few observers in 1919 had touched on what spelled the doom of the League and the treaty in advance. It was not the harshness of the treaty, nor the reparations, nor the debts, but the failure to provide for or even see the beginnings of what Julian Huxley has called the Expectation Revolution: "The hungry believe that they could and ought to be fed, the sick that they could and ought to be healthy, the illiterate and ignorant that they could and ought to receive a decent education." Blindness to these demands created a climate in which demagogues like Mussolini and Hitler might flourish. As John Maynard Keynes said, the "perils of the future lay not in frontiers or sovereignties, but in food, coal, and transport."[33]

Villard continued to ignore the differences between his staff and himself until the fight against the League was nearly over and the editors turned to domestic issues.[34] This may help to explain why it was relatively easy for him later to join ranks with men with whom he had little in common. In 1919 and 1920 Villard was obsessed with one objective and he was willing to call upon the resources of any group to achieve it.

Acclaimed as wild-eyed radicals by the notorious Lusk committee in June of 1919, Villard and his editors defiantly ridiculed the committee and continued their offensive.[35] *The Nation* published a supplement entitled "Out of his Own Mouth: The President in Opposition to the Treaty," which consisted of five pages of extracts in close type from Wilson's speeches during the war denouncing a harsh and punitive peace.[36] When MacDonald reported that the supplement had caused a great sensation abroad, Villard sent it to "a select list of fifteen hundred editors, congressmen and senators."[37]

MacDonald's correspondence from Europe indicates that he played a major role in formulating *The Nation*'s policy and providing moral support to Villard whenever he wavered. He told Villard that the way to insure against charges of sympathy for the Republican opposition was to publish a series of "strong constructive editorials, pointing out . . . how to get a real League of Nations, how to bring about the revival of trade and financial soundness, etc. . . . . Keep hammering away on Russia and against alliances for America . . . rub in the doctrines of the Fourteen Points as far as they can be given application." These, he wrote, "are the things that are having their effect here."[38]

On June 28, 1919, Germany accepted the treaty, shattering any hope for a new kind of peace. Villard wrote MacDonald the day before that the "foul deed is done and the Treaty will be signed tomorrow."[39] He came out with a blistering unsigned editorial entitled, "The Peace That Is No Peace," in which he stated that no "peace so wicked, so hypocritical, so contrary to every allied pretense can endure. . . ."

Villard repeated MacDonald's assertion that the "world is henceforth divided into two camps, radicals and reactionaries" and warned that the "real true revolution which is to free humanity is not yet begun."[40] His references to the "real true" revolution were couched in vague political and moralistic phrases and did not state the actual steps to be taken. His interest continued to be inspired more by the destructive value of the Leftist's critique than by any tangible programs they advocated.

Villard may have believed that a whole new conference was possible if America refused to ratify the treaty and League. MacDonald firmly held that the only solution was to defeat the existing settlement and start all over again "on the right lines." One historian felt that Villard, although opposed to the League, found it difficult to join forces wholeheartedly with the irreconcilables, [41] though whatever hope he may have held out for a new conference was short-lived. Charles T. Hallinan, an associate of Villard's in the American Union Against Militarism and a frequent contributor to *The Nation,* wrote Villard in August that *The Nation* should "present some kind of a plan for a treaty and a league and not just go along with those who are fighting the league on grounds of the right of withdrawal, sanctity of the tariff and the Monroe Doctrine." These were the aims of the reservationist group in the Senate who would accept the League and treaty if American sovereignty could remain unimpaired. Villard and *The Nation,* however, now grew closer to the irreconcilable camp— always protesting that their support was for different reasons. Villard replied to Hallinan that *The Nation*'s contribution was unfortunately but necessarily a negative one because the treaty was "so rotten." "The whole treaty should be cut off behind the ears and I hate to be the one to plan a new ribs and rump and tail. Why don't you try your hand at it?"[42] Hallinan accepted the challenge, and said *The Nation* should pressure Congress to pass a resolution calling for a new conference, held in a neutral city, with representatives to be made up by direct apportionment of the parliamentary bodies of belligerents and neutral countries. This conference should have the power of drawing up the peace with Germany and a League of Nations Covenant. Villard became impatient and replied that *The Nation* had ceased to urge the calling of another conference because it seemed "to us impossible of accomplishment." To William Allen White, on the same day, he put it more bluntly: "I come out against the whole dad blast thing, I want it in the junk heap once and for all."[43]

Villard was sensitive to the charge that he was joining his traditional enemies. He reported that he had only recently been charged with striking hands with Lodge. He recalled the famous anecdote of Maria Weston Chapman, who, during the Abolitionist fight, had marvelled that the good Lord used instruments in the cause that she would not have touched with a forty-foot pole. Villard, not to be outdone by this venerable crusader, remarked: "Sixty feet we always wish between us and Mr. Lodge. But our concern is not with him."[44]

Yet the nature of the struggle drew *The Nation* into the political orbit and with increasing frequency editorials appeared giving outright support to the conservative forces. Lincoln Colcord, for example, praised the Senate opposition to Wilson and attributed wisdom and idealism to men who were blatantly involved in a purely partisan struggle. Colcord wrote that much of the Senate opposition was "not on the basis of partisanship, and not from the point of view of bloodthirsty jingoism but on the score of [the treaty's] inherent injustice. . . ." He then asserted that "even a reactionary Republican is more liberal than a Bourbon Democrat and more liberal than a man who preaches liberalism and never keeps his word."[45]

A few weeks later, Albert J. Nock assured his readers that if America abandoned the League, it would not hurt the people of Europe. "If they were only left alone, they would prove quite able to help themselves." By the end of June Colcord, with tortuous logic, was presenting Senator Knox as a man fighting a brave battle for righteousness and asserting that Senators Joseph S. Frelinghuysen, Harry S. New, and Frank B. Brandegee were defending the people from an international conspiracy promoted by bankers and industrialists. Colcord praised the speeches of Senators James A. Reed and Hiram Johnson, who "wisely appealed" to a responsive audience by recalling "American history and traditions," and resorting to "the old familiar allusions, the simple appeal to love of country and wisdom of past days."[46] Such statements were hardly calculated to separate *The Nation* from the conservatives or to antagonize the most timid isolationist.

Villard was not in complete accord with all these utterances, but in the heat of the battle he too applauded "the gallant fight the Republicans are making against the League."[47] He wrote Ramsay MacDonald, "It is a curious fact that having started in mostly from political motives, they [Republican senators] have been swept away by the unrighteousness of the treaty and are more and more inclined to reject the whole thing."[48] Soon he was reluctantly praising Lodge's leadership. One wonders if Villard remembered his taunt to Tumulty at the sight of Wilson, Lodge, and Roosevelt clasping hands at the time of American intervention.

This flirtation with Lodge and his kind could not last. As the battle shaped up a more palpable solution presented itself.

Senator Borah, the leader of the liberal Republican forces, was an insurgent within the party; he agreed with *The Nation's* policy on many domestic issues. Borah was no friend of Senator Lodge but was irrevocably opposed to the treaty and the League. Villard and his editors could support Borah without qualms—he was opposed to the settlement for the "right reasons." Although Villard frequently denounced isolationism, Borah's distinctly isolationist tendencies did not seem to bother him. By the fall of 1919 *The Nation* was in the camp of the irreconcilables. Through Lincoln Colcord, a personal friend of the Senator, the editors kept in touch with Congressional strategy and provided Borah with an avalanche of material to aid him in the fight.[49] Borah, in return, managed to get the treaty document and proposed amendments and reservations to *The Nation* before they were received by the newspapers and other rivals. It was Borah who informed Villard that the international bankers were pouring a great deal of money into the fight in favor of the League. *The Nation* continually repeated this charge.[50] Villard wrote MacDonald that *The Nation* had developed warm friends in Congress, "namely, France, Johnson and Borah." Colcord bragged that the senators who were in revolt against the treaty were so dependent on *The Nation* for its extensive information that they watched for their weekly copies as a "schoolboy waits for *Youth's Companion.*"[51]

In aligning *The Nation* with the irreconcilable faction Villard rejected advice from men he held in high esteem. Lord Robert Cecil, for example, was one of the staunchest supporters of the Covenant and a liberal crusader for the kind of peace and treaty that Villard had advocated. When the treaty did not live up to expectations, he publicly criticized its failure, but he did not believe in abandoning the entire League and held little faith in the reconvening of a new conference.

Cecil, who was more sensitive to American domestic politics than Wilson,[52] warned Villard of the consequences of his position: "If it is not too late, let me implore you and all other men of good will to think very carefully before you destroy the only existing instrument, however imperfect, which remains to us for securing real pacification." Cecil asserted that most of the important figures in England had come to this point of view, except for the reactionary militarist group, implying that Villard was aiding those whom he despised most of all.[53]

It was too late. Villard was committed to the destruction of both the League and the treaty. He disagreed with Cecil's premise that it was either the League or a return to rampant militarism. "There is," he said, "another alternative—disarmament." This was the hope of the world and the only solution. It would not take a League to bring this about. On the contrary he charged that the League was opposed to disarmament. Villard made no suggestion as to how disarmament was to be achieved, but he repeated that he was not at all sure "that it would be disastrous for America to withdraw from the whole mess," while he was sure that it would "be disastrous if an effort is made to execute the League as it is now drawn."[54] Villard had similar exchanges with Jan Christian Smuts, an architect of the League, and with Fridtjof Nansen, the world-famous Norwegian explorer and humanitarian.[55]

The intensity of Villard's conviction is evidenced by a letter he wrote Senator LaFollette upon hearing that the Senator was about to make one of his speeches against American participation:

I hope with all my heart that you will speak not only against the covenant, which is such a travesty on the League of Nations we have all been hoping for, but against the Treaty itself. The more I study it, the more I am sure that it is the most iniquitous peace document ever drawn, that it dishonors America because it violates our solemn national pledge given to the Germans at the Armistice, and because it reeks with bad faith, revengefulness and inhumanity. Evidently Mr. Wilson and I do not use or understand words in the same way, for when he says the Treaty constitutes a new order, my mind stands still and I doubt my sanity, for to me, it not only retains the old and vicious order of the world, but makes it worse and puts the whole control of the situation in the hands of the international bankers. To my mind it seals the ruin of the modern capitalist system and constitutes a veritable Pandora's box out of which will come evils of which we have not as yet any conception.[56]

Villard was delighted with the delaying tactics of Lodge in the Senate. He believed that given four months, or possibly only two, the treaty could be beaten.[57] When Wilson decided to take the issue to the people, *The Nation*, acting like one of the Republican truth squads, ridiculed him weekly by picking apart his utterances and referring to him as an evangelist whose pretensions could hardly be taken seriously.[58]

Villard still feared Wilson's powers of persuasion and wrote Ramsay MacDonald that the President was having some success on the tour. There had been in America "a tendency to worship the presidential office, which makes it incumbent upon everyone to receive with rapturing applause whatever our temporary ruler says or does." The opposition that Villard noted during the President's tour was a healthful sign. Villard showed little compassion for Wilson's tragic collapse after his address at Pueblo, Colorado, at the end of September. He only feared that the President's illness might rally new suport for purely sentimental reasons.[59]

The Nation's half-hearted statement of sorrow contained a bitter reference to the regrettably low character of Wilson's campaign, which, they argued, should be pursued on a plane of "reason and not passion." Only a few weeks before, Colcord, in a tone hardly dictated by reason, referred to Wilson as an amazing charlatan who had robbed "America of its true and independent Americanism" and "prostituted the soul of the nation."[60]

The first *Nation* to appear after the defeat of the treaty in the Senate in November expressed satisfaction at the outcome of the vote, but apprehension over the causes of the defeat. The treaty was not "rejected squarely on the grounds of its inhumanity . . . but largely due to a group of partisans, most of them narrow nationalists with no adequate vision of true internationalism which the future holds in store for the world."[61] This belated statement of regret was notably unconvincing. *The Nation* a few weeks earlier, in an article entitled "A Covenant with Death," asserted that "it has been a profoundly encouraging sight to see men who turned against the Treaty at first for purely partisan reasons or out of a petty spirit of narrow nationalism, finally beginning to glow with the white heat of moral indignation."[62]

The editors now spoke of the need to pursue an international point of view and denied that the treaty's defeat meant return to the old isolation. They had aligned themselves with various factions fighting the treaty because to give in to those arguing for half a loaf would be to give in to political expediency. *The Nation*, said the editors, had faced the dilemma that all reformers must face, "namely that of laying aside principle and conviction and assenting to evil lest a conjuring vision of some terrible future prove a greater calamity."[63]

The article went on to say that the country had "rightly asserted in decisive tones its historical opposition to entangling alliances . . . it will not allow its friendliness or wealth to be used to pull European chestnuts out of the fire"—a statement likely to please the most ardent isolationist.[64] Another editorial, praising Senators Knox and Hiram Johnson for their vigorous repudiation of any League or treaty that would have "American boys fighting all over Europe," indicated that *The Nation* was having a good deal of difficulty maintaining its simon-pure position of theoretical internationalism.[65]

The Nation, under Villard's leadership, was attempting to have it both ways. They uncritically supported "liberal isolationists" like Borah and LaFollette for their efforts to defeat the treaty and League, but in their zeal also embraced men of much more conservative leanings such as Knox, New, and Frelinghuysen. At the same time they sincerely desired to dissociate themselves from the attitudes expressed by these men toward international affairs. As soon as the battle seemed won, they immediately became sensitive that their liberal position might be misinterpreted.

When the treaty, with reservations, came up again for a roll call in March 1920, it was defeated by a coalition of Democrats, who stood by the President's refusal to accept reservations, and irreconcilable Republicans. Ironically, the man whom Villard had called the great compromiser would not, as Villard might have put it, "budge an inch from principle." Accepting Villard's dictum against political expediency, Wilson did as much as Villard and the irreconcilables to defeat the treaty.

Publicly, Villard now talked of a new conference to bring about a genuine League of Nations including Russia, Austria, Hungary, and Mexico. If the League were remodeled to give assurance "that it is a democratic peaceful world organization, and not the device for the despotic and imperial control of human affairs," America would certainly join.[66]

When Villard attempted to inaugurate a vigorous crusade for civil liberties in the closing months of 1919, he invited Senator Borah to lead the fight in the Senate. He received little encouragement. Borah said that he could not fight against indiscriminate use of the injunction against striking miners or for the protection of civil rights because it would divide his disciplined ranks fighting the League. Villard wrote letters to his European Labor party friends describing the complete political decay in the United States. The liberalism of a few years ago was gone. There was no one to lead. He blamed it on the war.[67] At no time did Villard admit that perhaps he and his journal had played a part in creating the climate of political reaction, skepticism, and disillusion that prevailed. On the contrary, he stoutly defended his position.

William (Billy) Hard, *The Nation*'s Washington correspondent, gave classic expression to the feelings of those who had opposed the treaty to the bitter end. He wrote Villard a few years later for permission to take a leave of absence in order to write a book. The book was to be one that "no pro-leaguer could poke holes in," but also, "one that will give to all future historians the point of view of that little band of people who saved the country."[68]

CHAPTER TEN

Reaction, Revision, Reform

1920-1924

Villard soon learned that it is easier to maintain unity of purpose in a campaign to defeat a measure than to muster cooperation for a positive program. He had been swept into prominence as an articulate spokesman for the wildly divergent forces fighting the treaty and the League. By November 1920 the League had been pronounced dead. But the fruits of victory were bitter. The descent from the lofty idealistic rhetoric of Wilsonianism to the fatuous banalities of Warren Gamaliel Harding was more than the most hard-boiled dissenter had bargained for. Villard quickly dubbed him the "Marion marionette . . . a dummy, an animated automaton that moves only when the strings are pulled." It was an election by "disgust."[1] *The Nation* was riding the crest of the wave and Villard, in this moment of victory, was reluctant to put down the cudgel. He warned his readers that the election was not, as the successful candidate claimed, "a mandate against the League." *The Nation* would maintain its vigilance, for any day the "covenant of death" might raise its ugly head.[2]

But the League was dead. There would be, during the next decade, frequent skirmishes over issues of international law and jurisprudence, but the main fight was over. A pall of dullness and complacency enervated even thinking Americans.

Villard was not long in finding a new cause. In the fall of 1920 he was persuaded by an Irish patriot, Dr. Maloney, to help establish the Committee of One Hundred on Ireland, which eventually led to the American Commission on Conditions in Ireland. Although Villard tried to remain in the background, his support and good wishes were so well known that it was referred to as the Villard Commission. The committee proposed to institute an impartial investigation into the stories of atrocities committed by the British government in putting down the struggle for Irish independence. Although Villard insisted that he was concerned only with human justice, such a commission did, by its very nature, exploit the intense anti-British feeling in the Irish-American community and supported the old attack on the Versailles treaty as a hypocritical document.[3] The commission, which had such distinguished members as Jane Addams, Frederick Howe, Norman Thomas, and Senators Oliver P. Newman, George W. Norris, and David Walsh, was accused of being nothing more than a propaganda agency created by pacifists and pro-Germans to discredit Great Britain and disrupt Anglo-American relations.[4]

It was the kind of battle that Villard relished and he lent the good offices of *The Nation* personnel and presses to the enterprise, which ultimately produced a lengthy report, admittedly one-sided and damning to the British.[5] Most Americans, however, were tired, and this kind of wrangle interested few. The press made much of the commission and took Villard to task, playing upon his German-American background, his seditious pacifism, and Bolshevistic sympathies. All of the old recriminations, counter-accusations, and letters to the editor followed on schedule. Perhaps the wear and tear of such a ritual was debilitating even to Villard. He wrote Jane Addams that at times he felt "utterly sick" about the whole affair with its factional disputes and personal jealousies. He regretted the weakness of the commission's direction and the mistakes "of which we of *The Nation* as well as others are guilty . . . . I have often reproached myself for ever having asked you to join. Nothing I have ever done has focused such social pressure and intolerance on us as this."[6]

Yet Villard could not pass up the opportunity to stand before the mob, to denounce hysteria, to expose tyranny. Shortly after the Commission on Conditions in Ireland had completed its hearings, Villard insisted on meeting a speaking engagement in Cincinnati. Under the zealous leadership of the Reverend R. H. Stevenson, a Congregational minister, several civic and veterans' organizations banded together to protest his appearance. Stevenson warned the citizens of Cincinnati that Villard was one of those "who stir up trouble between capital and labor," a "member of the so called intellectual rebels. . . . A man of Villard's record has no right to stand in any forum where decent Americans will listen to him."[7] Such publicity encouraged Villard and he went to Cincinnati as scheduled. The hall was stormed by a group of veterans and at one point he was actually in danger. This kind of experience exhilarated him, and made him feel that he "was following in the footsteps of [his] grandfather. . . ."[8]

The episode satisfied Villard's need to live up to his heritage, to be a personal witness in the struggle to gain the good society. It gave *The Nation* publicity. But where did it lead? Villard, with deep commitment, described the good society, called upon men of good will to give their lives meaning by standing up for the truth, fighting bigotry and injustice. But he failed to advance a program toward the attainment of these objectives. He was so caught up in surface struggles that he had little time to probe. It is the problem of the true believer whose emotional commitment outruns his thought. Though exciting, the effort is exhausting, and the results are often inconsequential. Even Villard had doubts: "The trying thing is that everything like that, that I try to do, is so persistently misunderstood and misrepresented that every once in a while I feel despondent enough to wish to chuck the whole business."[9]

Villard was not alone in his feeling of discontent. Some of his editors grew impatient with his insistence on fighting the same old battles, denouncing the same old villains, calling up the same old noble standards. Henry Raymond Mussey warned Villard as far back as 1918 that the magazine would not gain any permanent recognition if it merely persisted in denouncing conditions and "knocking" the government. Subscribers wrote that they agreed with *The Nation*'s criticism of world affairs, but that a more constructive and well-defined policy was called for. Mussey insisted that what was needed was a firm commitment "on some of the pressing economic questions."[10]

Up to a point which was never quite clear, Villard agreed to accept significant innovations. In his speeches and articles there were frequent allusions to the great upheaval that had taken place as a result of the war. He was convinced that a reexamination of the whole basis of America's social life was needed. In later years he recalled that by 1919 he had "been emancipated from any smug liberalism and social blindness due to the ease and luxury" of his upbringing.[11] Shortly after his return from Europe, still flushed by his exciting experiences, he answered a letter from a disconsolate subscriber who charged *The Nation* with abandoning its traditional policies and embarking upon a socialist binge of the most radical and outrageous dimensions. Villard wrote that he believed in the right of private property and "the enforcement of the guarantees thereof." Nevertheless nationalization of mines and other industries might become necessary to meet new social conditions. Although in the past he had never accepted national ownership of the railroads, telegraph, and telephones, he had witnessed what was going on in Europe and England, and could not fail to see that similar measures might soon be found necessary in America. Of course, he was "not for forcible seizure of property, but legislative action."

Villard had come to realize that the "position of the working man has got to be radically changed in America to prevent the coming of such a revolution as is going on abroad." He assured his former reader that the danger in America was not radicalism, but the reactionary type of conservative mind which denounces every new idea and applies epithets to everyone who dares to think outside of conventional bounds.[12]

In the spring of 1919 he offered more specific and constructive suggestions. He supported federal abolition of child labor, which he had previously opposed, and he agreed to the desirability of government purchase of the railroads, which would then be run on a modified Plumb Plan, that is, by administrators representing government, the owners, and labor. He spoke vaguely of the "democratization of industry" and the need for the nationalization of such natural resources as iron and coal. At the same time he called for the simplification of the government structure at every possible point.[13]

In fact, Villard sounded very much like his old adversary, Theodore Roosevelt, who, upon leaving office in 1908, had recognized that economic problems would become paramount, pointing out that his problems had been moral ones. Villard realized that the times called for technicians, system-makers, and economic theorists, but he interpreted his own role as that of guardian of the moral conscience. He hoped to leave the discussion of difficult technical questions to his staff. *The Nation* was tolerant of many views but intellectually committed to none.[14] Because in those days a magazine's editorial policy was often synonymous with the personal views of its owner and editor, Villard was repeatedly attacked for indecisiveness by patrons and readers advocating one panacea or another.

Members of the staff insisted that the magazine must make up its mind on a program and stick with it. Mussey, Villard's most persistent critic, demanded that *The Nation* move further to the Left and accused Villard of being bound by old prejudices and unwilling to break with the past.[15] There was some truth in Mussey's charges. Villard expressed a willingness to support government ownership of unworked mineral land, but he added significantly, "I think we ought to try for a scheme of private ownership before going into the evils of government ownership, those evils being chiefly political, and the inevitable killing of any initiative." Villard was worried that the magazine was already going "very fast towards a complete break with the old *Nation* tradition; a little going slowly now may not harm." Villard wanted more leisure to think about these new departures.[16] He was struggling to keep abreast of the times but his pace was not sufficient to appease his editor.

Mussey was dedicated to a kind of Christian guild socialism leading to the establishment of a cooperative commonwealth. His pacifism and humanitarian instincts appealed to Villard, but he had little administrative talent and seemed to Villard to have vague and impractical notions about how to manage a weekly journal. Villard often attacked the business mentality for its tawdry motives, but when it came to his own affairs he had great respect for common sense, practical reality, and business efficiency. Mussey had no use for Villard's "practical" considerations if they led to a cautious and evasive policy. In the summer of 1919 Mussey, in his most quixotic vein, suggested that Villard abandon his control of *The Nation* and turn it over to the stockholders, giving each an equal vote in deciding policy. He was disappointed that Villard refused to take even a beginning step toward his own economic position: "You want *The Nation* to be your paper, to reflect your ideas to make propaganda for the particular things in which you chance to be interested in." Mussey then indicated what he would do if he had more to say about the policy:

> We should throw the wages and profits system overboard . . . substitute for it a system of cooperative industry . . . oppose banking as a means of profit making and favor every type of cooperative credit arrangements. . . . I would favor the elimination of private income from the ownership of natural resources.[17]

Villard could entertain such proposals in the abstract, but he took a dim view of Mussey's idea of starting with the management of *The Nation*.[18] Mussey, however, was not to be dissuaded by any "twaddle about private property" and loss of initiative: "I am opposed to anybody running any business because he happens to own its stocks, land, labor, credit. . . . I would stand for the freeing of them all by pitching the present outgrown system of ownership on the rubbish heap where it belongs. . . ."[19]

Villard tolerated Mussey's vagaries, but he was forced to take seriously the demands of *The Nation*'s leading financial supporter, Francis Neilson. Neilson, a former British M.P., had come to America and married Helen Swift Morris, heiress to a meat-packing fortune. His particular plan for the reorganization of society was the single tax, although he did not like that label and always referred to it as a plan for the "taxation of the site value of land." The Neilsons had placed Albert J. Nock on *The Nation*'s staff and paid his salary. Because of this and financial contributions of over $30,000 annually, they felt they had a right to participate in shaping editorial policy. Neilson agreed with *The Nation*'s policy on the League, the treaty, free speech, and civil liberties, and with "the moral and religious tone" of the magazine, but *The Nation* lacked a genuine economic policy. It was superficial and not getting to the root of things.[20]

Villard was in a quandary. Readers and contributors also prodded him.[21] He confided to several friends that he was not equipped to pass judgment on all of these issues. He wrote to Neilson: "I am very weak both as to finance and economics." He insisted, nevertheless, that *The Nation* did have a sound policy—"Free trade, no government ownership of ships or railroads, no Socialism, no special privileges, these seem to me the basis for a pretty sound economic policy."[22] Such an answer hardly satisfied Neilson and it would have infuriated Mussey. In November 1919 the Neilson forces left *The Nation*, taking Nock with them, to establish *The Freeman*, which became a radical single tax journal. In the spring of 1920, when Nock's *Freeman* first appeared, Villard editorially welcomed it to the ranks of liberal journalism. Nock quickly replied that *The Freeman* was not a liberal magazine: "You make your appeal to the Liberals we make ours to Radicals."[23]

It is true that Villard had always made quick decisions, but in the past he found it easy to reconcile them with his heritage. Now he lacked confidence and was reluctant to allow his editors responsibility with the family enterprise. Villard wrote MacDonald, who was still in Europe, that he missed his advice, that the entire staff was split, and that he felt deeply his incompetence on many matters: "Probably the fault is altogether mine. I am not temperamentally the man to head a staff or big enough or well enough educated to do so."[24] He pleaded that "no editor should be asked to pass upon all these questions and to take fundamental ground all at once on the reorganization of society."[25]

Villard's difficulties with his staff involved more than disagreement over specific political and economic positions. The barrier of restraint that had separated him from downtown bohemianism in the past, although partially undermined, still remained. In 1925 Villard was 52 years old. Lewis Gannett, associate editor, was 34; Joseph Wood Krutch, drama critic, 32; Mark Van Doren, following in the footsteps of his older brother Carl as literary editor, only 31; and Freda Kirchwey, the managing editor, still in her early twenties. Ludwig Lewisohn was a doddering 43 but his spectacular amorous life justified his inclusion among these youthful spirits who had invaded the antiquated offices overlooking the sedate churchyard of St. Paul's on Vesey Street. The comradeship between the aging Villard and his young and spirited crew had been forged out of the war experience. Although they had not all opposed the war, they were all disappointed in its results. As long as the repudiation of that war remained a burning issue Villard and his new recruits had, or so it seemed on the surface, much in common, but as it receded, the differences in background, temperament, and age became apparent.

Most of these young intellectual rebels who staffed *The Nation*, served their apprenticeship in the Village, wrote for the little magazines, and combined an interest in politics with an intense dedication to experimental forms in literature and the arts. Harold Stearns stated their case succinctly in his erratic yet revealing anthology, *Civilization in the United States:*

> We have no heritages or traditions to which to cling except those that have already withered in our hands and turned to dust. One can feel the whole industrial and economic situation as so maladjusted to the primary and simple needs of men and women that the futility of a rationalistic attack on these infantilisms of compensation becomes obvious. There must be an entirely new deal of the cards in one sense; we must change our hearts. For only so, unless through the humbling of calamity or scourge, can true art and true religion and true personality, with their native warmth and caprice and gaiety, grow up in America to exorcise these painted devils we have created to frighten us away from the acknowledgement of our spiritual poverty.[26]

While Villard hesitatingly called for consideration of political innovations, these iconoclastic rebels demanded experimentation in art, poetry, morality—in life itself. For Van Doren, poets need not be uplifting, pastoral, and serene but should "plunge into thunder, provided they write with haunting power."[27] Above all there should cease to be a dichotomy between a genuine social conscience and an aesthetic conscience. Joseph Wood Krutch, who by the end of the decade became the apostle of doom, recalled that in the early years of the twenties he and his fellow editors felt that nothing stood between them and a "brave new world" except the "traditions, prohibitions, and inhibitions of a happily moribund past."[28]

How could Villard with his graying hair, his almost military posture, his unbending sense of propriety, expect to become a member of, let alone control, this band of unruly puritan-baiters? He still frowned on intoxicating spirits and feared that an unintended slip revealing that he occasionally enjoyed a cigarette would disappoint his mother.[29] Affectionately, sometimes condescendingly, known as "the boss" or O. G. V., he attempted to maintain an almost paternal relationship with his staff, while struggling to allow his editors complete freedom. He wanted to be in the swing of things and often affected a show of tolerance to demonstate his willingness to accept modernity.[30] At other times their defiance of decorum led to outbursts that unsettled him and the staff. He feared that defiant behavior would only confirm the charge that liberalism unavoidably led to a "relaxation of morals." The advocate of reform and innovation must be as pure as the driven snow.[31] Because he knew little of the new poetry, art, and literature, he preferred to risk the reputation of his magazine on more pressing political issues. Other departments continued to appear in *The Nation* because they were a part of its tradition. Freda Kirchwey recalls that he would often burst into an editor's office waving a letter from a kind old lady subscriber in Dubuque whose sensibilities had been offended. All the editors at one time or another suffered under these attacks but Van Doren and Miss Kirchwey bore the brunt most often. Van Doren's choice of poetry was "queer," "difficult," or worse yet it was not "hopeful."[32] When Van Doren accepted a poem by Babette Deutsch, who was politically Leftist (which was acceptable) and moderately avant garde in poetry (which was not), Villard dashed off a memo to Van Doren expressing his objection to the scandalous phrase "as dozing bitches break their dreams to bark." "I object to this new poetical license in which we speak of bitches. There is a dignity about our paper that must be upheld. . . . I think some of [the poetry] execrable and I wish to print none when you cannot get poetry up to our standard."[33] Van Doren bore these suggestions with good-humored patience but on one occasion when Villard invaded his office with the usual complaint, the mild-mannered editor looked up from his desk at the red faced "boss" and shouted, "Mr. Villard you don't know a god-damned thing about poetry."[34] Villard's fits of cantankerousness always passed. Van Doren continued to publish the poetry of Miss Deutsch, Maxwell Bodenheim, Robert Graves, Hart Crane, Robinson Jeffers, and Allan Tate, and to defend the works of the new writers, Theodore Dreiser, H. L. Mencken, Sherwood Anderson, Sinclair Lewis, and others.[35]

Villard submitted to and even appeared to enjoy a jocular show of disrespect expressed by his youthful associates. Often when he scolded a member of the staff he prefaced his remarks with an apology for his "old fogey point of view." When informed that a scion of one of the city's most prominent families had been exposed in a flagrant case of financial fraud, Villard exclaimed, "I can't believe it. Why he is an old Harvard oarsman."[36]

Villard had trouble not only with the aesthetic tastes of his staff, but with their private lives as well. He bore Albert J. Nock's eccentricities, even tolerating the editor's refusal to give any home address. It was rumored he did not want his nocturnal alliances disturbed.[37] Ludwig Lewisohn, probably not the most reliable source, has nevertheless left a revealing explanation of why Villard tolerated the flamboyance of some of his flock. On a short trip together Lewisohn began to relate the lurid details of his personal life, which at the moment were bringing him, and indirectly *The Nation,* notoriety in the Hearst press. Although sensitive to Villard's acute discomfort, Lewisohn was confident that "the boss" would stand by him and not throw him to the mob. Lewisohn detected Villard's fear that his world was tottering and his unconscious grasping for the "snug brief comforts of some compromise." Finally Villard broke into a winning smile and concluded: "A man of your artistic temperament will always be in hot water." The stereotype was established; Lewisohn was an artist and everyone knows that artists are different. Although Lewisohn's analysis seems accurate, he failed to see the clichés in his own romantic conception of himself.[38]

Krutch referred to his contemporaries as "gay crusaders" who were fundamentally optimistic and confident that liberalism "would triumph and . . . create a better world."[39] This Villard could understand. But their brand of liberalism involved the revolutionary principle that to create one had to destroy.

Villard could not condone a brutal rejection of the past. Krutch has described this conflict. At one of the editorial luncheons at which politics was usually discussed, the guests were three members of the British Labor party and, incongruously, D. H. Lawrence. As the editors earnestly discussed conditions and spoke of ameliorative programs, the courtly Villard noticed Lawrence sitting in sullen silence. He politely asked the author what he thought they should do "to save the world." Lawrence blanched and, as the younger members held their breath, he "replied with measured ferocity: 'I thought, Mr. Villard, you understood that I hoped it would go to pieces as rapidly and as completely as possible.' "[40]

It is remarkable that Villard remained flexible enough to maintain these associations for so many years. In many cases it was the innocence of the rebels rather than his own innocence that made a genuine rapport impossible. Both sides, nevertheless, contributed to the creation of a journal of opinion. Villard provided stability and leadership while the young rebels searched for the "significant gesture" of defiance, to give meaning to their lives. He occasionally demanded that they understand who was boss, and threatened to have all proposals for new departures pass over his desk. In the long run they were delighted with the considerable freedom he gave them.[41] Krutch recalls that at times he failed to appreciate how "liberal" Villard was "in just that respect where liberalism of the present day is most likely to fail—I mean in his genuine tolerance of opinions different from his own."[42]

Villard did submit to changes in the literary tone and format but the magazine continued to reflect his personal imprint. He held fast to his conception of the role of a liberal journal. At the beginning of the decade he made his position clear during a campaign to raise funds for the future support of the magazine. The depression that followed the war threatened to destroy *The Nation*. The drain on Villard's personal resources was alarming. To buttress his financial reserves he established a *Nation* foundation. He asked influential supporters to underwrite the paper for a period of three years, when, he felt, it would be self-supporting. Since most of the potential patrons that Villard solicited were liberals of his own generation,[43] he made it clear that he intended to reject the more radical approach favored by many of his critics. In a confidential report sent to potential benefactors Villard noted that *"The Nation* in two short years has assumed the leadership of liberal thought in the country."* He assured them that the magazine would fight any future proposals to join the League and continue to call for total disarmament. As for domestic issues, *The Nation* still stood for cooperative and democratic control of industry, including the railroads. "It has, and will continue to oppose with unfailing courage and unflagging zeal, government by injunction and terrorism."

Villard concluded, *"The Nation* stands, in short, for the old-fashioned Americanism and will apply to new situations the old principles modified by the facts of today." *The Nation* rejected socialism but it did accept the idea that there was

a need for a new world and a new order from which special privilege will have disappeared with resultant contentedness and a wider and juster distribution of wealth. It is afraid of no new idea because it is new, but it is American to the core in the spirit of the America of Wendell Phillips, Charles Sumner and Abraham Lincoln. No modification of this policy is contemplated or will be entertained by its present board of directors.[44]

This rhetoric dismayed the younger rebels. Villard, however, managed to maintain his youthful staff and to channel the magazine's efforts toward two major campaigns directed toward a rejuvenation of America's moral virtue. At the same time they were compatible with the younger dissenters' desire to repudiate the past and to retool prewar progressivism.

The first was support of the revisionist school of journalists and historians, who, with almost obsessive diligence, were bent upon proving that America's ideals and humanitarian impulses

were betrayed at home and abroad when she was enticed into
the war. The second concerned Villard's and *The Nation*'s
participation in the Convention for Progressive Political Action, which presented Robert LaFollette as an independent
candidate in the presidential election of 1924. Both offered
Villard and *The Nation* the opportunity to continue the negative campaign which had so successfully attracted readers during the first two years of its career, as well as to present a seem-
ingly positive program of reform.

In 1919, when the Senate was engaged in repudiating Wilsonian idealism, Lincoln Steffens wrote to Hutchins Hapgood:

> I sat on the fence watching the Peace Conference and laughing
> at the four men who looked so small on the great throne of
> God where they sat themselves. It was the funniest sight man
> ever saw. Nothing in art or history ever touched it. One had to
> laugh quietly, however, the world was taking it seriously.[45]

During these years of disappointment the persistent image of
the American "sucker" developed. Not only had Wilson, the
naive schoolmaster, been outwitted but the American people
had been taken. They were led to believe that they were fighting a war for democracy and freedom when, in fact, they were
engaged in sordid intrigue and international chicanery. It was
natural that those who opposed America's involvement from
the beginning appeared as Cassandras whom history was to
vindicate. Villard and his *Nation* played this role to the hilt,
and even published old editorials from their pages which had
predicted the events that were daily coming to pass.[46]

Villard rejoiced in the increased prestige that the revisionists were giving the pacifists and liberals. He wrote Joseph
Sturge, "We pacifists are again able to speak publicly and
find ourselves on the winning side."[47] To a critic of *The Nation* who was angered by the magazine's constant carping,
Villard replied:

I feel that America ought never to have gone into the war because the right was not clearly on one side. Personally I do not think there is much difference between any of the belligerents.

Villard still believed that the German government was probably most to blame for the outbreak of hostilities, but he still argued that the system of diplomacy dedicated to the balance of power had been the cause of the war and all participants had played the game.[48]

Although there were a number of reasons for Villard's sympathy toward the revisionists, personal vindication was one of the most compelling. He had been accused of traitorous activity and of cowardice. Revisionism, as it developed, charged that America's intervention had been a colossal blunder which caused the wasteful slaughter of thousands of innocent boys. "Never were lives more uselessly sacrificed. . . . It would have been better if they had been murdered on Broadway," Villard wrote to Ray Stannard Baker after the revisionist thesis had become popular.[49] Revisionists also charged that none of the Allies had fought for idealistic objectives. They repudiated the war guilt clause in the treaty, which, by implication, had indicted the Germans as a nation. The nationalistic historians were charged with perpetrating a monstrous falsehood.

Revisionism did more than appeal to Villard's pacifism and his sympathy for the German people. Its attack on international power politics and its castigation of war profiteers indicted imperialism and reaction.[50] Villard wrote, as early as 1917, that the President had been acclaimed "by every munitions maker, every agent for big business—all the evil forces combined." Seven years later, at Wilson's death, he repeated the charge verbatim in *The Nation*, adding only "war profiteers" to the list.[51]

The great majority of revisionists in the 1920's were liberals or progressives. Their association with the forces of movement in all countries made revisionism from the start more of a

155

political issue than an academic problem.[52] Revisionism served liberals and progressives in the same way that the bloody shirt had served conservatives in the 1880's and 1890's, only now the shoe was on the other foot—those who had supported the war were the nation's betrayers.

The issue of war guilt and the subsequent revisionist theories were initiated by European liberals and radicals. In 1914 the Union for Democratic Control had denounced the idea of Germany's sole guilt. E. D. Morel, one of the leaders of the movement, wrote in 1916 that the genesis of the war was to be sought not in original sin on the part of the German government or nation, but in "a universal reign of fear."[53] Francis Neilson's *How Diplomats Make War*, published in 1916, had a profound effect on American historians. Neilson had written Villard in 1919 that the system of secret diplomacy not only was responsible for the war but also had caused the "numbing and blinding of the wit and understanding of men whose intellect should have been sharpened by the terrific events which have brought ruin to Europe." It was Villard's wholehearted acceptance of Neilson's ideas that induced the former to aid *The Nation* so lavishly.[54]

Revisionism had its adherents in France, Germany, Austria, and Russia. The revolutionary governments in Russia and later in Austria and Germany, anxious to cast aspersions on their predecessors, rushed to make public their war archives with their accounts of intrigue and double dealing. It should be remembered that it was Villard who had tried in 1918 to give wide circulation to the Bolshevist revelations of deals between the Czarist regime and the Allies. In addition to the official documents, a great number of important figures in the defeated countries immediately published memoirs, which they hoped would relieve them from the burden of sole guilt.

These writings eventually found their way to America and Villard dedicated himself to publicizing them. He was joined by *The New Republic*, which, after its recantation, spent much of its space repudiating its former position. *The Dial* and *The*

Freeman soon joined the ranks of journals devoted to revision-ist interpretations. *The Nation's* biweekly *International Sup-plement* seemed to be the American clearing house for Eu-ropean government documents and revisionist articles and re-views. The secret treaties once again became the subject of sharp controversy."[55]

Revisionist history in America dealt with two major issues: responsibility for starting the war and the real reasons for American intervention. When these historians began to probe the causes of America's entrance, they developed the conspiracy thesis, implying that the munitions makers and the financiers had encouraged the country's participation. The repudiation of the traditional idealistic interpretation did not become widespread until the end of the twenties. Yet from the begin-ning pacifist journals such as *The Nation* held the conspiracy thesis; Villard could claim that he had exposed the conspiracy as early as 1914.[56]

Sidney B. Fay of Smith College was the first professional American historian to take up revisionist history seriously. In 1920 he published a series of articles entitled "New Light on the Origins of the War." Fay's scholarly articles made judicious use of the documents that had been released and were pri-marily directed to other historians.[57] Albert J. Nock's series of articles in *The Freeman*, entitled "Myth of a Guilty Nation," attracted widespread attention among journalists interested in using the revisionist thesis for political purposes. Unlike Fay, Nock felt that Germany's share of the guilt was "inconsider-able" compared to that of the French and Russians. Nock went beyond the divided guilt arguments of Fay and the early Eu-ropean revisionists and portrayed Germany as an innocent victim.[58]

With some chagrin Villard noted the widespread interest in his former editor's work. He wrote to J. A. Hobson, the British economist, asking him to take up the "whole question of the re-molding of public opinion as to German war guilt."[59] Hobson delivered according to specifications. He blasted the "sole

157

guilt" clause as an act of extreme hypocrisy and charged that it was responsible for the evils that plagued Europe. He attacked the unrealistic reparation demands of the French and the English and enthusiastically supported an independent and impartial inquiry into the war guilt question.[60]

In the spring and early summer of 1922 Villard visited Germany. On his return he published a series of articles on conditions in Europe and especially in Germany. Villard described a nation on the verge of economic ruin. The people were demoralized. Crime and degeneracy were increasing. He was shocked at the caliber of the theatre and reading matter, the bulk of which he considered pornographic. It was impossible to buy the works of Goethe and Schiller; he dealt at length with the rise of prostitution in the French-occupied zones. Villard's premise was that all of this was due to the rapacity of the treaty of Versailles and, in particular, to the extreme brutality and blindness of the French, who were more interested in the complete destruction of Germany than in reparations. Conditions in Germany and Europe confirmed Villard's conviction that war was the sum of all evils. "If Theodore Roosevelt were living today and could travel Europe from end to end, I do not believe that he could honestly find one single beneficent result from the war in any country. . . . The whole standard of living and, therefore, of morals and manners and ideals has gone down in Europe."[61]

Villard's articles presented a vivid and sordid picture. The degree to which his judgments were accepted by important officials may be seen in a letter written by Alanson B. Houghton, the American Ambassador in Berlin:

> I am reading your articles on Germany with a good deal of interest. I have had in mind the last dozen years that you were somewhat of an extremist. But I want to say that your statements regarding Germany are not only scrupulously fair, but are even understated in fact, and that your presentation is so restrained and so without emotion that I wonder at it.[62]

By 1922 the revisionist campaign began to take on a new dimension with the publication of John K. Turner's *Shall It Be Again*. Turner had frequently reviewed for *The Nation* since 1919, and was an avid devotee of the conspiracy thesis. He had little interest in the deceit of the Allies. His book was the first devoted to showing that Woodrow Wilson put America into the war to save the banking interests. *The Nation* was delighted with Turner's work. Ernest Gruening, the new managing editor, reviewed it with high praise. It might be biased, but it was the right kind of bias "out of favor for America's most cherished principles. If it be propaganda, it is propaganda only for the spirit of Washington, Jefferson, and Lincoln."[63]

In the fall of 1922 Frederick Bausman's *Let France Explain* appeared. It was published in England because no American publisher would accept it. In a letter to Villard, Bausman related that his work was written out of a "profound conviction that France combined with Russia to start the war for purposes of revenge and unfortunately had succeeded in wrecking one of the great modern states."[64] Villard reviewed Bausman's book favorably but sarcastically added that "Bausman's scholarly work will probably be dismissed as the product of a 'pro-Kaiser Dutchman.' "[65]

The Nation broke into the elite of the revisionists with what one historian of the school called "two epoch making articles" by Lewis Gannett, an associate editor. Gannett was a militant Quaker who had served with the Friends Service Committee in Paris during and after the war. He had, as a college boy, taken part in summer seminars, conducted by Norman Angell at Cornell, on the evils of war and its inability to settle international questions.[66] In October he presented to *Nation* readers "They All Lied," and in the *International Supplement*, "Documents of International Deceit."

The first article was a careful digest of all the literature available on the causes of the war. The second was a compilation of important French documents recently released. His conclusion was that the sole guilt of Germany was a "grim legend." One must "cast aside nationalistic charges and feel only general contempt for the international race of diplomats." Since there was divided responsibility (Gannett did not accept the tendency to relieve Germany of all guilt) then one must concede that "the Versailles treaty is built upon a lie and its A to Z revision is not merely a matter of economic necessity but of common justice and common decency."[67]

The works of Turner, Bausman, and Gannett all appeared on the eve of the French invasion of the Ruhr and became important source material for liberals, pro-Germans, and others who protested the French action. A strong anti-French feeling developed in America and *The Nation* contributed to this antagonism. Villard wrote weekly articles describing the French as insane and blind to the consequences of their actions. They were intent on "blood money" and were not as stupid as their policy seemed. Their intense desire to destroy the German nation would ultimately destroy all of Europe.[68]

Various responsible politicians now dared to show sympathy to Germany and to denounce the French. Borah wrote, "I am sincerely interested in this Ruhr invasion. I look upon it as a crime, a crime against peace, against humanity and against international decency."[69] Senator Robert Latham Owen, speaking before the Senate in December 1923, called for all the documents to be brought out of hiding. He placed the responsibility for the war on France and Russia. As for Germany, he remarked: "The German militants did not will the war"; they were forced into it by the persistent mobilization of France and Russia, which was tantamount to a declaration of war.[70] *The Nation* enthusiastically supported Owen's demand for a congressional investigation. Only two years earlier when M. Alfred Michaelson, a representative from Illinois, suggested the same thing, he was denounced as a traitor.[71]

The most persistent champion of revisionism was Harry Elmer Barnes, a colleague of Sidney B. Fay's at Smith. Barnes had little respect for Fay's cautious academic attitude.[72] In 1922 he wrote a long article for *The Nation* on the nationalistic and unscientific approach of American historians.[73] In 1924 he burst into the field of outright revisionism with a vengeance by contributing to *The New Republic* the longest book review in its history. Essentially it was an attack on American historians in general and Charles D. Hazen and Raymond Turner in particular. Barnes charged that their textbooks, *Europe Since 1815* and *Europe Since 1870*, failed to take any note of the new documentary material related to the cause of the war.[74]

Villard was delighted with Barnes's attack. He wrote an article entitled "Historians and the Truth" which began, "Three cheers for Harry Elmer Barnes," and thereby inaugurated a lifelong friendship. Barnes responded by assuring the editors that *The Nation* "alone of the distinguished periodicals of the country has shown consistent courage and determination" in bringing historical truth to light.[75] In 1925 Barnes's famous *Genesis of the World War* placed the blame on France and Russia and relieved Germany of guilt. It was awarded a place on *The Nation's* honor roll.[76]

Villard was more interested in gaining acceptance of the divided guilt theory than in proving France or Russia more guilty than Germany or Austria. In the spring of 1923 Simeon Strunsky, a former editor on *The Post*, accused Villard of supporting Franco-Russian responsibility for the war "in a minor key." Villard replied that *The Nation's* editors had persistently placed the major burden on Austria, "that Germany, Russia, and France shared a lesser degree of responsibility, that the whole system would have produced war but that Austria fired the train. . . ." Villard did stick to this for some time, but his increasing antagonism toward the French and his rationalizations for Germany are evidenced by a remark he wrote to his friend, H. L. Mencken: "You are aware of course that it has been firmly established that the French have invaded Germany fourteen times, while Germany has taken the offensive only seven."[77]

Revisionism gained popularity through the 1920's. By the 1930's revisionists had established the conspiracy thesis and provided ammunition for the famous Nye committee. The movement explains, in part, the growing popularity of *The Nation* during these years. *The Nation,* by opening its pages to the revisionists, became, as one historian has declared, a kind of "Wailing Wall" for penitent liberals who had supported the war.[78] Just as many Germans in the 1950's showed a desire to see the gruesome ordeal of Anne Frank portrayed on the stage, so Americans who had been caught up in the patriotic idealism of 1917-1918 demonstrated a desire to cast off impurities by denouncing what they had held so dear.

The revisionist campaign of *The Nation* brought it into a close, working association with the major political reform movement of the twenties—the progressive movement led by Robert LaFollette. When LaFollette was campaigning in the primary for renomination to the Senate in the summer of 1922, Villard supported him in a significant way. Although he approved the Senator's domestic record and applauded his attack on the conservatives of both parties, he stressed that LaFollette's return would "show that the masses of the people are beginning to come out of the hypnotic state in which they were placed by Woodrow Wilson and the war mania, and are beginning to sense how they were lied to, deceived, and misled in the name of democracy and humanity."[79] Villard greeted LaFollette's success with enthusiasm.

> Only five years ago this man was being denounced from one end of the country to the other as a traitor . . . . the Senate nearly expelled him . . . men demanded his arrest. He has gloried in his shame. Incredible as it seems it now looks as if the plain American people were falling away from the true faith about the war and were beginning to follow those benighted ones, pacifists and others, who treasonably declared that we had no place in the war, and that no good could come out of it for us or humanity.[80]

Villard felt that every victory for LaFollette was a victory for himself and *The Nation*—and for the revisionist theory. In the same article that congratulated LaFollette he praised Bausman's book, *Let France Explain,* which seemed to him to support LaFollette's return to power and influence in the Senate.[81] This connection between revisionism and the growing power of the progressive bloc in the Senate and House was not so far-fetched. It had been *LaFollette's Magazine* which ran in serial form Albert J. Nock's "Myth of a Guilty Nation."[82]

After the victory of a number of progressive insurgents in both parties in the November congressional elections, Villard wrote Philip Snowden, just elected to Parliament, that there were encouraging signs in America—"three anti-war senators have just been elected to Congress."[83] The success of Joseph Lynn Frazier in North Dakota, Henrik Shipstead in Minnesota, and Smith Brookhart in Iowa meant that the liberal bloc for which *"The Nation* has called for the two years past" had arrived and "is in the saddle."[84]

The success of the progressives no longer made it necessary for *The Nation* to lend support to such economic conservatives as Lodge and Knute Nelson. There now existed a group of men whom *The Nation* could endorse without qualification on international as well as domestic issues. The days of the awkward alliances were over. It was an ideal situation.

Statistics on the source of progressive strength and on *The Nation*'s circulation support the suggestion that much of the popularity of these new progressive senators as well as of *The Nation* was based on lingering ethnic prejudices rather than ideological commitment. Both had remarkable support in the heavily German-American populated centers in the Midwest. The Audit Bureau of Circulation reported 5,103 subscribers in 1922 in the Midwestern states and only 6,013 in the North Atlantic states, where the magazine was published and sold on the newsstands. There were more subscribers in Wisconsin than in New Jersey.[85] Villard was aware of pro-German sympathy. He wrote Charles Nagel, a prominent lawyer in the German-American community in St. Louis and Taft's conservative Secretary of Commerce, that *The Nation* "had the greatest opportunity of any publication to be an interpreter of the New Germany to America." Nagel obligingly financed a series of advertisements in the St. Louis German language paper, the *Westliche Post*.[86]

Villard, to be sure, was hopeful for the future of LaFollette and like-minded senators in the 1920's. Nevertheless, there is no question that much of the progressive vote in 1922 and 1924 was, in fact, not liberal at all but a politics of revenge of German-Americans.[87] Although Villard was committed to LaFollette's domestic program, with some exceptions, his enthusiasm was no doubt partly inspired by the personal vindication that LaFollette's postwar career afforded him. Villard preferred Borah for the leadership of the progressive insurgency. He wrote Ramsay MacDonald in 1923 that if Borah decided to bolt the Republican party, he would go out on the stump for him. Borah's circumspection was really more acceptable to Villard than the agrarian radical tradition that still characterized LaFollette's progressivism. But Senator Borah's political independence had become conspicuously lacking in election years. As Hamilton Owens, editor of *The Baltimore Evening Sun,* put it, Borah "speaks with righteousness, votes with the boys and bursts into tears." Throughout his career he threatened apostasy, encouraging his independent supporters, but in the end he placed party regularity above all other political virtues. LaFollette could be counted on and Villard played a prominent part in the early plans of the insurgent Progressive program led by the Senator from Wisconsin.[88]

In December 1922, Villard attended a meeting called by LaFollette to map liberal strategy. Villard, caught up in the movement, considered briefly running for senator on a progressive ticket in New York. William Allen White and Senator Borah advised him against it, saying that he would sacrifice his position as an independent journalist and jeopardize the prestige of *The Nation*.[89] Nevertheless in 1924 it was rumored that he was being considered as the Wisconsin Senator's running mate. Nothing ever came of this, and when the Montana Senator, Burton K. Wheeler, was nominated, Villard stumped the East with him.[90]

Villard and his editors supported most of the specific planks in the Progressive platform. *The Nation* had long since come out for government ownership of the railroads although Villard still referred vaguely to some scheme of "democratic operation."[91] Villard now supported the federal child labor law advocated by LaFollette, agreed with his program for a tax revision placing more of the burden on higher incomes, and supported most of the proposed legislation to ease farm credit and to create large-scale cooperative enterprises. *The Nation* endorsed the pledge of an amendment allowing Congress to override Supreme Court decisions as well as to abolish the lifetime terms of federal judges.[92] Villard's only criticism was LaFollette's weakness on the tariff; he was opposed to schemes to make the tariff work for the farmers as it did for manufacturers. This violated the moral basis of free trade and verged on political expediency of the worst kind.[93]

The progressive platform made very few departures from traditional Midwestern progressive principles of thirty-seven years: anti-monopoly and a return to open competition were still the main issues. Villard noted this staleness in LaFollette's program when he covered the convention in Cleveland. He remarked, after the Senator's acceptance speech: "It seemed to many of us that it was harking back a long way to return to the enforcement of the Sherman Anti-trust act. . . ." He conceded that the economic and industrial situation had gone far beyond control through the imprisonment of "a few trust heads and the dissolution of a few more trusts." "We cannot," he warned, "return to the era of the small businessman if we would." Villard felt that it would have been much more effective if LaFollette had underplayed the old agrarian rhetoric and emphasized his most important planks "such as the government ownership of all water power, and super power undertakings, and government ownership of all railroads. These are

the planks of which Wall Street is really afraid." Still Villard
was carried away by the mere fact of LaFollette's emergence as
a serious candidate: "The man from Wisconsin, hated, despised, abused, and derided; the man whom some of his associates tried six years ago to drive out of the Senate as a pacifist
and pro-German, has received the highest compliment which
could be paid to him short of the Presidency itself." It was
almost as if Villard himself had received the nomination.[94]

The symbolic meaning of LaFollette's candidacy and the
plank in the platform calling for a national referendum on war
declaration compensated for what Villard recognized as a
paralysis of imagination. During the heat of the campaign Villard's editorials began to sound like LaFollette's speeches.
They might have been written in the 1890's and certainly no
later than 1912: "The truth has reached more and more people that [this] is no new and dangerously radical campaign, but
the renewal of the old fight against the 'invisible empire.' "
Villard hoped for the return of government to the plain
people.[95]

The program which Villard enthusiastically supported in
1924 was in large measure "a throwback to the Populists and
the Greenbacks even more than to the Bull Moose." Much of
its support reflected a heartfelt desire to retreat from the
anxieties and frustrations of a complicated urban industrial
society. LaFollette's supporters hoped to return to the old
agrarian democracy. And yet given the political situation in the
1920's the progressives were the best alternative available.[96]
Because these nostalgic longings buttressed Villard's position
on foreign affairs, he was able to put aside his anxiety over the
program's shortcomings. In response to the insistence of Villard
and Burton K. Wheeler that LaFollette devote more time to
questions of foreign policy, LaFollette merely transferred the
language of his domestic criticism to foreign affairs.[97] The
plutocrats were at the root of all the world's problems: "The
treaty of Versailles which we were asked to ratify was a treaty
of financial imperialists, of exploiters, of bankers, of oil

monopolists." The fateful blunder had been Wilson's failure to treat the belligerents as equals. Villard was hearing his own words and he dutifully reported the text in full in *The Nation's International Supplement*.[98]

Villard insisted that LaFollette was not an "absolute" isolationist, a claim that was increasingly difficult to support in view of the Senator's record and his speeches. "International cooperation in the cause of freedom and liberty" was supported, but there was no plank advocating active participation in any existing body of international composition. Villard held that LaFollette would be "ardent in espousing any reasonable plan for disarmament. He would, nevertheless, oppose our immediate unreserved entrance into the League of Nations if he were President—wisely and honestly in our judgment."[99]

By August Villard realized that the campaign had little chance of success. He complained of the poor organization, the lack of money, and the amateurish approach of many of the most dedicated. He wrote his wife that "Privately the leaders do not, of course, expect victory." Nevertheless he maintained an optimistic front in the pages of *The Nation*. The prairies were catching fire. The election might be thrown into the House because LaFollette would keep any man from obtaining the necessary majority. But LaFollette won only one state —his own.[100]

In Chicago on February 21, 1925, the Convention for Progressive Political Action met again. It was called months before to establish an official third political party. Instead the C.P.P.A., disillusioned by defeat, pronounced itself dead. Labor abandoned the idea of political action, the Socialists wanted a party based upon class lines, and in the end only the middle-class reformers remained. They made an attempt to keep the movement alive by planning for a convention in the fall to establish the Progressive party. Villard, one of the most persistent of the diehards, insisted that the defeat was unimportant. He compared the progressive movement to the Labor party movement in England and told his readers that it would take years of third party activity to expect victory.[101] True supporters "do not, cannot, lose heart, we can only see the need for greater and greater efforts, for persistent, continued, and devoted patriotic service to the end that all people shall see where salvation lies and where is the high road to American ideals."[102] He worked diligently through 1925 and 1926, participating in a number of proposed drafts for platforms to be presented at a national convention, which was never called.[103] His interest turned toward the foreign policy aspect of the movement. This was not without a sense of realism.

The liberal movement during the Harding and Coolidge years was, for the most part, unsuccessful in stemming the tide of economic conservatism at home. But all was not lost. Senator Lodge died and the chairmanship of the Senate Foreign Relations Committee went to Senator Borah, the man Villard really wanted to lead the progressive movement in the first place. Villard noted that Borah saw eye to eye with him on disarmament, outlawry of war, and opposition to the League and the World Court. He was sure that Senator Borah would rise "to the opportunity to serve well his country and the world."[104] Thus, while the progressives failed miserably on the home front, Villard's principles received increasing appreciation in the field of foreign affairs.

CHAPTER ELEVEN

The Search For Peace

1921-1928

Senator Borah's elevation to the chairmanship of the Senate Foreign Relations Committee was one indication of the increasing prestige and popularity of Villard's position on foreign policy. His efforts to replace conservative domestic policies had ended in discouragement and frustration. As a by-product of that conservatism, however, both major parties began to accept the pacifist and liberal repudiation of "power politics" and to substitute a policy of moral pressure for collective security. Disarmament, international courts, the outlawing of war, greater popular influence in foreign policy decisions—all measures advocated by Villard—became slogans of the day.

Villard wrote J. A. Hobson in 1925 that *The Nation* was being "treated with much more respect by the old conservative papers." He had recently been overwhelmed by a letter from Ellery Sedgwick, the editor of *The Atlantic Monthly*, which described *The Nation* as " 'incomparably the best weekly paper in the country,' something he never would have said had he believed it two years ago." *The Nation*'s circulation, including subscriptions and newsstand sales, was over 33,000 and on the rise.[1] Foreign developments since the end of the war would have justified Villard's calling this a pacifist era.

In speeches and editorials following the 1920 presidential election Villard set forth a comprehensive program for the achievement of international peace. He called for total disarmament, initiated by a conference of the United States, Great

Britain, and Japan, to put a stop to the naval race for mastery of the Pacific. A world court, independent of the League of Nations and composed of the victors and vanquished alike, would settle international disputes and work in cooperation with a parliament of mankind. He envisioned a world government which would outlaw war.[2]

Villard insisted that the principle of coercion be rejected. He was not against alliances. On the contrary he was enthusiastically for alliances, but "alliances in good works," not of collective force to implement undemocratic and secret agreements.[3] Diplomats had "created a wilderness and called it peace," but the rule of force still governed the world—was, in fact, the basis of international politics. For once, Villard argued, idealism and practicality were the same. With the discredited League dead, Americans at last could practice "the teachings of Jesus."[4] Shortly after Villard published these views Senator Borah presented a resolution calling on the President to request a conference with Great Britain and Japan to discuss disarmament.

Curiously, Villard's claim that his program was compatible with practical politics seemed true to less idealistic men. The Republican party had come to power repudiating Wilsonian foreign policy. Harding was ambiguous about the future policy of his administration, but many influential figures in the party implied that a Republican victory promised some sort of substitute for the League; there was also a strong faction opposed to the continuation of military expenditures. Borah's resolution was not received with enthusiasm by the Republican majority in December 1920, but by the middle of the following year, under pressure to present some alternative to Wilsonianism,[5] Borah's resolution seemed to provide an expedient solution to the growing split in the party. The Republicans could replace the Democrats as the champions of peace and, at the same time, appeal to a large segment of the population that was weary of the high tax burden necessary to maintain continued naval expansion.

Disarmament also provided a possible solution to international problems. Relations between England and the United States had become increasingly strained over the Anglo-Japanese alliance made at the beginning of the war. The United States was openly hostile toward Japanese expansionist aims exhibited during the Versailles conference and the old alliance was embarrassing to the British. In addition, Great Britain's economic position following the war hardly allowed for a continued naval race. If the British could promote an agreement among the three powers that would maintain the status quo in the East and begin a naval disarmament plan, it would be to their advantage.

Practical politics both at home and abroad and the idealistic clamor for disarmament brought about the Republican reduction of military expenditures. Absorbed in the return to normalcy, Americans were eager for any policy that relieved them of the responsibility of thinking about world affairs.

Secretary Hughes decided to call a conference, including the other major powers, France and Italy, as well. Villard chose to ignore the aspect of expediency that motivated the administration. Once a conference met, public opinion would take control and force the diplomats to go much farther than they planned.[6] Shortly before the conference was called he organized a meeting in New York of the editors of the main liberal journals to combine efforts to exert pressure on the administration.[7]

Villard informed his readers that no greater opportunity had ever been presented to mankind. President Harding could "associate his name forever gloriously with greater service to all the world than has ever been achieved by any other modern ruler." He wrote Borah that only three or four words from Harding demanding total disarmament would establish him "as one of the great figures of the world and as the saviour of Europe."[8]

Villard's enthusiasm was more than Albert Jay Nock, the skeptical editor of *The Freeman,* could stand. He ridiculed Villard and his editors for refusing to discuss the power struggle behind the call for the conference. Villard charged Nock with betrayal of an agreement to "force a larger policy" on the administration. Nock countered that *The Nation* was "misleading the public as effectively as though it were pretending that the plague of pellagra could be stayed by the beating of tom toms."[9] Villard was not as naive as Nock claimed. He conceded privately that he did not entertain high hopes for the conference but that he was willing to support it in the hope that "we may get a half or even a quarter loaf."[10] Coming from a man whose entire philosophy had always repudiated the half-a-loaf rationale in the past, Villard's statement was strange indeed.

Villard realized that *The Nation* could not continue to thrive on destructive criticism. He accepted Republican propaganda that pictured the Washington conference as a new and more efficient "peace conference," which would rectify all the blunders of Versailles, because he was sure the power of public opinion would force the Republicans to keep their word.

Villard's optimism was short-lived as it soon became apparent that the delegates would refuse to consider the reduction of land and air power. He ridiculed "the stupid old Republican gang" for neglecting to place "a woman or a labor representative or any true peace lover on the delegation. The youngest member of the group is considerably over a hundred years old mentally and all are living in the period of 1890."[11] Editorials recalled the shadow of Versailles as Villard foresaw "a reactionary lot of conclusions sweetened by a few pious words." The problem was not armament limitation but preventing the "human race from committing suicide." If it were impossible to get the European nations to accept total disarmament, then America should act unilaterally. Villard was certain that the "moral forces of every other country would compel their people to follow in our footsteps."[12]

Villard was as enthusiastic as any observer when Hughes opened the conference with an exhibition of daring which placed control in American hands. Abandoning the traditional clichés, Hughes committed America to a specific and practical plan of naval disarmament, which was put in such a way as to force the other conferees to follow suit. "Not in modern times," wrote Villard, "has there been so clear and so astounding and so brilliant a feat in statecraft." It was, the lead article in *The Nation* proclaimed, "A Great Beginning."[13]

Villard felt this conference was a thousand miles in advance of that nefarious gathering at Versailles. He compared the official pomp and ceremony at the Paris conference of "diplomats and generals who had done their share to plunge Europe into war, and having plunged it into hell, did not know how to extricate it until civilization faced complete disaster," with the unrestrained "freedom and freshness of America." The balconies were packed with "people who lived and breathed, who responded to sentiment, who did not hesitate to charge the atmosphere with their own emotions, to applaud and to cheer and to let the conferees know where they stood." This was Villard's ace in the hole. Hughes may have acted out of political expediency to maintain the status quo, but public opinion would demand that "we go on with the policy in the matter of land disarmaments." The men in Washington would become the pawns of world opinion, forced to abandon traditional caution in response to the great moral pressure.[14]

The conferees at the next meeting accepted the principle of Hughes's plan, but with evasive qualifications. Villard, more acute than many observers, detested their quibbling and castigated the weasel words of the Japanese Ambassador and the charming but disappointing remarks of Balfour.[15] Villard was reluctant to take the renewal of old charges of secrecy and imperialism seriously,[16] but as the conference deliberated it became apparent that the meeting was largely designed to preserve the balance of power in the Pacific through an intricate system of alliances or agreements.

Villard obstinately refused to abandon hope. He looked with satisfaction on any turn of events that diminished the stature of the authors of the Versailles treaty. He repeatedly attacked the French for their demands that commitment of military support, in the event of future German aggression, be attached to any disarmament program.[17]

Villard, embittered by the American refusal to accept outlawing of the submarine and her willingness to allow the further building of cruisers, recorded "compromise of principle number 2478" and denounced the dealings of traditional diplomats. It was now Hughes's "extraordinary stupidity in worshipping the opinion of naval experts" that caused the difficulty. The "littleness of [the] diplomats and statesmen" appalled him. They were "for all the world to see like children squabbling over the number of green and white marbles they had." The issue was so simple: "The way to disarm is to disarm."[18]

The agreement to fix the tonnage of capital ships at a ratio of 5 (U.S.), 5 (Britain), 3 (Japan), 1.67 (France), 1.67 (Italy) was predicated on a series of treaties designed to stabilize the Far East and the Pacific. The Nine Power treaty was merely an extension of America's Open Door policy. Since America had never shown any inclination to support this policy with force, the new treaty merely broadened the base of a diplomacy of platitudes relieving America of the responsibility of leadership. The most important and controversial agreement was the Four Power treaty between the United States, Great Britain, France, and Japan, which dealt with realities and was essential to any disarmament plan. The participating nations were bound to respect one anothers' rights in the Pacific. Article Two was the stickler. It stipulated that if "the said rights are threatened by the aggressive action of any other power," the contracting powers would arrive at an understanding "as to the most efficient measures to be taken, jointly or separately, to meet the exigencies of a particular situation."[19]

This clause brought forth a battle cry from the old irreconcilables. It skirted dangerously close to collective security. Senator Borah had feared this when it had been agreed to include a Pacific parley with the disarmament conference. Villard, for a brief moment, had questioned Borah's intransigence, but he returned to the fold. Article Two of the Four Power treaty was similar in intent to Article Ten of the Covenant,[20] and he now supported Borah and Hiram Johnson in their insistence on some reservation, denying American commitment to any use of coercion, before ratification. *The Nation* concurred: "There is a dangerous hint of force in Article Two . . . a definite affirmation that the U. S. commit itself to no act of force of war is imperatively demanded."[21]

It was poetic justice that Henry Cabot Lodge was called upon to defend the treaty. He denied that it was an alliance and argued that America must not be overcome by distrust and allow herself to "sink back into sullen solitude, a prey to dark suspicions, a hermit nation." Lodge's defense had little effect upon Villard and the opposition. They were not satisfied until the Foreign Relations Committee insisted that American ratification contain the reservation that Senators Borah and Johnson had demanded. Villard wrote that insofar as any amendment could "sterilize an obnoxious treaty the Four Power Treaty is bettered by the reservation. . . ."[22]

The treaty, as finally accepted with the reservation, was, in effect, no more than a gentleman's agreement. Disarmament advocates had attempted to ignore the *Realpolitik* underlying any international agreement. The result had been the emasculation of any genuine step toward disarmament.

Encouraged by the defeat of collective security, Villard turned his attention to another basic objective in his program of peace as an alternative to the League of Nations—the "outlawry of war." This phrase had been coined by an ambitious, civic-minded Chicago lawyer, S. O. Levinson. Levinson was a conservative in domestic affairs and believed in the power of law to solve chaos and violence. Spurred on by a profound faith in the evolutionary concept of progress, Levinson developed a detailed plan for the outlawry of war which he presented in

December 1921, while the disarmament conference was in session.[23]

Levinson's specific plan contained three main ingredients: a codification of international law, the outlawing of war, and the establishment of a world court to settle disputes between nations. Levinson envisioned a court independent of the League with compulsory jurisdiction over all disputes which were international in nature. It would not make the pernicious distinction between "justiciable and non-justiciable disputes," which Levinson considered a euphemism for protecting national honor and vital interest.[24]

Villard had been in contact with Levinson for some time. Levinson was one of the more substantial financial supporters of *The Nation* during the fight against the League in the Senate.[25] In 1918 and again in 1920 Villard editorially supported outlawry. Levinson credited Villard and *The Nation* with initiating the movement and assured Villard that if the magazine's support brought forth criticism he was prepared to refute all objections.[26]

When Levinson's plan was circulated at the disarmament conference, Villard had only one objection—the plan failed to disavow the right of self-defense. Levinson had conceded that a nation could maintain a military force adequate for defense based upon the "citizen soldiery" plan used by the Swiss. To Villard this amounted to universal military training.[27] Levinson soon discovered that Villard's criticism reflected the feelings of many pacifist and peace groups. He wrote Villard, "I have decided to eliminate the citizen soldiery feature from our outlawry program. To this you have largely contributed. It seems that notwithstanding its intention to be pacifistic, it is taken as really militaristic, not only by you but by many of my co-workers."[28]

The outlawry movement became swallowed up in the great debate over America's possible adherence to the protocol of the Permanent Court of International Justice in Geneva. In order to reassure the irreconcilables, who charged that the Court was inextricably connected with the League, Secretary Hughes offered a number of reservations guaranteeing that America's participation would involve no legal relations with the League or assumption of any obligations under the Covenant. This inducement was not sufficient to satisfy dyed-in-the-wool League-haters. In their desire to thwart the administration's program they seized upon Levinson's scheme. On February 13, 1923, Borah offered a resolution for the outlawing of war which was a verbatim statement of S. O. Levinson's plan.[29]

Borah's maneuvering and rejection of the administration put Villard on the spot. Villard had not seen Levinson's plan as a means of sidetracking American participation in the World Court. *The Nation* had previously criticized the administration's reluctance to join the Court: "It was a tragedy that had its roots in America's justified opposition to the covenant," but nevertheless the editors advised American entrance.[30] Villard was reluctant to abandon his previous support of the Court, but there is more than a suggestion in their correspondence that Levinson considered that his financial contributions to *The Nation* entitled him to direct editorial policy on the question of the Court and the outlawry program.[31] When he prepared an editorial in February, he noted Levinson's objections, but he refused to abandon cautious approval of the Court: "For all the Court's defects the United States was not justified in holding aloof from it and we so stated editorially on February 15, 1922. There is no political control here as in the League itself, no commitment to the policies of a few great powers." Villard added that the editors "rejoice that Mr. Harding and Mr. Hughes have moved at last and we shall be disappointed if, after considering the matter during recess, the Senate does not follow the suggestions of the President and ratify the program."[32]

Levinson's infuriated reply came on schedule. He expressed astonishment "that a man of [Villard's] progressive mind and . . . thorough grasp of old world diplomacy should fall for this proposition." Villard replied that he was not going to change his stand. He knew his editorial would "bring on the wrath of God with you playing God. But, as we stated in the editorial, we took our position a long time ago. The sin was committed last winter."[33]

Villard's stand on the Court in 1923 was his only flirtation with any existing international organization throughout the twenties. His acceptance of the Washington treaties was not a compromise because they were not related to the League in any way, but the Court was a product of the Covenant. Apparently Villard had accepted the Hughes reservations assuring that America would not be committed to any policy of collective coercion.[34] It is obvious, however, that he was unhappy in his new role as the man of expediency. His sudden opposition to Levinson and Borah was more the result of chance than of conviction. In order to extricate himself, he wrote Levinson that he was planning to ignore the issue. He considered it dead.[35]

The major parties also tried to bury the Court controversy as the 1924 presidential campaign approached. They gave vague endorsement, but managed to delay debate until December 1925. This gave Villard ample time to consider his apostasy. He decided to return to the ranks. On December 9, *The Nation* admitted that it had previously "leaned" in the direction of joining the Court, but it now felt that the Hughes reservations were not sufficient. America must see to it that the Court would be backed by no power other than the moral force of world opinion. The United States "must condition its entry on effective agreements that neither the Court, nor the League nor any of its members shall have power to enforce the decrees of the tribunal by war, or by economic pressure of any kind."[36]

Villard was utterly confused by the Senate debate over international legal questions of advisory opinions, Court jurisdiction, and the relationship of the League to the Court. He turned to Professor Edwin Borchard of Yale for help in the preparation of an article which would state *The Nation*'s position once and for all. Borchard, a staunch opponent of the

League, was on the way to becoming an expert on international law dedicated to promoting American isolationism. He was, like Villard, very anti-French.[37] Borchard prepared a memorandum on the Court with a technical analysis of all the arguments pro and con. Essentially the Court was intimately attached to the League, which was a political machine founded on force, and it would use force to carry out even advisory opinions. The whole advisory opinion system was "the trap through which the League can exercise control over the United States like any other country." Having exhausted all the current arguments, he suggested that Villard state that:

> *The Nation* is for a Court with obligatory jurisdiction in legal questions; a Court absolutely and completely separated from the political League; a Court which can give no advisory opinions to the League or the Council, but only to the nations that may request them; a Court whose decisions under no circumstances be enforced by any political machinery, public opinion being its only sanction. If the League Court cannot conform to these proposals of a genuine Court, *The Nation* is opposed to the United States entering the World Court.[38]

Villard thanked Borchard for his help.[39] On February 3, 1925, an unsigned editorial appeared, written by Villard. It dealt almost entirely with the question of force, but repeated, in similar phrases, the paragraph written by Borchard. Villard added that a court not based on force was right and proper, and would also be effective. If any nation did not accept the court's decrees, "it would face world wide odium and reproach, but even such a refusal would be only a temporary setback to a Court rightly organized and avowedly conducted with entire faith in the public opinion of the world."[40]

Villard had returned squarely to the pacifist position of a moral imperative. By returning to pure principle he was able to avoid serious discussion of technicalities and also avoid coming to grips with the concrete problem at hand. He wrote William Hard that he intended to call a halt to all discussion of the Court, since he felt "his readers were 'bored stiff' by the discussion."[41]

Villard continued to support Senator Borah and the irreconcilables who managed to have a fifty-page list of reservations tacked on to America's acceptance, which went even beyond the objections that Hughes had anticipated. It stated that the Court "should not, without the consent of the United States, entertain any request for an advisory opinion touching any dispute or question in which the United States has or claims an interest." In effect, the United States proposed to remain aloof from the responsibilities and obligations of League membership but to maintain an equal veto power with the nations making up the League Council.[42] When the forty-eight member nations met in conference and demanded clarification, Coolidge decided that the question of membership was closed, and in an Armistice Day speech, 1926, he announced that he saw no prospect of American adherence to the Court.[43]

Villard considered it a great victory for Borah and anticipated the Senator's candidacy for the presidential nomination. America would at last have "a first rate intellect in search of the Presidency."[44] He rejoiced that the country had remained aloof from "the daily intrigues and quarrels of Europe" and stated that America should hold to "the historic doctrine of keeping out of entangling alliances and political commitments. Let us keep to our shores politically."[45]

Despite these sentiments, Villard still proclaimed *The Nation*'s internationalist position. In January 1926, shortly after the vote on the Court, Villard insisted that *The Nation* had no sympathy with those "who opposed the Court and the League from the narrow and chauvinistic points of view. The editors of *The Nation* do not fear alliances in good works with other nations—they are not afraid to be called internationalists"; they look "forward to a parliament of man and the cooperation of all nations not only to outlaw war, but to grapple unitedly with the monstrous evils of the world."[46] Villard was not being disingenuous; this statement was consistent with the pacifist approach to foreign policy. Villard, unlike Borah, Hiram Johnson, and others of the irreconcilables, had no fear of sacrificing American sovereignty. He did not worry that a compulsory court might have jurisdiction in the Caribbean, and he had no desire to preserve the Monroe Doctrine.[47] The practical effect of his firm opposition to the League, however, was to support almost to the letter the isolationist position.

Villard continued to search diligently for an alternative to collective security and became interested in other lofty schemes that prompted Samuel Flagg Bemis to refer to this period as "The Fool's Paradise of American History."[48] No discussion of this search and the continued policy of peace by proclamations of good will and faith in humanity is complete without mention of the most famous example—the "international kiss" known as the Kellogg-Briand Peace Pact.[49]

Villard wrote during the Washington naval conference that the delegates' failure to do away with the means for chemical warfare and the submarine "cast a dark shadow over the world." Nevertheless "that cloud will have a silver lining if by reason of this failure men's hopes turn from the *utopian dream* [of arms limitation] to the practical possibilities of abolishing war" (italics mine).[50] Why Villard should view arms limitation as more utopian than the abolition of war is not entirely clear. *The Nation*'s exhortations hint at the belief that only when war became unthinkable would peace be assured.[51] The solution to the world's problems was to replace the martial spirit with the pacifist spirit and idealists applauded the war novels of Ernest Hemingway and John Dos Passos, in which the heroes became nauseated at such words as "sacred," "glorious sacrifice," "loyalty," and "honor" in praise of the martial spirit.[52]

Aristide Briand, the French Foreign Minister, had for years devoted himself to constructing a wall of bilateral agreements to encircle Germany. Briand's obsession with the next war made Villard detest him as the most militant of the traditional European diplomats.[53] When amateur diplomats James T. Shotwell and Nicholas Murray Butler brought tidings of America's intense desire to abolish war, Briand saw a chance to place the United States in the position of censuring any future aggressor against France by means of a bilateral treaty. Such an agreement might insure that America would, under no circumstances, enter in a war against France.[54] The Kellogg-Briand Pact, like the Washington treaties, was the product of a strange combination of popular idealistic sentiment and the shrewd manipulation of world politics. The first stage in its development was almost entirely the work of amateur diplomats urged on by peace groups, the clergy, and the League advocates, who viewed any rapprochement with the member states as encouraging. The administration, under Coolidge, the State Department, under Kellogg, and the Senate Foreign Relations Committee, under Borah, viewed the whole affair with suspicion and distrust. Kellogg was infuriated when Briand directed his appeal to the American people, by-passing the normal channels of diplomacy. At one point, driven to a frenzy by the "naive meddling of do gooders," he remarked that the peace leaders were a set of damn fools.[55]

When men like Borah and Charles Clayton Morrison, the editor of *The Christian Century,* advocated broadening the pact into a multilateral agreement, Briand's whole purpose was destroyed.[56] It would now be just another toothless, platitudinous proclamation. Briand had exploited the idealism of the reformers for his purposes, but two could play at that game, and Borah used the concept of outlawry to outwit one of the shrewdest diplomats in Europe.[57] The Republicans had just suffered a diplomatic defeat with the refusal of France and Italy to take part in the Geneva disarmament conference called by Coolidge to extend agreements initiated at Washington. They might now revive the wonderfully simple and popular slogan, "the outlawry of war," and enter the presidential campaign of 1928 as the champions of peace and freedom.

During the preliminary stages leading up to the Kellogg pact, *The Nation*'s editorials were lukewarm and suspicious. They encouraged the idea of discussion but Villard lacked the enthusiasm he had exhibited at the time of the Washington conference.[58] Villard's friend, Alanson B. Houghton, wrote him in June 1928, only a month before the multilateral pact was signed at Paris, that *The Nation* was "underestimating the value of the Kellogg Pacts" and stressed its beneficial appeal to the "plain people." Villard replied that he was eager to talk to Houghton because he was "quite conscious that *The Nation* has not done itself proud on this issue. That is my fault and I need help to obtain a clear understanding of it."[59]

Villard did understand the issues involved in the debate over the pact, but there were a number of reasons for his lack of enthusiasm. Villard's Francophobia and his belief that the French were primarily responsible for the failure of the recent disarmament talks made him suspect any agreement with France. More significant was his waning enthusiasm for the beneficence of public opinion. During the fight over World Court reservations Villard wrote that Senator Borah was a man of integrity and principle, and he would not succumb to the clamor of public opinion.[60] This was the same public opinion that he viewed with such hope during the Washington conference. After the Senate approved adherence to the Court with reservations, Villard wrote Senator Norris that he thought if there had been a secret ballot the senatorial vote would not have favored the Court.[61] Villard's position was contradictory. He spoke of making any commitment to war subject to national referendum.[62] At the same time, when popular opinion did not represent his views, he spoke of the need of a secret ballot.

A more important reason for Villard's half-heartedness was his belated realization that idealism was being used by practical politicians for partisan advantage. He could no longer have faith that the mobilization of popular pressure might overwhelm the strategists. Levinson, anxious to see his plan become a reality, wrote Kellogg that "aside from the humanitarian aspects of the matter it has great political potentialities. After the factional differences created by the contest over the league and the court, a simple clean cut opinion would rededicate the great Republican party as the party of abolition [of war]."[63] Villard recognized this partisan motive.[64]

When Charles Roden Buxton wrote Villard that English liberal leaders were enthusiastic about the prospects of the pact, Villard replied that he doubted if the statesmen involved really wanted peace.[65] The proof of the pudding was in the administration's simultaneous support of a naval cruiser bill. This struck him as the most patent hypocrisy, and proved to him that the Kellogg pact was a sham. During the Senate debate over ratification he wrote that "a vote for the Kellogg Pact is like a vote for the Ten Commandments—perfectly safe and in no wise affecting the existing state of the world."[66]

Villard's accusations were justified by Vice President Dawes's statement to reluctant senators that the antiwar treaty and the cruiser bill, taken together, constituted "a unified policy of the United States."[67] Villard heaped scorn and abuse on his previous champion, Senator Borah. He spoke of the man's wretched leadership and his willingness to descend from principle in order to see that the Kellogg pact passed, not because he was interested in the pact, but as a feather in the hat of the Republican party. He demanded that the unreliable Borah be dropped from the roster of independents and progressives.[68]

Villard's specific criticism was directed against the pact's approval of wars in self-defense and it was valid. A pact outlawing war that left the definition of war up to each nation was a patent absurdity. On the other hand, Villard did not advocate any machinery to define aggressive war or to punish transgressions. If the signatories had not mentioned self-defense in their reservations, there is nothing in Villard's indictment that indicates he would have disapproved of the pact. The signatories had not come to that state of mind where the concept of any

184

war for any purpose was unthinkable; this was, according to Villard, the tragic failure.[69]

If Villard had stopped to view the course of foreign policy, he would have seen that in one sense his position had been substantially supported. In no decade in American history did popular opinion play a more decisive role in foreign affairs than in the ten years preceding the Kellogg-Briand Peace Pact. Villard pleaded for greater recognition of the practicality of the pacifist position and of the superiority of the "ethic of Jesus" over force as a means of obtaining peace. Never had lip service to moral righteousness received greater currency than in the nineteen-twenties. The Washington conference, the World Court issue, and the Kellogg Peace Pact rested entirely on an ostensible belief in the good will of men. In no previous decade had the pacifist had greater prestige. Pacifism was adopted by a great majority of the clergy, by students, and by politicians.[70]

In 1916 Wilson had remarked that "if you say 'we shall not have any war,' you have got to have the force to make that 'shall' bite."[71] Villard had bitterly resented this statement and the entire Wilsonian concept of collective security. By 1928 those responsible for the course of American foreign policy had virtually accepted Villard's position and repudiated Wilson. They made sure in every qualification of every agreement that there should be absolutely no force to make the "shall" bite. But Villard felt that the spirit of his position had been betrayed by opportunists who did not have faith in the principles they espoused. It was extremely difficult in the light of the record to maintain the tenuous distinction between his theoretical internationalism and the narrow chauvinism of so many of his allies.

Villard refused to modify his position. In 1927, even after recognizing some of the humanitarian achievements of the League, he told John Palmer Gavit that as long as the League "stands for war and the Treaty of Versailles, I have got to be an outsider."[72] When Allan Nevins wrote that *The Nation* had lacked sanity and balance during the war and asked Villard if he did not regret some of the harsh things that he had said about Wilson and the League, Villard replied:

> I regret nothing I have ever written about Woodrow Wilson or the League of Nations. On the contrary I am sharpening my pen for a biography of Wilson and—confidentially to you— I should like to call it, "The World's Greatest Criminal." As for the League, I am happy to record its progress and give it full credit for every good thing it does. But I cannot close my eyes to its very great defects and the fact that it is still deeply involved in that body of death, the Treaty of Versailles.[73]

Here was the moral imperative again—the insistence on principle regardless of the cost. He had tried to work with the prevailing powers but they had failed him. At his best his criticism expressed an ethical urgency which was badly needed in politics, both domestic and international. Since the major parties had betrayed the true spirit of pacifism, the only solution was to attempt once again to create an opposition party. The impulse that forced Villard to vote for the Prohibition party in 1908 and 1916, the Socialist party in 1920, and the Progressive party in 1924 once again drove him on in his search for a genuine reform party that would represent his views on foreign policy and, at the same time, support vigorous liberalism at home.

CHAPTER TWELVE

New Directions
1928-1932

In the first decades of the twentieth century many reformers began to realize that their faith in political equality and economic freedom had failed to measure up to the challenge of America's industrial growth. The progressive mind, Louis Hartz wrote, "is like the mind of a child in adolescence, torn between old taboos and new reality, forever on the verge of exploding into fantasy."[1] As late as 1925 the inspiration for Villard's reformist zeal was the righteous indignation he felt at the corruption of nineteenth-century liberal ideals. The problems plaguing American society were still, for him, questions of moral turpitude, not fundamental failures of the system. In the early twenties he cautioned his adventurous editors to go slowly in their demands for drastic innovation. The system was not a failure—it was the men who exploited the system who were to blame.

Villard made no pretensions of radicalism. He was drawn into cooperation with Left-wing groups largely because of their pacifist leanings. During the hearings of the commission on Ireland he answered a critic by insisting that *The Nation* "is not even socialistic much less extremely radical, except perhaps in its pacifism." He quoted the appraisal of Henry Nevinson, editor of the London *Nation,* who described Villard's magazine as "a conservatively liberal paper." In frustration Villard added: "It is annoying to us who know that we are not radical, not even socialistic, to be constantly portrayed by ignoramuses as extreme radicals, thereby classifying us in the public mind with the I.W.W. and the advocates of bloody revolution, with whose views as you know we pacifists have no sympathy whatsoever."[2]

Villard advocated encouragement of Socialist groups in Europe to ward off a Bolshevik revolution. He hoped that certain strategic concessions could be made to save the free enterprise system from its own folly. He gradually conceded that modifications would have to be made to meet the complexities of a new era, but he hoped it would not be at the expense of traditional values. What disturbed Villard was that *laissez faire* liberalism had contributed to the creation of a system in which the old virtues of diligence and honesty were not rewarded. Sagacity, the shrewd deal, and the short weight were more often than not the requirements of success. If the New Deal technicians on the horizon were devoted to saving an economic system, reformers of Villard's vintage were more intent on saving *McGuffey's Reader*—not necessarily the narrow provincialism and rural prejudice of McGuffey's code, but the fundamental values. Any modification of the system should insure that the old virtues receive their proper reward.

In 1929 Villard attacked progressives, who were intent on using the tariff to aid the farmer, for failing to see the moral issue involved. He insisted that free trade would do more than anything else to "purify our whole political life."[3] In every liberal economic measure he came to support, his emphasis was on its ethical merits. Disarmament was wise from an economic point of view, but more important, it reflected the attitude of the good samaritan. To Villard the politician who backtracked and compromised might be intellectually incompetent, but much worse than that, he was morally corrupt. The question of character was always at the root of things.

It is this evangelical perfectionist spirit that has caused Villard to be labeled an "old-fashioned liberal."[4] In 1932, when even Villard had suspicions that the capitalist system had failed, he still wrote: "I have not lost faith in Democracy or the workability of our institutions, provided they are adjusted to modern economic, social and political conditions. The fault in my judgment has been less with the economic and political system under which we have lived than with the men who have been chosen to work it."[5] Many contemporaries viewed him as a "self-righteous schoolmarm"; others, like Mencken, expressed good-humored disbelief at Villard's almost "boyish innocence." In 1928 Mencken wrote: "Villard near sixty? It is impossible to imagine it. He will always be of the age that dreams of honest politics—i.e., edible cobblestones, white blackbirds—and leaps to the summons of high adventure."[6] While younger critics were scoffing at everything from mom to the New England town meeting, Villard wrote of "the pure, sound, gold that lies underneath the commonness of exterior, the commonplaces of much of our rural and small town multitudes."[7] Heywood Broun, a flamboyant iconoclast recently fired from *The New York World* and quickly recruited by Villard, remarked in the pages of *The Nation* itself: "It is a curious piece of casting which finds [Villard] head, and also body, of the most effective rebel periodical in America."[8]

The description of Villard as a curious phenomenon, a relic from an older age, is understandable. Nevertheless, his flexibility and growing willingness to face issues squarely have not received just recognition. Villard declared in a telegram on behalf of the Committee of One Hundred supporting LaFollette's candidacy in 1924: "We believe the time has come for a New Deal."[9] His conception of a new deal was diluted by the nostalgic overtones that characterized the LaFollette campaign and tinged with personal vindictiveness. Four years of cynical exploitation of idealism by politicians and diplomats made Villard realize that there must be more fundamental reform. The progressives in both major parties who represented his views on foreign affairs inevitably remained within the sterile stalls of party orthodoxy on domestic issues, and he was intent on enticing true progressives away from party allegiance.

Unfortunately 1928 was a poor time to start. The pure gold

of the small town multitudes had lost its lustre. Important issues at home and abroad were buried under an avalanche of
bigotry, ignorance, and nationalism. Villard had trouble in
forcing attention beyond the frightful bogeys of "Rum, Ro-
manism and Tammany Hall."[10] Hoover, he felt, was nothing
more than the impotent representative of a defunct political
party. He would bring no change in affairs. The man had stood
mute in the face of sin and corruption for nearly eight years.
Villard admired Al Smith for his courage and forthrightness.
He also felt that the election of a Catholic would do much to
break down the walls of prejudice. But Smith was a product of
Tammany, and had deliberately selected a man like John J.
Raskob of the DuPont and General Motors empire, and a regis-
tered Republican, to run his campaign. This confirmed Villard's belief that the Democratic party was as sterile and bankrupt as its opponent.[11]

There was the question of prohibition. Villard still observed
the pledge of abstinence made to his mother as a college boy.
Despite pressure from *The Nation's* staff to play down the
superficial struggle between the wets and the drys, the issue
did have meaning for Villard. In 1924 he still felt that the
Volstead Act had "done more good than harm."[12] In 1928 he
wrote Franklin Roosevelt, whom he supported for governor,
that he was "struggling desperately" to bring himself to "support Al but I cannot see myself through the maze yet. I think
the Democratic party is done and finished, and I am somewhat
on the other side of the wet issue and so my difficulty of decision is very great."[13] This was not inconsistent with an
important stream of progressive thought that looked upon
prohibition as a powerful reform measure that would aid in
breaking down corruption and lifting the worker out of his de-
graded position. Many former progressives supported Hoover
on the basis of Smith's disapproval of the Eighteenth Amendment.[14]

For these reasons Villard straddled the fence in the campaign
of 1928. His logical choice should have been Norman Thomas.

He conceded that the Socialists' platform was "far more that of *The Nation* than any other."[15] Norman Thomas was a contributing editor of *The Nation,* his name was on the masthead, and yet the magazine refused to endorse him. As late as September 26, 1928, Villard still failed to make a choice. In an article entitled, "Should the Liberal Vote for Smith?" Villard rejected the endorsement of Smith by a committee of former LaFollette progressives. He remarked that the "Progressive vote was not deliverable in bulk." He denounced Hoover as a former engineer turned party politician that no liberal could possibly vote for. He then praised Smith for his frankness on prohibition—at least people knew where he stood. There was no sign, however, that Smith would "take big business by the throat." Significantly he remarked that Smith's program stopped short of "firing the blood of true progressives. He doesn't go the whole distance on water power, he does not use the words, 'government operation', which is the crux of the problem." In 1924 Villard had studiously avoided the idea of actual government operation of any private industry. Villard went on to say that Norman Thomas was closest to the principles for which *The Nation* stood. Unfortunately "the menace of Hooverism will weigh so heavily on thousands who would like to make him their choice" that they feel they must support the Democratic candidate. *The Nation*'s editors, he concluded, would leave it up to the conscience of the progressive voters whether to vote for Smith or Thomas.[16]

Villard appealed to Herbert Croly to join in a campaign to explain why progressives couldn't vote for Hoover. Croly replied tersely that this was obvious to most informed liberals.[17] Only old line progressives like Jane Addams, Carrie Chapman Catt, and Ruth Morgan, who supported Hoover because of the prohibition issue, couldn't see the light. *"The New Republic* will be intent on informing its readers why it must support Smith."[18]

Norman Thomas found Villard's editorial insipid, illogical, and without political courage. He felt that it was absurd to concede that both major parties were useless, that the complete death of the Democratic party was all to the good, and then fail to support his candidacy. As long as *The New Republic* and *The Nation* "remain so pathetically grateful for any sign of grace in the candidates of the old parties," it was doubtful that a third party could gain recognition. Villard replied meekly that "the whole campaign is so befuddled by the issues of Tammany Hall, prohibition and Catholicism that it is utterly idle to spend any time on the more fundamental progressive issues."[19]

Thomas angrily pointed out that during the hysteria of the war Villard had not found it idle to treat the issues—"You are a Mr. Facing Both Ways supporter of doubtful value." He unjustly charged Villard with taking a position designed to increase circulation and influence: "I should not write to you at all except that you profess to want to help a third party and neither I nor anyone who has spoken to me—I never bring the matter up myself—believes that you are helping a third party."

Villard was painfully hurt by the accusations of his long time friend. He denied the charge and pointed out that his straddling of the issue caused criticism from all sides. But Thomas's criticism bared the real problem: Villard did want a third party—but not one that went under the name of socialism. He told Thomas, "If I shared your belief that by coming out for the Socialist party now I would best further the formation of a new third party, I should unhesitatingly come out on your side. But I cannot."[20] Villard stated his position in a letter to Ida Crouch, a member of the party:

> I am willing to grant that I find nearly everything in the last socialist platform satisfactory to me, but I am, nevertheless, firmly of the belief that no party can get ahead in America under the name Socialist. I am only interested in starting a new third party which may have, as a matter of course, three-fourths of the aims of the Socialist party but which will be free of the Marxist stamp. I believe that such a party is under way,

192

and I sincerely hope that the Socialist organization will become a part of it.[21]

Villard told a dinner audience honoring *The New Leader,*
the Socialist organ, that "Socialism, pacifism, and internationalism are words that have a taint upon them." Although
the last two had stood for the greatest kind of humanitarian-
ism, "our common enemy, the militarists, the imperialists, the
exploiters of labor and the masses, have succeeded in poisoning
public opinion." Villard advised his audience, if they were
truly interested in promoting their objectives, to abandon
allegiance to the name of socialism and join with liberal progressives in the formation of a new third party.[22]

Although Villard did not come out for Thomas, he was
driven by Thomas's criticism to deal with the fundamental
issues of the campaign. He made his position clear in an editorial published shortly before election day. Norman Thomas
was the only candidate that was dealing with "the economic
question which the public ought to be discussing—control of
the government by organized wealth." He asked whether the
people should rule in America. Great human issues were
involved: protection of labor through a system of "adequate
old age pensions, insurance against sickness, accident and unemployment" was imperative. The lawmakers "are capable of
drafting legislation to make Wall Street safe for the most
gigantic speculation of modern times, but no one can provide
a bill . . . to function when millions are out of employment.
No one is planning, outside of the socialist party, for greater
industrial democracy and greater economic justice."[23] Villard's
reference to over-all planning was in accord with the demands
of younger liberals such as Paul Douglas, Stuart Chase, and
others who were criticizing their progressive colleagues for
pseudo-realism and refusal to look ahead.[24] Villard closed with
a ringing demand that *Nation* readers realize that:

A thousand wrongs in American life cry out for redress, but we
are told to consider how rich and happy we are and how we

can add to that happiness at the expense of other peoples. . . . Those are right who declare that the battle of freedom and conscience must be fought anew in every generation. It will be fought and so will the struggle as to whether the United States is to be the property of a favored few or of the great masses of the American people whose labor and whose toil create the wealth we have.[25]

Villard still could not bring himself to endorse Thomas and he refused to allow his staff to do so, although most of them favored him.[26] Freda Kirchwey, in a minor act of defiance, let her name appear on a *New Republic* straw vote favoring Thomas. Villard simply could not make up his own mind between a vote of protest and one of political expediency. Early in October he wrote his son Hilgard: "I am not going to vote for Smith. I shall vote for Thomas or not vote at all." Villard did finally vote for Smith in a desperate effort to defeat Hooverism. To his friend Ramsay MacDonald he described the anguish he felt: "In the last few days of the campaign Hoover drove me into coming out personally for Smith. Yet I hated not to support Thomas whose platform was far more that of *The Nation* than any other, but as long as there was a hope and there seemed to be a good one at that time in October, I felt I must do my bit to make it real. . . ."[27] In preparation for a miracle if Smith were to be elected, Villard wrote a victory editorial:

No more extraordinary victory . . . against him were concentrated all the forces of bigotry and snobbery. . . . It is the victory of the man in the roundhouse, and on the roadbed, the laborer in the mines, the clerk in the grocery store . . . No corporations have, we hope, a strangle hold on him. . . . We are under no illusion as to the Governor's limitations. We have not forgotten that he heads a party composed of utterly diverse and incompatible elements. . . . We have often hoped that it might die and yield in its place a newborn party of progress. . . . Today we can do no else than give thanks for the defeat of Herbert Hoover and the whole of the reactionary and corrupt Republican party.[28]

The fantasy of preparing that denunciation of the major parties was the only joy that Villard took in the campaign. A few weeks after Hoover's election he decided that his refusal to endorse Thomas had been a mistake. "I look back on the campaign with unmixed horror, and without the least satisfaction in my own part in it; in fact, I think I handled it worse than any campaign I have ever been in."[29] Villard had voted out of political expediency for the lesser evil and it seemed as though he had thrown his vote away.

Villard's absorption in domestic issues and the resulting frustrations did not dampen his interest in foreign policy. *The Nation* kept a sharp lookout on the European scene and week after week predicted disaster if America did not take a more active and responsible position in international affairs. This did not mean that Villard or his editors advocated joining the League. "The United States enter the league? Sometime in the distant future, but not now."[30] Nor did *The Nation* show any renewed interest in the World Court.

Although reaction and political sterility seemed firmly entrenched at home, Villard was encouraged by Hoover's Memorial Day address, in which he spoke with seeming sincerity of a renewal of disarmament negotiations and also made some guarded statements about readjustment of German reparations.[31] His hope was buttressed by the victory of the Labor party in England and the elevation of Ramsay Mac-Donald to the office of Prime Minister. In a letter of congratulation he told MacDonald that his success had "sent an electric thrill through every progressive and socialist in the country." In *The Nation* he wrote that it was "a glorious victory for labor —not only for progress in Great Britain but for Progressives all over the world."[32]

Villard hoped that MacDonald's appointment would give vitality to the new organization of progressives in America, the League for Independent Political Action, which he had helped organize in December 1928. It hoped to draw all non-Marxists from the Socialists to liberal Democrats into one

195

organization. He felt certain that with such important figures as John Dewey, Paul Douglas, William Du Bois, and Norman Thomas working for the cause the possibilities for a new and powerful third party were good.[33]

In view of these important developments abroad and their implications for the American political scene, Villard made plans to spend some time in Europe. *The Nation* was in good shape. The circulation, including newsstand sales, had reached 40,000 and was gradually increasing. During the period May 1928 to May 1929 the magazine had actually made a profit.[34] Villard had consented to the modernization of the format, which allowed for more drawings and cartoons, and even tolerated the frivolity of Heywood Broun's column although he was dubious about its taste. The *Nation* Foundation, now *The Nation* Incorporated, was made up of a number of substantial stockholders whose interest and generosity relieved some of the strain on Villard's personal finances.[35] The magazine was far from a money-making proposition but it did begin to look as though it might pay its own way. Villard contemptuously referred to *The New Republic* as a "kept journal" because of its dependence on the Willard Straight fortune. "In the long run a paper that has to be supported loses its effectiveness."[36] Although Villard was never adverse to soliciting financial support, it was a point of pride with him that generous benefactors should eventually receive a return on their investments. Throughout his editorship he could never consider *The Nation* a liberal philanthropic enterprise. He needed to prove that he was not an idealistic aristocrat dabbling in liberal politics but a good businessman and competent journalist.

Although Villard appreciated this relative financial security, the staff was in a normal state of turmoil. Freda Kirchwey was apparently sampling the temptations of the Jazz Age. Villard complained that she was burning the candle at both ends and needed a rest.[37] She was released from her responsibilities as managing editor and was temporarily assigned the lighter duties of literary editor, filling the vacancy left by Mark Van

Doren, who had returned to Columbia. There was some criticism of her "Greenwich Village" approach to literature, but Villard, while conceding her faults, defended her as "efficient and up to date." She was not dull and did not "think every review was sacred" as Van Doren had.[38] The literary editorship remained in a state of flux until Henry Hazlitt settled into the job in 1930.

Villard searched for a good managing editor whom he could depend upon during his extended absences. He always hoped that Lewis Gannett would take the job and assume the chief editorship when he retired. Gannett, however, decided to leave *The Nation* for the more lucrative and more stable atmosphere of *The New York Tribune*.[39] Villard called upon the erratic Henry Mussey to leave his position as professor of economics at Wellesley College and return as a vice president of *The Nation* corporation and managing editor. Mussey made it clear that he would not be Villard's "hired man" and warned that he would leave if Villard maintained his paternalistic attitudes. So eager was Villard to have done with the negotiations that he apologized for past disagreements and gave Mussey assurances that he would have a free hand. Mussey rejoined the staff in June 1929.[40]

Villard sailed on July 3. He planned to spend the summer traveling with his family and also to participate in a month's tour of Soviet Russia under the sponsorship of the American-Soviet Chamber of Commerce. *The Nation*'s enthusiasm for the Soviet regime had increased throughout the twenties. Whenever Red-baiters raised a hue and cry about Soviet politics, *The Nation* came to their defense. When responsible critics questioned the more brutal aspects of Soviet methods to enforce political conformity, *The Nation* published sympathetic rebuttals. Its pages were filled with lengthy articles on various aspects of the Soviet society and its industrialization advances.[41] Every year *The Nation* dedicated a November issue to sympathetic accounts of developments in Russia since the revolution. In November 1927, during the tenth anniversary celebration, *The Nation* devoted an entire issue to "The Land of Hope." One unsigned article began "Ten years ago something new was born into the world—something fresh and alive, infectious and creative."[42] Significantly Villard made no contributions. Louis Fischer was *The Nation*'s correspondent for most of this period. His articles throughout the decade and until late in the thirties were enthusiastic about the "Soviet experiment" and apologetic for its failures. Like so many Americans discontented with the "dull normalcy" of the Harding-Coolidge era, the "Soviet promise stimulated [his] imagination." In 1925, with tortuous logic, he explained away the existence of "Political Prisoners Under Bolshevism" by attacking the "hit or miss campaign" of the enemies of Soviet Russia "who do not hesitate to stoop to exaggeration and falsification, and attack alike what is good and bad. . . ." He was sorry that "some very good, sincere and sentimental people make themselves the tools of these implacable foes of the Union of Soviet Republics."[43]

Villard as editor continued to deny the charge that *The Nation* staff was a pack of "hard-boiled Bolshevists."[44] Although he continued to deplore the brutality and tyrannical methods of the Soviet leaders, he too was not immune to the compelling need to counteract the prejudice and virulence of reactionaries and he went out of his way, as he had during the revolution, to emphasize the good side of the Russian "experiment." Sometimes this proved to be difficult. When news reached America of the wholesale executions "for sabotage and counter-revolution" as a result of trials in 1929 Villard wrote: "The only credible thing about it is that the Soviets seem to be telling the world of the killings they authorize. But they must not be surprised if the killings produced injurious resentment abroad."[45] Villard was not well enough informed to become involved in the factional machinations of the Trotskyite and Stalinist disputes that filled the pages of *The Nation* and absorbed the interest of radicals in America. His interest was in the diplomatic recognition of Russia regardless of the internal conditions in that country.

In October 1927, in an interview with I. I. A. Kitten, the editor of *Rusky Golos,* New York's largest Russian language newspaper, Villard had stated his case on the question of Russian recognition. He placed the blame for America's refusal to recognize Russia on Woodrow Wilson, who inaugurated the policy of watchful waiting during the Mexican revolution in 1915:

> It is one of the worst things that Woodrow Wilson did to institute the modern idea that recognition of a foreign government is an ethical weapon—something to be given or withdrawn . . . according to whether we like or dislike the particular government with which we happen to be dealing. I believe in the historical American policy that any established de facto government is entitled to recognition without reference to morals or methods at home. Personally I do not happen to like the communist government. I am still a democrat and opposed to government by oligarchy or a party or a group upheld by a checka and the terrorism of dictators, but my dislike of that government has nothing to do with the question of recognition. Russia is in the family of nations and should be recognized, and we should deal with her as we do with Italy—whose government seems a bit more detestable than that of the Soviet Republic.[46]

It is strange that Villard, who so frequently spoke of moral sanctions and the power of the organized opinion of mankind, should be so ready to abandon diplomatic recognition as an ethical weapon. Russia's proclamations on peace and disarmament had much to do with his position.[47] At no time in the twenties or early thirties did Villard ever view Soviet peace offensives as anything but genuine.

His analysis of Russia was not confined to contrasting the differences of America and Russia toward disarmament. Villard had a set speech entitled, "What Should our Attitude Toward Russia Be?" He gave this repeatedly from 1927 until eventual recognition in 1933. He denounced the growing combination and consolidation of industrial power in the United States and charged that it was merely a kind of back door to Soviet principles in the interest of the few rather than the many: "Our capitalist system is breaking down under the circumstances, and I feel very strongly that the world is under a strong obligation to the Bolshevists who essayed the communist experiment." America, he demanded, "must view Russia in the spirit of a scientist who pursues the quest of the remedy for cancer."[48]

It was in this frame of mind that Villard undertook his tour of Russia in the late summer of 1929. He recorded his experiences in a long series of articles entitled, "Russia Through a Car Window," which appeared in *The Nation* immediately following the stock market crash in October 1929. Their simultaneous juxtaposition with a series of articles by Stuart Chase, "Prosperity, Believe It or Not," explaining the failures of the American economy, points up the tendency of liberals to look at Russia through the dark glass of American shortcomings.[49]

Villard's initial reaction to his Russian tour was one of admiration mixed with confusion, but after a month of reflection, he was ready to put his thoughts down on paper.[50] His articles, like those of other liberals and radicals who made the pilgrimage during these years, are remarkable more for their revelation of the author's aspirations for America than for any factual description of actual conditions in Russia. Villard's articles are all the more remarkable given his political background and tradition. He continued to criticize the tyrannical oppression of political freedom, but he was greatly impressed with the vitality of the Russian government and its people. He repeatedly compared Russia with America, suffering under the initial shock of the Wall Street debacle. In the light of the confusion and chaos at home, Russia appeared all the more purposeful and dedicated to a worthwhile goal.

In almost every case criticism was leavened with admiration.

"The Russians are on their way. By means of force, by the use of exiles and drastic executions, by the use of all the methods of repression to which Mussolini resorts so freely and so basely, but with this difference, the Bolshevists are working for the good of the masses of the working people." He was astonished at the lack of graft and corruption.[51] "It is a gallant, far sighted magnificent effort to rebuild an ancient commonwealth and to bring relief and happiness to one hundred fifty million souls."[52]

Villard preached to Americans about the public parks, museums, recreational facilities, health services, old age insurance, pensions, vacation resorts, and other benefits for the workers: "Any capitalist state could, if it wished, give all the benefits listed above to the workers, if it could bring itself to the belief that the workers, and not those who are already rich and privileged are the chief concern of an enlightened state."[53]

In his conclusion Villard was quick with a reminder that liberals could not be expected to show uncritical sympathy for a government which "resorted to the methods of Caesar, Cromwell, Nicholas and Mussolini." He could not accept the arguments of apologists who believed that the end justified the means. "For myself I can see no compromise on this question; no argument which shatters the intensity of my belief that those who take the sword shall perish by the sword."[54] Nevertheless Villard's distrust of Russian tyranny was more than balanced by his enthusiasm for the Bolshevist achievements. He wrote Sophia Sturge: "We were thrilled by the experience, I particularly. While I cannot approve of a regime that bases itself on violence and force and is constantly exiling people who do not agree with its economic theories, I am impressed by the vigor and vitality of the government and the unselfishness of the leaders. They have a wonderful Christian vision."[55]

Many other honest and intelligent Americans had much the same reaction as Villard. John Dewey, who also visited Russia in 1929, was enthusiastic about Russian experiments in education and wrote that he had never seen such "happily and intelligently occupied children." He was impressed by the idealistic dedication of the government and the people. Critics failed to see that there was "an enormous constructive effort taking place in the creation of a new collective morality." He sensed, as did Villard, an almost evangelical motivation: "I feel as if for the first time I might have some inkling of what may have been the moving spirit of primitive Christianity."[56] In every case the judgments of these visitors must be seen within the context of conditions in America. Many saw the power of the collective will as an antidote to the doctrines of rugged individualism and free enterprise.

Villard's dilemma is hardly unique: he was a twentieth-century liberal who had accepted the potentialities of collective action through governmental control and regulation, which he hoped to incorporate into the system without sacrificing individual freedom and initiative. He was never, to be sure, in the camp of the fellow travelers, but to label him "the proto-type of an older liberal" who could not abandon the nineteenth-century tradition of *laissez faire* merely because his conscience forced him to temper his enthusiasm with reservations is an arbitrary use of political labels.[57] It is misleading to distinguish between generations of liberals by the degree to which particular individuals accepted or rejected the Russian revolution and the Soviet government. John Haynes Holmes, Roger Baldwin, and many other close friends of Villard became fellow travelers. Holmes recalled, "We liberals permitted ourselves to condone wrongs that we knew must be wrongs. . . . We accepted covertly if not openly, the most dangerous and ultimately disastrous idea that can lodge within the human mind, namely, that the end justifies the means."[58] Some younger liberals such as Max Eastman, Joseph Wood Krutch, and Edmund Wilson, who demanded domestic reforms, shared Villard's profound skepticism of the Russian example.[59]

In spite of his reservations, Villard was not adverse to ridiculing opponents of recognition by scoring American failures as opposed to the alleged achievements of Russia. When Matthew Woll, an A.F. of L. leader, suggested putting an embargo on trade with Russia, Villard remarked that the Soviet workers were hardly more slaves at forced labor than American labor, "which dances to the tune of the capitalist piper upon whom depends how near or how far from the line of bare subsistence the American worker and his family lives."[60]

As the depression deepened, Villard argued that Russian recognition would be a great boon to the economy. He saw nothing to fear from exchange in trade, ideas, and people. The overriding fear of the "Communist menace" was doing irreparable harm both at home and abroad. He conceded that it would be impossible for Red baiters, like Congressman Hamilton Fish of New York and Matthew Woll, to see any good in Russia but "besides the bloody and bad side there is a great deal of fine idealism, a genuine desire to uplift humanity. . . ."[61]

Not long after the stock market crash the question of Russian recognition became more and more controversial. Ironically, there was much business support for renewal of diplomatic relations.[62] In an entire issue devoted to the question, in May 1932, *The Nation* cited many important business executives who favored the renewal of diplomatic relations.[63] Commercial reasons compelled business leaders to join liberal forces who had been in the fight for more than a decade. The popular press also supported the movement, with the Scripps-Howard chain leading the way. *Colliers* and *The Literary Digest* presented articles favoring recognition. Ivy Lee, the public relations man for Standard Oil, proclaimed that "the most significant fact about the Russian regime is the personal honesty of the men in charge."[64] American businessmen had carried on a significant volume of business with the Russian trading company, Amtorg, for many years. By 1930, after Russia launched its first five year plan, the United States was the chief exporter to the Soviet Union.[65] Villard and many businessmen agreed with Paul D. Cravath, an influential corporation lawyer, who argued that "when the government encouraged business with Russia, it owed citizens the duty of protecting this trade."[66]

Diplomatic relations were renewed in 1933 for commercial and strategic reasons. Secretary Hull later told Molotov that his support for recognition was primarily motivated by "the great need for cooperation between our two governments during the years ahead for the purpose of promoting and preserving . . . peace in the world." Ambassador Bullitt recalled that "both the President and I were convinced that Hitler would eventually make war unless England, France, and the Soviet Union should stand together against Nazi aggression. The primary objective was to prevent the launching of another World War by Hitler."[67] It is doubtful whether liberal pacifists like Villard or eager businessmen like Lee understood the motives of Hull, Roosevelt, and Bullitt, nor would Villard have been sympathetic to them. Villard and *The Nation*, however, played an important part and, when recognition became a fact, Bullitt wrote Villard, "My dear man you must realize that this recognition is as much due to your efforts to promote sanity in this country as to the efforts of any other human being, and I hope you get some personal satisfaction out of the result."[68]

Villard was chagrined. In *The Nation* he reported that there had not been a peep out of the anti-Reds, not even from that strange team, the Daughters of the American Revolution and the American Federation of Labor, both of whom had vociferously denounced the policy.[69] It was a disappointing victory.[70] On November 24, 1933, a dinner was held in New York City in honor of Ambassador Litvinov, celebrating the renewal of diplomatic relations. *Time* magazine reported that "the big warm room buzzed with the voices of General Motors' Sloan, General Electric's Gerard Swope, Ford's Sorenson, Pennsylvania Railroad's Atterbury, Thomas A. Edison's son, Charles,

Theodore Roosevelt's son, Kermit, Owen D. Young, Henry Morgenthau, Sr., and dowagers galore."[71] Villard disgustedly wrote: "Not a liberal editor appeared on the dais and hardly a man or woman who battled for recognition, when to do so was to invite contumely, insult and abuse."[72] Villard complained to Lillian Wald "that the whole affair was purely a business one in the interest of getting good will for the Soviets."[73] So a crusade of a decade, motivated by humanitarian ideals and a belief in free trade as a means of promoting international harmony, was adopted in the end as a method of shoring up the sinking American economy and was embraced for expedient and strategic military reasons.

Hoover's opposition to recognition of Russia did not endear him to Villard; nor did Villard have any respect for other aspects of the administration's foreign policy. He did greet initial moves toward disarmament with enthusiasm, but after Hoover named the members of the American delegation to the London conference, he once again charged that the administration obviously had no intention of pursuing a vigorous policy.[74] When the conference bogged down in an attempt to equalize English and American naval forces, Villard blamed the failure on the lack of any pacifistic motivation and the obstructionism of experts representing the big navy bloc.[75] Again the admirals were solely responsible and should be shipped to Pitcairn Island and forced to fight it out with their own bare hands.[76] Stimson's frank announcement that the American delegation had not been sent with a specific plan in mind led Villard to describe Hoover's administration as government by abstention.[77]

Villard blamed the failure of the world disarmament conference, which met in Geneva in 1932, on Hoover's lack of leadership and the French government's obsessive desire for security agreements. He denounced France for being opposed to the entire world. Villard felt that the administration should take leadership of the conference, work out agreements with other nations, and if France refused to cooperate, she should be ignored.[78]

Villard was also disheartened by the administration's approach to debts and reparations. He had advocated the cancellation of the war debts almost since the signing of the Versailles treaty. In the fall of 1930 Villard went to Germany on an extended leave of absence from *The Nation*. He remained in Europe eight months. During that time he gathered material for *The German Phoenix,* a book on the German Republic.[79] The main thesis was that Germany had been forced to the brink of disaster by the Versailles treaty. In articles sent to *The Nation* he warned that, if nothing was done to relieve the financial chaos in Germany, the entire European continent would collapse.[80] He accused Hoover of preaching a doctrine of futile American isolation from world affairs and he advocated a conference of heads of state.[81] Villard, while in Europe, tried to persuade Ramsay MacDonald to call the German and French leaders to a meeting. He argued that their revocation of reparations would force America to adopt a policy of debt cancellation. Upon his return to America in the spring of 1931, he continued to call for a conference.

In June of 1931 Hoover did call for a moratorium on debts and reparations, largely to protect private loans in Germany and Austria. Borrowers relieved of their reparations payments might not default on their private obligations to American bankers. Villard, aware of the reasons for the moratorium, nevertheless greeted it with wild enthusiasm. He wrote his wife that he had been vindicated: "The mere announcement that the President has begun to busy himself with international affairs, with a view to cooperation and aid would send a thrill of hope and encouragement around the world. It may really mean the turning point in the world's history. Certainly we may easily be able to date the recovery of the world from its depression from the date of this action."[82]

Villard's enthusiasm was short-lived. He soon realized that

Hoover never considered the moratorium in relation to a broad program of economic cooperation and efforts toward disarmament. In December the House passed the requested moratorium with a proviso stating that it in no way implied subsequent cancellation or even reduction. Villard placed the blame on the President, who had spoken so often about America's ability to work itself out of the depression alone that he had encouraged the legislature to tie his hands.[83]

Hoover had failed; he refused to use the economic collapse of the world to push constructive policies. The final degradation was the administration's stand on the tariff. It approved the highest tariff bill in American history. Villard called it "a crime against humanity," the treacherous swindle of gigantic proportions. Hoover's justifications and evasions, since he had advised a revision, only proved to Villard that the man was, indeed, a pitiful figure.[84] To make matters worse, progressive senators acquiesced wherever the tariff touched the interests of their constituents. With this betrayal Villard gave up all hope of any reform under the leadership of the two major parties. He wrote in the fall of 1930: "If we are to do anything else but drift, we must realize that the competitive system has failed at many points." America must, out of necessity, "formulate far reaching economic and political programs to deal with the new situation." He warned reformers in Congress that the "days of tinkering, and of stopping leaks and patching, and of taking one timid step in this direction and that are over."[85]

CHAPTER THIRTEEN

A New Deal

1932-1935

Villard's criticism of both Hoover's administration and the Democratic opposition indicates a continuing change in his political philosophy. By the end of the twenties he had little faith left in the piecemeal depression measures of either party. He soon became a supporter of the positive welfare state, and accepted wholeheartedly the programs of the New Deal. Yet James Burnham sees Villard as a neo-Jeffersonian duped by the New Deal's promises of a return to prosperity, who soon became disillusioned with the concomitant government encroachment on the rights and liberties of the individual. On the other hand, the liberal Max Lerner, noting Villard's criticism of labor violence during the sit-down strikes, his opposition to the Court-packing plan, and his protest vote for Norman Thomas in 1936, classifies Villard as a champion of lost causes—a man always on the fringe of the reform movement who turned away in horror from the give and take of majority politics.[1] A recent scholar of the period, William Leuchtenburg, writes that Villard was not a representative twentieth-century liberal but a special case: "While most of his fellow liberals were concerned with mobilizing majorities and increasing the power of the state in the welfare field, Villard, I feel, while he shared many of these views, also was concerned far more than other liberals with the menace of the state or of concentrated power. He thought of the reformer in the way of Garrison or John Brown—the individual against the state or the mob."[2]

These judgments are misleading in the light of Villard's political beliefs in the thirties. He came to rejoice over the extension of federal authority and the rejection of rugged individualism and *laissez faire*. It was his contention that government must be responsive to the majority of its citizens. When he opposed the state, he did so because he felt that it had failed to do just that. Anti-statism is not incompatible with modern liberal thought except when it is advocated in behalf of a vested minority. This is not to say that Villard rejected the rights of the minority. He rejected the *privileges* of a minority when they were not extended to the mass of the people. Villard as a liberal was a staunch defender of these rights and he attacked the state when it encroached on fundamental civil liberties.

Villard's liberalism was genuine and compatible with the mainstream of liberal thought in the early thirties. Admittedly he arrived later than some of his younger colleagues, but he did arrive and was unquestionably in the swing of things. Villard's course during the period between the bankruptcy of the Hoover administration and the development of the New Deal programs reveals reasons other than an inability to cast off old political inhibitions for his subsequent break with the New Deal.

Villard was convinced by 1931 that the capitalist system as represented by the Harding, Coolidge, and Hoover administrations had proved inadequate to the challenge of the depression: "The evolution of capitalism has given ever increasing opportunities for the selfishness and greed of the average human being in industry and politics and these traits are bringing down the structure. We in America have learned the bitter lesson of uncontrolled individualism whether rugged or otherwise." The business mind had failed. For all its reputed ingenuity and ability to adapt itself to conditions, it lacked vision and imagination in a time of crisis. Businessmen had no answers, "no plan, no economic program." He referred to Hoover's assurances that things would take a turn for the better as the vague "inanities of the happiness boys."[3]

Although Villard had refused to give Norman Thomas his support in the presidential election of 1928, he supported him in 1929 for mayor of New York against Fiorello LaGuardia because of LaGuardia's membership in the Republican party. By 1931 Villard was a leader in the League for Independent Political Action. He acted as treasurer and insisted that it be not merely an advisory body on legislative programs but pave the way for a third party in the campaign of 1932.[4] He continued to encourage progressive legislators to bolt from the old parties. In an article entitled "Headless Washington" Villard wrote that the progressives were as bad as Hoover with their stop-gap measures and their refusal to map out a long-range program.[5] Villard made it clear that he was no longer interested in the 1924 progressivism of LaFollette. When the Senator's son Philip ran for governor in Wisconsin, Villard wrote that he hoped he would approach the state's economic problems as a modern progressive: "These evils cannot be cured by the program and philosophy of the elder LaFollette. It remains to be seen just how far the son is abreast of the times."[6]

In February 1932 Villard criticized "A Four Year Presidential Plan," advocated by the League for Independent Political Action, because "it was not built around some central policy," it only called for "piecemeal measures," and was "not radical enough or impassioned enough for the existing situation."[7] He complained that America had not adopted the British tradition of genuine discussion of political theories and principles. Only a well-organized and comprehensive long-range plan would save America from the demagogues of either the Left or the extreme Right.[8] As the days wore on, a new word, "planning," appeared in Villard's political vocabulary, and he gradually recognized the need for a government of experts to deal with economic affairs.

In an article entitled "The Challenge of 1932" Villard warned that Americans would have to go a long way in making over their processes of government: "We shall have to face

the blind and bitter opposition of many who do not realize
that the prevailing system has broken down, that the doctrine
of rugged individualism is today a joke, that the kind of
leadership we have leads only to despair. . . ." A few weeks later
Villard contributed to a series in *The Nation* entitled "If I
Were Dictator," in which he developed tangible steps toward
reform.

International relations were of prime importance and could
not be separated from the domestic crisis. Disarmament as
a method of economic recovery was imperative. As for the
admirals and generals, he would ship them all off to Guam,
where they might prepare for war to their hearts' content.
All American troops stationed in the Caribbean and the
Philippines would be withdrawn. He would inaugurate a
system of free trade. America would cancel all debts. Russia
would be recognized immediately. An international conference of heads of state would meet to discuss economic problems. On the domestic scene Villard, as dictator, would see to
it that the poor received adequate medical care, dental service,
and other basic welfare measures through federal subsidy
financed through savings on military expenditures as well as
through increased taxation for the higher income brackets
and drastic inheritance taxes "preventing the transference of
swollen fortunes from one generation to another."

As for Mr. Hoover "and other talkers of economic non-
sense," Villard vowed that he would set aside the island of
Yap where they would be required to "meet every morning
and evening and inform one another that prosperity was just
around the corner." In Mr. Hoover's absence Villard would
establish government operation of the railroads, pipelines,
telegraph, telephone, radio, mines, oil wells, water power, and
all other natural resources. "I should endeavor to create social
control of institutions as a source of funds for progressive social
policy." Villard said he would frankly imitate the Russian
policy by stressing above all else "the welfare, the prosperity,
and the happiness of the plain people. . . . Instead of making

the government for the well-to-do and the rich, I would make it a government primarily concerned with the welfare of the lowly classes and I should let the rich go hang."[9]

In addition to the permanent programs designed to reduce working hours, Villard's plan envisioned a "scientific plan of unemployment insurance, and a vast public works program which would help immediate problems." His program was designed as "a general overhauling of the economic system," not simply caring for the unemployed of the day. The problem as Villard saw it was not overproduction but "underdistribution." All this is a far cry from his 1920 rejection of the "evils of government ownership . . . the inevitable killing of any initiative."[10] Villard went far beyond the L.I.P.A., which envisioned public ownership only for utilities. His approach was consistent with the liberal pragmatic call for a drastically modified capitalism rather than with the radical's desire to do away with the entire American economic system.[11]

Week after week Villard ridiculed Hoover's evasion of the problem of immediate federal relief.[12] In the summer of 1931 he demanded editorially that Hoover call a special session of Congress to consider federal aid to the unemployed. As for those who argued that direct relief demoralized character, Villard noted that the guardians of the national fibre never felt that government grants to needy corporations had an evil effect "upon the character or practices or initiative or self-reliance of the several corporate managements."[13]

In September, when *The Herald Tribune* rejoiced that Ramsay MacDonald, head of a coalition government, agreed to a reduction of the "dole," Villard defiantly answered that "the British millions who have learned that the government owes them a living are right. Any government which fails to keep its citizens from starvation will not and should not last overnight." Villard announced, "If but one ringing word came from [Hoover] that no American man, woman or child should die of starvation . . . our whole morale would be uplifted."[14] "Can anyone," he questioned, "really assert that we should stop at anything to save American lives, to prevent disaster, and preserve the American Republic?" Villard suggested a new slogan for the Republican party: "Millions for business not a cent for the jobless."[15]

By June 1931 it was apparent to Villard that Governor Franklin Roosevelt would be the commanding figure in the Democratic party. Villard had supported Roosevelt for governor in 1928. He considered himself a friend of Roosevelt's and predicted as far back as 1910 that the man would some day be president. Nevertheless, when Roosevelt appeared on the horizon as the front runner Villard began finding fault with him. Roosevelt was, like Smith, in the party of Jacob Raskob. He had not demonstrated significant qualities of leadership in Albany and had pussyfooted in his dealings with Tammany.[16] Roosevelt informally threw his hat into the ring in his annual message to the New York state legislature in January 1932. The message only confirmed Villard's belief that the Governor was "a charming person, an increasingly astute politician able to pull with reformers, the Republican party, Tammany Hall, and a man who does not advance the cause of reform one whit."[17] He was obviously paraphrasing Walter Lippmann's caustic observation that Franklin Roosevelt was "a pleasant man who, without any important qualifications for the office, would very much like to be President."[18]

He found the Governor's speeches during the spring of 1932 evasive. In May, resorting to an old polemical weapon, he published in *The Nation* "An Open Letter to Governor Roosevelt" in which he stated the public's disgust of "political flim-flam." Roosevelt had ignored "a glorious opportunity for leadership" and consequently was losing the support of many former friends.

Villard then directed a series of questions to the Governor, asking for yes or no answers. Did Roosevelt favor a protective tariff? Did he advocate repeal of the Eighteenth Amendment? Did he favor cancellation of war debts? Finally, and most important: Would the Governor "advocate direct government relief so that America may not starve to death alongside of warehouses bursting with food?"[19] With feigned innocence Villard sent along a note with the proofs of the article: "This goes to you with the best personal wishes and in the belief that it is the best political advice which could be offered you by Oswald Garrison Villard."[20]

The Governor, vacationing in Warm Springs, apparently did not get the article for some time. Villard claimed that he had given it to Raymond Moley, who promised it would be delivered by personal messenger. By the time Roosevelt did respond, Villard had already published an endorsement of Norman Thomas and a bitter rejection of Roosevelt. Roosevelt, irked by constant criticism, often from sources of expected support, did not feel the need to be tactful. He was dismayed that Villard in his more mature years had not discovered "some way to be more truly useful to his country." When the proofs and the letter had reached him he mused: "I bet a new hat that Oswald merely published that query for rhetorical or journalistic effect and that even before I get a chance to answer him he will have a leading article damning me up and down and advising his readers to vote for Norman Thomas. I won the bet." Roosevelt seemed delighted not to have to relinquish the dilapidated fedora that he wore for good luck. In a less jocular tone he recalled that he had once written another editor:

> I suppose God, in His wisdom, feels that there are some advantages in creating people who condemn you if they don't agree with you on each and every one of the fifty-seven varieties of important political, social or economic problems—but it is hard to understand what practical value these fellows give in bringing the support of intelligent persons to public officials who are at least more honest, progressive, and useful for a nation than those in power.[21]

Roosevelt was certain that Villard agreed with him on more matters of national policy than with any other candidate of the major parties. He hoped Villard would be satisfied in voting for his "good friend," Norman Thomas. Roosevelt closed with the remark that he did not "care a rap" whether Villard agreed with him or not just as long as he did not "print anything misleading as to fact."[22] Villard, in righteous indignation, stated that he had merely offered the Governor "the best opportunity you have had for expressing yourself on the questions of the day."[23]

Some Roosevelt detractors on the Left felt that his alleged weakness might inspire a greater effort to promote a third party. Norman Thomas wrote Villard that he had no doubt that the Governor would get the nomination so there was little reason to celebrate except that "it may facilitate the effective confirmation of the new political realignment we have been talking about. . . ."[24] Apparently Villard was losing his faith that this would be the year for the cooperation of liberals of all persuasions. Only a week after Thomas's letter Villard wrote Mussey, who was making the pilgrimage to Russia, that he felt there was a demand for a third party but that neither he nor Devere Allen, the editor of *The World Tomorrow*, had the money or the time to devote to the cause.[25]

As hopes for a third party dwindled, Villard showed a growing weariness. He told Hobson after a visit to his farm in Connecticut that he had looked at "those lovely hills and the sweet old home where I am so happy . . . and I think what a fool I am to try and carry on the liberal fight; and then I look at my fine boys and I am determined to go on."[26]

Going on meant abandoning the futile effort to form a progressive third party and backing the candidacy of Thomas. Devere Allen, a supporter of a progressive third party, joined the Socialists and threw his support behind Thomas. In May many participants of the League for Independent Political Action decided that the only thing to do was to come out for the Socialist candidate. The Thomas and Maurer Committee of One Hundred Thousand was headed by Paul Douglas and its officers included John Dewey, Reinhold Niebuhr, and

Villard. Intellectuals who flocked to the call included Elmer Davis, Henry Hazlitt, Lewis Gannett, Stuart Chase, Joseph Wood Krutch (all contributing editors to *The Nation*), W. E. Woodward, Stephen Vincent Benet, Robert Morss Lovett, Van Wyck Brooks, W. E. B. Du Bois, Ben Huebsch, Kirby Page, Franklin P. Adams, Alexander Woollcott, Deems Taylor, George Gershwin, Eva La Gallienne, and Edna St. Vincent Millay.[27] *The New Republic,* under its new editor Bruce Bliven, and *The Survey Graphic*, still edited by Paul Kellogg, joined with *The Nation* in supporting Thomas.

To many of the younger intellectuals on the Left the support of the Socialist candidates by well-meaning progressives and idealistic academicians reduced the Socialist party to little more than an association of do-gooders. John Dos Passos remarked facetiously that joining the Socialist party would have "just about as much effect as drinking a bottle of near beer."[28] Granville Hicks recalls the hysteria during the campaign when many intellectuals, feeling that they stood at the crossroads of civilization, decided to support the Communist party. Many of them did so without enthusiasm, as a last resort. A friend gave to Hicks a fairly typical justification of his own decision:

> It is a bad world in which we live, and so even the revolutionary movement is anything but what (poetically and philosophically speaking) it "ought" to be: God knows I realize this as you do and God knows it makes my heart sick at times; from one angle it seems nothing but crime and stink and sweat and obscene noises and the language of beasts. But surely this is what *history* is. It is not made by gentlemen and scholars, and "made" only in the bad sense by the Norman Thomases, Devere Allens and John Deweys.

He conceded that Lenin, John Brown, Cromwell, Marat, and "others who have destroyed and built up" were probably dreadful men. He was convinced that it was necessary in order to avoid pain, disenchantment and "even worse (treachery to ourselves) . . . to accept proletarian and revolutionary leaders and even theorists for what they are and must be: grim fighters in about the most dreadful struggle in all history—*not* reasonable and 'critically minded' and forbearing and infinitely far-seeing men."[29]

This sense of urgency prompted such men as Hicks, Malcolm Cowley, Newton Arvin, Edmund Wilson, Theodore Dreiser, Sherwood Anderson, Sidney Hook, Matthew Josephson, and others to sign the revolutionary manifesto, *Culture and the Crisis*, in support of the Communist candidates, William Z. Foster and James W. Ford. They warned their weak-hearted friends that the Socialist party was merely the "third party of capitalism." Throwing caution to the winds, they announced:

> We have aligned ourselves with the frankly revolutionary Communist Party, the party of the workers. . . . The Communist Party stands for a Socialism of deeds, not of words. . . . The Communist Party is the only party which has stood in the forefront of the major struggle of the workers against capitalism and the capitalist state. . . . The Communist Party proposes as the real solution of the present crisis the overthrow of the system which is responsible for all crises.[30]

The reformers, the pacifists, and independent liberal editors such as Villard found the appeal of Thomas and the Socialists a far more heady brew than Dos Passos had. True, they were for reform, not revolution—but it was fundamental reform. They did not accept the "omelet theory"—that because one had to break eggs to make an omelet, one necessarily had to break heads to make a revolution.[31] Thomas represented a streamlined, up-to-date, less rigidly doctrinaire Socialist party. The Socialists' constructive and practical program promised long-range social and economic planning to ward off future breakdowns. In supporting Thomas, Villard wrote that, while he still hoped that a new third party might endorse the Socialist candidate under another name, *The Nation* would stand by its endorsement. Thomas stood head and shoulders above any other potential candidate in force and vision and if the country were to "choose men for their respective worth he would undoubtedly head the poll."[32]

Villard attended both the Republican and Democratic conventions. As in the past he was scornful of "the obscene proceedings." Hoover's nomination proved that there was not "a vestige of statesmanship, not a shred of courage" in the Republican party. The "Democratic trough at Chicago" was equally deplorable. Villard wrote Ratcliffe that if Roosevelt "had merely taken as his platform that no American man, woman or child shall starve while there is a dollar in the treasury and flamed that message out in every direction, he would sweep the country." In *The Nation* he stated: "If the nomination had been awarded on the grounds of great intellectual capacity, of proved boldness in grasping issues and problems, of courage and originality in finding solutions, the honor would never, never have gone to Franklin Roosevelt."[33]

The growing crisis and the administration's inaction made Villard certain of a Roosevelt victory. Contrary to his argument in 1928, he insisted that a protest vote demanding more radical change was necessary and vital to the American political process. He quoted Norman Thomas approvingly: "The only way to throw your vote away is to cast it for somebody you don't really want and then get him." Villard pleaded with readers to cast their votes "for a new and square deal." No liberal could really believe that the election of either Hoover or Roosevelt would mean anything more than "a little patching here and a little patching there on a machine which cannot be made to work efficiently." He cited an unnamed Democratic politician who predicted at least 3 million votes for Norman Thomas. Villard felt this would "make the old parties sit up and take notice and encourage those who desire a third party without the Socialist name." By October Villard was desperate and no longer cared about the disadvantages of the Socialist label. He quoted Elmer Davis: "If you can't swallow the name 'Socialist,' if you prefer to vote for the kind

of politicians we used to think we could afford in the fat years
—well God Save the United States."[34]

Villard greeted the Roosevelt landslide with mixed feelings.
He could not restrain his delight over the crushing defeat of
Hoover. On the other hand, Villard felt that Roosevelt toward
the end of the campaign had become even more evasive: "His
sickening wobblings on the tariff . . . his pathetic belief that he
has outlined a big constructive program . . . only reveals his
ignorance, the callowness, yes the juvenility of his mind." The
editors of *The New Republic* echoed his sentiments: "This is
an election in which we can find more satisfaction in rejoicing
at defeats than at victories."[35]

The small vote for Thomas was disappointing but after a
week of analyzing the returns, he decided that the overwhelming rejection of Hoover was not due solely to the depression.
It indicated the dissatisfaction of the great mass of people with
the character of the Republican administration. He felt sure
that many more liberals would have voted for Thomas if the
horrible possibility of Hoover's re-election had not frightened
them into choosing the lesser of two evils. Liberalism was not
defeated. There was even reason to feel vast satisfaction over
what had taken place. Americans before long would realize
that they could not just swing back and forth between the two
major parties. It was the duty of all liberals to step up their
activity and to unite in the sole aim of opening the bursting
warehouses to starving Americans.[36]

Villard's spirits were not dampened by regrets after this
campaign. In fact, he felt a sense of satisfaction in the role *The
Nation* had played. In an article on October 7, celebrating the
centenary of Godkin's birth, Villard noted that the former
editor had made his mark:

> Why not? He was a crusader, his soul was his own, his pen
> untrammeled. All his life having ideas and faiths, he would
> say what he wished, when he wished, fearing no man, yielding
> only to the truth. What richer, happier, more useful life could
> any desire.[37]

This was Villard's ideal and surely a bit of unconscious self-praise. Villard was proud that *The Nation* during his editorship had not succumbed to political expediency. Its criticism of the American political scene had been constructive and enlightened, and judging by the company he kept in the last campaign, Villard had kept abreast of many of America's most politically sophisticated liberals. He had nothing to be ashamed of. When a subscriber of more than thirty years praised his editorship, Villard responded modestly that the paper had achieved about 50 per cent of what he had hoped for when he took it over. Although he could never make his peace with some of the aesthetic tastes of his editorial associates, who had effected what he considered "the lowering of style, and at times the tone" of the magazine, he felt that he had carried on in the spirit of Godkin and his uncle, Wendell Phillips Garrison, despite the drastic changes that had taken place during the last decade:

> You see we went into a new world in 1914 and there had to be new methods of approach, not new ideals, but new applications of old principles. The old laissez-faire spirit in which I grew up under the teachings of the two great founders of *The Nation,* and my own father has had to yield to the altered situation of the world.[38]

He asked his correspondent to remember how much more complex the world was now than in the days of the old *Nation:* "Perhaps the remarkable thing is that *The Nation* has not been worse."[39] He was capable of this gracious humility because of the new sense of confidence, achievement, and self-esteem he had acquired—even before the campaign of 1928—over his record as editor of *The Evening Post* and *The Nation.* In the long run he felt he had been steadfast in his principles and his papers reflected these virtues. He was no longer an object of derision but accepted by his colleagues and by important figures in government and education as one of the more effective liberal editors in the country.

Although Villard always hoped for a greater circulation than he was ever to achieve, he knew that the influence of a journal of opinion depended mainly on reaching well-educated and well-informed readers.[40] When *The Post* fought the Democratic boss, James B. Hill, during the 1890's, Hill is supposed to have lamented: "I don't care anything about the handful of Mugwumps who read it in New York. The trouble with the damned sheet is every editor in New York State reads it." The new *Nation* under Villard received a similar accolade from an entirely different source. Frank P. Walsh, the liberal lawyer, once called *The Nation* "the greatest mystery in American journalism." At a time when its circulation was not more than 27,000, he contributed an article on the railroads. At the same time he published a similar piece in his syndicated column for the Hearst papers with a circulation of nearly 10 million. He never met a man who had read the article in the Hearst papers, but on the day *The Nation* hit the newsstands, his telephone rang incessantly: "People who counted, editors, assorted reformers, and lobbyists pro or con read *The Nation* and reacted to it. They had to to keep up."[41]

Henry Mencken, who seldom missed an opportunity to lampoon the liberal journals, respected Villard as a professional journalist. He laughed at "the bunch of do-gooders down there. ... Krutch still has baptismal water behind the ears, and Freda Kirchwey thinks it's heroic to overlook adultery." Nevertheless, Mencken conceded that he read every issue because there was something worthwhile, something in it he couldn't find anywhere else.[42] He was astonished by its influence:

> *The Nation* is unique in American journalism, for one thing: it is read by its enemies. ... That is, the more intelligent of them—the least hopeless minority of them. It is to such minorities that *The Nation* addresses itself, on both sides of the fence. It has penetrated to the capital fact that they alone count— that the ideas sneaked into them today will begin to sweat out of the herd day after tomorrow. ...[43]

This kind of praise from hard-boiled professionals gave Villard great comfort and led him to reassess his personal evaluation of himself. He felt that he had not asserted himself enough and had underestimated his own talent and ability: "Coming into the office under such great men as Godkin and Horace White, and such first rate editors as Garrison, Clark and Ogden, I had an apprentice's feeling about them, an inferiority complex probably. At least it never occurred to me until years later that I might rank with them."[44] In 1930 he wrote to Ernest Gruening that he now knew that his "journalistic judgment and aptitude was better than any of those men and far superior to Ogden. . . ."[45]

This sense of achievement came in the late twenties and early thirties when he was beginning to contemplate retirement from his duties as editor-in-chief. Since 1928 he had been looking for a competent journalist with his general views to replace him. Villard wanted *The Nation* to continue to reflect the spirit of one individual. After failing to persuade Lewis Gannett to return and take over, he consulted with Morris Ernst, the civil liberties lawyer, about possible successors. Devere Allen, Dorothy Thompson, and several others were approached but in each case negotiations fell through.[46] Eventually he decided to turn the helm over to an editorial board made up of the most promising members of his regular staff.

From 1928 until his retirement in 1933 Villard took extended leaves in Europe, partially to test the ability of his protégés. Publicly he expressed confidence in the younger editors: "It is going into younger hands, four admirable younger people, all of whom are brilliant and making fine names for themselves."[47] Privately, he frequently doubted that they could manage without his guidance and his devotion to *The Nation* tradition. Often when he was away he complained that the magazine lacked "punch and vitality. . . . The 'boss' is needed to give them courage and steady them down." After returning from one such absence he noted a quick rise in newsstand sales. He boasted to his wife, "You can see that the 'boss' is needed on the job again."[48]

Toward the end of 1932 the arrangements were concluded. The active management of the paper was turned over to a board of editors consisting of Freda Kirchwey, Joseph Wood Krutch, Henry Hazlitt, and Ernest Gruening. Villard maintained his majority stock holdings and was to continue to write a weekly column for a fee of $500. When times improved he was to receive $1,000. His column was to be absolutely free of editorial supervision.[49] Villard still expressed concern over *The Nation*'s future. Shortly after the announcement he wrote Felix Frankfurter that it was impossible for him to be completely satisfied with the arrangement: "Frankly what worries me is whether the editorial page will keep up the vigor and the passion against injustice and be able to express it as it has in the past. . . . Not one of the four who have taken over the paper has either my political knowledge or interest and, I am afraid . . . the paper is going to drop down to the level of *The New Republic*."[50]

Villard's fear of a change in *The Nation*'s approach was justified. The magazine had been an extension of his own personality, and without his active control it would not be the same. Ernest Gruening wrote about Villard's coming retirement:

> Whatever may be the result, and however considerable the contributions of his fellow editors to *The Nation*, it stands today as a Villard monument, wholly consonant with the journalistic traditions of four generations. Its virtues . . . and its vices (sentimentalism, moralizing, and occasionally biased and inaccurate presentations) are alike Villard's. For twelve years it has been dedicated to the perpetuation of principles which are representative of the worthiest striving in the American experiment. It has left an imperishable mark on contemporary thought. With all its internationalism, it has

kept alive a peculiarly American spirit and tradition of independence and decency in an epoch of great confusion. The credit is chiefly Villard's.[51]

Villard's concern for the future was more than offset by the relief of unburdening himself of the editorship. He was at last free of the grinding details of management. He assured William Allen White and H. L. Mencken that his pen would never cease. Although he was committed to write the weekly column in *The Nation*, he looked forward to getting started on long neglected literary projects. He wrote James Kearney, former editor of *The Trenton Times*, that publishers were "hot for his memoirs, hot for the life of Godkin and *The Nation*, hot for the Woodrow Wilson . . . hot for the life of Wendell Phillips. . . . If only there were three of me."[52]

Villard's gratification for professional recognition was accompanied by a personal satisfaction in his family. In the last years of his active management of *The Nation*, when the magazine had fewer financial and editorial problems, he was able to devote more time to his wife and three children, Dorothea, Hilgard, and Oswald, Jr. His two sons, unlike their father, were good students. In 1928 Hilgard had gone to Yale, "throwing overboard the family tradition." He graduated with honors, and earned an M.A. from Cambridge (England) and a Ph.D. from Columbia. Oswald, Jr., made a fine record at Hotchkiss School. He was elected to Phi Beta Kappa at Yale, from which he was graduated magna cum laude in 1938. Dorothea studied at Smith and Barnard and made her New York debut in 1926.[53]

In 1923 Villard bought an old farm house on the edge of the beautiful Berkshires in Watertown, Connecticut. Rockledge Farm consisted of eighty acres of woodlands and about thirty acres of tillable soil when Villard purchased it. Through the years he bought up considerable surrounding property and added wings to the house. At first Villard approached the farm with much the same attitude he had *The Nation;* he wanted it to pay for itself, but he was never completely successful in running it as a farm.[54] In time Villard, reconciled to the impossibility of making such a farm pay, liked to relate the story of the man who offered his guests milk or champagne, explaining: "Take your choice, they cost me the same!"[55]

Villard deeply loved Rockledge Farm, a "sylvan retreat" where he felt he could escape the crusades and causes that continually beckoned him.[56] It was a fine old house and Villard entertained frequently. In addition to *Nation* weekend parties—the Krutches and the Mark Van Dorens lived in nearby Cornwall—guests included old family friends, Garrison relatives, and, on one occasion, Ramsay MacDonald. Neither his wife nor his children shared his enthusiasm for Rockledge, however. Julia Villard did not really like to leave New York except in summer and complained of the inadequate hired help. Oswald, Jr., built a radio station on its highest hill from which he talked to radio hams as far afield as Poland and Borneo. But Hilgard—who inherited the interest in boats that led his father to found *Yachting* magazine—wanted to get back to salt water and eventually bought a summer home in Edgartown, Massachusetts. Rockledge was sold before Villard's death in 1949.[57]

For a man of Villard's position a country home, extensive travel, and his children's education were necessary obligations, and he did not stint to see that they were done properly, although in his business dealings he had a widespread reputation for penuriousness. Contributors to *The Nation* often complained of the token payments they received; the salary scale for full-time staff members was hardly lavish. R. L. Duffus in 1927 saw more than a little irony when he wrote that *The Nation*, which "waxed strident in behalf of the exploited workingman, exploited its literary workers . . . when it accepted their pen products at a cent a word."[58] This was another manifestation of Villard's deep-seated need to prove that he was not merely the inheritor of a great fortune but a competent businessman in his own right.

Reports of Villard's fortune were probably magnified and he spent a great deal of it without return in keeping *The Nation* alive. But, despite his frequent protestations of financial difficulties and his complaints that the depression had greatly reduced his income,[59] he continued to live very comfortably indeed. He had a normal weakness for material things. In September 1929 he hired a chauffeur to drive his Cadillac. He subsequently owned a sporty Packard coupe, and when each of his children came of age, he provided them with sports roadsters. He spent a great deal of time studying the virtues of one vehicle as compared to another, and at one point had a particularly painful decision over the purchase of a La Salle instead of a Cadillac.[60]

R. L. Duffus wrote that Villard was a genuine champion of the poor and downtrodden but "he prefers to keep them at a distance until they have bathed and changed their underclothing."[61] It is to Villard's credit that, unlike many less effective dilettante reformers of the thirties, he refused to affect a manner entirely alien to him. He remained his own man. He wrote with some cynicism about criticisms of his editorship of *The Post* and *The Nation:*

> A man can make a national name for himself as a radical journalist if he is born absolutely poor and sleeps on the floor of his composing room. He cannot when he is the son of a railroad president, and the inheritor of wealth. My circumstances made me play ball with the Wall Street men, but that could never be reconciled with editing a gadfly weekly, or even as dissatisfied a liberal daily as the *Evening Post.*[62]

That was in 1931. By 1933 the congratulations upon his retirement and the expressions of concern about the future stability of *The Nation* had mellowed Villard. On the night of February 28, 1933, at a dinner for *Evening Post* alumni, he received confirmation of his success. He was presented with a medal for the "individual who has shown the greatest courage in journalism." Former associates, who had denounced him as traitorous in 1917 and as a Bolshevik sympathizer in the twenties, now came to honor him. Villard was overwhelmed by the celebration. Not quite two weeks after the evening held in his honor, he wrote Hilgard, at Cambridge:

> I wish I were getting younger, but I can truthfully say that my spirit is just as young as it has been for years and that I am sure I have cast off many inhibitions in the course of time and am freer than ever. . . . My enthusiasms are not dimmed even by the tragic era in which we live. I want awfully not only to keep young, but to live on for some time to see that my sons are well established in life and their sister too, and to watch how some of the problems that are facing us are worked out.[63]

Villard and a great many other Americans were determined to cast off the pall of fear, embrace new departures, and support a new President, who, if vague about just what he would do, promised he would do something. The first hundred days were exhilarating. Although major problems still remained, Franklin D. Roosevelt had restored the country's determination. Will Rogers, after only a week, announced that the country was behind Roosevelt: "If he burned down the capitol we would cheer and say 'well, we at least got a fire started anyhow.'" Walter Lippmann, whose pre-inaugural pessimism had equalled Villard's, announced, "in one week the nation, which had lost confidence in everything and everybody, has regained confidence in the government and in itself." Villard could hardly believe that the man in the White House was the same man he had known as Governor in Albany.[64]

Villard sailed for England shortly after the inauguration, and upon his return he was astonished at the changes. He confessed relief that he was no longer an editor who would have to judge the soundness of all the measures being put through Congress. On the other hand he felt the editors of *The Nation* were being too cautious and picayune in some of their criticisms. They might show "a little more jubilation." He did not mean that he accepted everything, but who could fail to admire the child labor law, the minimum wage, and other provisions of the National Recovery Act? Villard was even more excited over the "mental revolution" in America: "To come back to America and hear no more of Hoover, no more of rugged individualism, no more complaints that government is delving too far into private business," this change had come "with a speed that defies belief." Villard noted that "no one can tell us how far . . . we shall get out of it, but the great and wonderful fact remains that, whether they know it or not [the] world has dropped out from under [the] Babbitts, our great capitalist rulers."[65]

Villard had called for a man who would "lead America out of the wilderness." He was now ready and willing to proclaim Franklin Roosevelt that man. As the days of the new administration wore on, Villard's criticism was mild and entirely from the Left.[66] He supported the NRA labor codes but, in August 1933, he said that the President still hesitated to transfer the economic power from the hands of the privileged few to those of the masses." Villard wasn't at all sure how far the President was willing to go. Certainly, he added, there was little evidence that Roosevelt had any "comprehensive far reaching program . . . there is still no promise that the basic industries, through which Wall Street power maintains its stranglehold upon us, shall be nationalized—not even the railroads or the banks."[67] Villard was willing to wait, however. He defended the brain trusters against the ridicule of the conservative press; at long last, the "idealists" had come to the front. He was ecstatic over the appointment of A. A. Berle, Rexford Tugwell, Frances Perkins, Harold Ickes, and his old friend, the vintage progressive, Frederick C. Howe. He could not suppress his "unholy glee" that supervision of the power industries had in part passed into the hands of the college-bred brain trust. Of one thing Villard was sure—the visionary brain trusters could hardly do worse than the practical men of business who preceded them.[68]

After a year Villard set down what he considered to be the

lasting achievements of the first year of the New Deal, noting particularly the "change in *spirit* from a government by and for big business to a government dedicated to the public welfare." The recognition of the right of labor to bargain collectively with representatives of their own choosing was a step in the right direction, but Villard was sure that its achievement would still have to be fought for in the years to come. The revitalization of the union movement, "the rescuing of the members of the American Federation of Labor from the follies and stupidities and narrowness of purpose of their own leaders" and the spreading of the idea of unions from the automobile industry to chorus girls was an encouraging sign. Significantly, Villard applauded "the beginning of national planning of industry in the United States by the Federal Government, and the control by it of the exploitation of the individual by predatory interests and human greed; the supervising of competition; and the management of great combinations of capital in the interest of the consumer and of the general public."[69]

Villard headed an organization called the Social Policy Committee on the Future of the NRA, which presented a protest to the President on April 27, 1934. It demanded that the administration be firmer with the big corporations, ban all company unions, force compulsory arbitration on management as well as labor, and crack down on all violations of the codes on working conditions. Villard soon accepted the Brandeis position that the plan of the NRA to encourage big business to regulate itself had failed and therefore the government should adopt a more coercive policy to restore fair competition. This may have been a less imaginative view than that of the national planners who had established the NRA, but it was held by a great many liberals and Socialists, and it would be misleading to interpret Villard's antagonism toward the NRA as evidence of a return to the old *laissez faire* liberalism.[70]

Villard's attack on the NRA does not indicate a deep-rooted anxiety about the "menace of the state." One cannot deny, however, that from 1934 on Villard and many other liberals were increasingly apprehensive about the growing power of the executive branch. What they feared most was that a powerful executive could plunge the country into war. Over the years, much of Villard's criticism of government authority was directed not against domestic policies but against measures to strengthen national defense. Whether under McKinley, Theodore Roosevelt, Wilson, or FDR, Villard's criticism was usually related to the President's control of American foreign policy and the danger of war.

When Villard's old foe of the National Security League, Stanwood Menken, charged that *The Nation* undermined the state, Villard replied:

> I want to break down reverence for the state when it sets up to control the conscience and personal liberty of individuals, if only because the state has of late in all countries degenerated into the control of the destinies of the people by two or three irresponsible men, drunk with power and all too often deliberately crooked like Mussolini. . . . Reverence for the state? Lord, what has the state been and what is it today in the United States, but big business personified? What was it in Germany? What is it in Italy and Spain? Why should we reverence it? It is meant to be the servant of the peoples, and it has become their master and beyond control slaughters millions at its will.[71]

This was an affirmation, not a condemnation, of the positive welfare state. It is compatible with nineteenth-century liberals' castigation of government by the rich, and with Franklin D. Roosevelt's denunciation of "economic royalists."

In 1917 Villard insisted that the government was preparing for war on behalf of the vested interests and not in accordance with the desires of the people. In 1936 he made the same charge. This, not a lingering fondness for *laissez faire*, was the source of his disillusionment with the New Deal.

In the early years of the New Deal Villard demanded forceful leadership, "not only because he is head of the party, but because he is head of the nation." He often cited two of his bitterest foes, Theodore Roosevelt and Woodrow Wilson, as fine examples of presidential initiative and liberal leadership in domestic affairs.[72] Only when Villard began to see dark clouds on the European horizon did he begin to distrust that leadership. The haunting refrain of 1917, "He put us into the war," returned as he watched Roosevelt's masterful direction of Congress and its passive acceptance by the people.

As the New Deal years went on Villard expressed concern over the possible spread of Fascism to America. He noted the speed with which some bills were rushed through Congress before the peoples' representatives even had time to read or understand them.[73] As early as 1933 he spoke on the topic "Are We In Danger of Dictatorship?" He pointed to the "enormous powers concentrated in the President. Certainly it is undeniable that merely because of an economic disturbance we have done something absolutely contrary to the spirit of our institutions." He suggested that it might be tempting to many who lacked fibre to "go on and make over our republic into one of these new states—the so-called fascist corporate state." He denied that he was accusing Roosevelt of dictatorial aspirations, but he insisted that Americans must take an active interest in the government and its processes and not just accept everything without question.[74]

These statements, taken out of the context of Villard's lifetime devotion to the peace movement, have confused the issue and supported those who deny him his rightful place in the liberal ranks of this century. Suspicions of underlying conservatism ignore his devotion to New Deal objectives and his criticism of the New Deal from the Left. Villard's failure to reconcile his pacifism with his liberalism does not place him outside the liberal tradition. It does point up the failure of any theoretical absolute to solve the human dilemmas of the 1930's. The very rigidity of Villard's deeply felt humanitarian principles proved inadequate in the face of imminent disaster.

CHAPTER FOURTEEN

A Surrealistic World

1933-1936

One is compelled to agree with those who describe the course of international events in the thirties as madness and incredible folly—and yet that madness and folly seem inevitable. Men consciously skirted the issues and tried desperately to suppress facts they knew to be true.[1] Year after year they retreated from one bastion to another until finally they admitted that of the alternatives open to them—appeasement or defiance—both were horrible, but one was less horrible. Oswald Garrison Villard's failure and defeat in the 1930's was his inability to realize that America had no choice that was not tragic.

In September 1931, Japan invaded Manchuria, repudiating the Nine Power treaty and the Kellogg pact as well as the League Covenant. Villard was quick to call for "preventive measures" and applauded the Stimson doctrine declining recognition of any territorial acquisition obtained by force. Villard rejoiced that it was finally being understood that instead "of war being nobody's business, it is everybody's business."[2] In January 1933, after another violent "incident" in North China, he asked if the great powers, including America, were going to "sit back with hands folded." He favored a more positive action than nonrecognition and called for an American embargo on the shipment of arms and ammunition. Japan's aggression was an affront to humanity and if the other great powers failed to act America should act unilaterally—"it would be a magnificent gesture of disapproval."[3] Most Americans, however, considered economic sanctions too dangerous. "The American people," asserted *The Philadelphia Record*, "don't give a hoot in a rain barrel who controls North China."[4]

Villard's concern extended beyond the crisis in the Far East. He was among the first to see the menace of Fascism to the entire world. During the late twenties, when many Americans regarded the new regime of Mussolini with interest and even admiration—it was efficient, the trains ran on time—Villard was soliciting funds to help fight the dictator and was publishing denunciations of him and his government. He wrote to Gaetano Salvemini, an anti-Fascist professor: "The trouble is that all the Americans who return from Italy spread the gospel that Mussolini is the most wonderful of men and that Italy is an earthly paradise. This makes it especially hard to get money from the monied people, for as you know they wish Mussolini to succeed."[5] Thomas Lamont, of the J. P. Morgan firm, told a meeting of the Foreign Policy Association that he was not a politician and knew little about the merits or failings of Fascism, but as an economist he could safely say that Italy under Mussolini had less unemployment, had reduced the government debt, and had ended inflation. "We all count ourselves liberal I suppose. Are we liberal enough to be willing for the Italian people to have the sort of Government they apparently want?"[6]

Mussolini's drive and energy appealed to a wide variety of Americans. Hearst wrote, after a visit with the flamboyant dictator: "He is a marvelous man. . . . It is astonishing how he takes care of every detail of his job."[7] Liberals, radicals, and avant garde writers were also fascinated by the Duce and admired his repudiation of bureaucracy, red tape, and the irritating obstacles presented by democratic inhibitions. Lincoln Steffens, writing in 1931, was particularly delighted with the dictator's scorn for liberal scruples. Disillusioned now with the Russian solution, Steffens thought Mussolini possessed the magic key. By 1931 liberalism was an epithet used to characterize the timid and ineffective who were obsessed with old-fash-

ioned ideas about political freedom and civil liberties. Mussolini was accomplishing things and liberty was only relative:

> Don't we always abolish liberty when we are afraid or in
> trouble? Isn't liberty a psychological matter? Isn't it some-
> thing that depends not on laws and constitutions, but upon
> our state of mind? Isn't liberty a measure of our sense of secur-
> ity and nothing else? Like democracy, like honesty, like peace,
> liberty has to be founded in economic arrangements that
> abolish fear.[8]

Some old-timers continued to make a fetish out of constitutional and legal machinery but all they ever got was formal
freedom. For true freedom one must abandon "political liberalism" for "progressive radicalism." Hard-boiled politics was
the rage.[9] Henry Miller claimed to despise Mussolini's program but added with admiration, "The man who sticks to his
guns has the world at his feet. . . . Mussolini's politics is real
politik. That's something in a world of cagey bastards, of pussy
footers and stinking hypocrites."[10]

Ezra Pound, who eventually gave outright support to the
Italian Fascist, expressed the growing cynicism toward the liberal democratic mentality in a letter to Upton Sinclair, after
his unsuccessful campaign to end poverty in California:

> I would have done anything in my power to get you in. BUT
> you are a God damn fool. You got a mind like an old family
> photograph album. Any idea you get stays. You are just as set
> and incapable of thinking as that triple shit Villard (who is
> possibly dishonest). You are not a monomaniac but a polo-
> maniac with a number of fixations.[11]

This curious admiration for power reflected discontent with
American conditions and evidenced little understanding of the
phenomenon it praised. Although most liberals and radicals
saw Fascism as the greatest menace of modern times, their enthusiasm for fundamental change often led them to exalt

power and force as the only means of achievement. Villard was suspicious of these means. If this worship of getting things done were transferred to the international scene, it would only lead to war and he saw the precedent for his fears in Germany.

Villard was as well informed on the history of the Weimar Republic in 1932 as any journalist in America.[12] He was one of the first to warn Americans that its failure would mean the rise of some form of totalitarianism. While Americans were absorbed in their own domestic crisis, waiting for the inauguration of Franklin D. Roosevelt, Villard was fearfully recording the fortunes of Adolf Hitler. A few months after Hitler was made Chancellor of Germany, he wrote his son that he had "a very straight story that the French government [had] sounded out the English as to whether they had not best smash Hitler and Germany immediately before he builds up a great military power." Apparently Villard was not adverse to aggressive action or was willing to look the other way this time, for he added, "I really shouldn't blame France if it did—given its belief in the worthwhileness of force."[13] In the fall of 1934, after his son wrote from Germany that he had recently seen Hitler and he looked peaked after a recent automobile accident, Villard replied, "I cannot but feel that if something should remove him now, some accident, it might mean the saving of millions of lives, for I feel strongly that he will precipitate another war if he continues."[14]

In the winter of 1933-1934 Villard undertook a speaking tour across the country. His theme was the menace of Hitler and the need to reassert the value of democracy. In March 1934, Villard warned:

> The Hitler Government presents a challenge, and if it persists, it will see to it that the world faces and answers that challenge. There will be no escape from it. We are to choose once more whether we are to be free men or whether we are to be human beings enslaved. For me there can be no compromise. I shall remain true to our American faith as long as I have eyes to see, ears to hear and lips to speak. . . .[15]

235

In the fall of 1933, when Hitler abandoned the Geneva disarmament talks and made clear that Germany would soon
leave the League of Nations, Villard insisted that the former
Allied nations must decide whether they would move against
Hitler immediately or wait until he had "organized a more
efficient nation in arms than the world has yet seen." He called
upon them to present a unified economic, diplomatic, and social boycott of Germany. He did not advocate the use of force,
but he was sure that, given the unstable nature of the dictatorial regime, economic boycott and nonintercourse would be
powerful weapons in discouraging the "barbarity of Germany." America must take bold leadership in this program to
encircle Germany with "united world opinion."[16]

As Mussolini's designs on Ethiopia became known in 1935,
Villard stepped up his demands that "all methods short of war"
be undertaken by the League nations to stem the increasing
tide of aggression. If Mussolini were allowed to continue un-
hindered it would mean "the end of all the peace machinery
created since the World War." He wrote that strict economic
sanctions must be applied at once: "I am well aware that
boycotts and sanctions are acts of war and that they may well
lead to war, but grave risks must plainly be taken in this situation." Villard immediately reassured his readers that he had
not changed his

> belief that war is the sum of all evil, that it can never be any-
> thing else than a disaster and never yet has produced good
> results. I feel that the nations involved are more than justi-
> fied if they attempt now, even at the risk of war, to find a
> substitute for it in the economic boycott, in measures short of
> war provided they go into the undertaking with the deter-
> mination that they will refuse to be drawn into actual hos-
> tilities even in the face of overt attack.[17]

Some of the implications of his previous position had gradually come home to Villard. But at the same time as he recognized the necessity of possible belligerent action, he revised

his opinion of America's responsibility. His strong advice clearly applied only to "the nations involved." He avoided any mention of America's role. He advised other nations to risk war but not to resist if war resulted. This was the first sign of a creeping hopelessness in Villard's thinking that was to lead him into a mire of sophistry from which it was impossible to extricate himself.

Villard's change in position was complete by the time Hitler occupied the Rhineland in March 1936. He severely criticized the French and Great Britain for their policy of appeasement, but quickly added that fortunately he was not compelled to decide who was in the wrong. He was certain, though, that "the time has come for *the League and the former allies* to act with great vigor and with the same daring and aggressiveness with which Hitler has acted. . . . There must be a united front . . . or Germany will impose its will on all of Europe" (Italics mine).[18] His reference to "former allies" was a clever loophole. He was well aware of the technical distinction insisted upon at the time of American intervention in 1917 which had made America an "associated" power and not an Ally.

Villard made a further retreat during the debate over the American neutrality laws in 1935. From the very beginning of his awareness of Hitler's operations and the general tension in Europe and Asia, Villard had taken grim satisfaction in reminding his readers that these problems were the bitter fruit of the iniquitous treaty of Versailles. In his 1931 study of the Weimar Republic he charged that "Adolph Hitler is as much the creation of the wicked Treaty of Versailles as is the economic crisis in which the world flounders."[19] With each new aggression Villard recalled Wilson's rebuff of the pacifists in 1917.[20] Soon a senatorial investigating committee took up the refrain.

Villard was among the earliest and most enthusiastic supporters of the Nye committee.[21] The committee began its long and detailed investigation in September 1934 ostensibly to uncover the role of the munitions makers and financiers in influencing American foreign policy. Although the committee was concerned with present conditions, the investigators naturally turned to the years preceding the first World War, exposing the huge profits of the armament industry and the relationship of the industry to America's decision to intervene. Villard was happy to cooperate with Senator Nye by digging up material for the investigation. He hoped the committee would propose sufficient legislation to insure that the "merchants of death" did not involve America in another war.[22]

The widespread popularity of Gerald Nye's committee indicates the degree to which revisionist historians were accepted by 1935. When Walter Millis published his revisionist work, *The Road to War*, its jacket promised readers a sensational exposé of "the frenzied years of 1914-1917 when ... a peace loving Democracy muddled but excited, misinformed and whipped to frenzy embarked upon its greatest foreign war. . . . Read it and blush, read it and beware."[23] Villard found Millis's book "extraordinary and useful. . . . No one can read that volume and not be convinced. It is an absolute justification of the pacifist position." "I never dreamed that I should live to see the time when public opinion in the United States would be practically united in recognizing that we were lied to and deceived into going to war ... and when Congress would actually put a stop to those processes by which Wilson, House, Lansing and J. P. Morgan and Company brought us into the war." He looked forward to a rigid arms embargo and strict neutrality legislation.[24]

The Nye committee's primary purpose was legitimate and worthwhile. But the committee, encouraged by the press, oversimplified the problem by implying that American bankers, financiers, and munitions makers were solely responsible for America's entry. This fostered the naive belief that, if the sale of munitions and the extension of loans could be prevented, America would be safe from the possibility of involvement in another war. The investigators resurrected the old charges of British and French duplicity and encouraged animosity toward the only nations arrayed against the real threat to world security—Italy and Germany. In short, once again there was an attempt to portray all the foreign nations as equally insidious and to destroy all distinctions in an effort to buttress the argument that America must avoid any involvement.

In the debate over proposed neutrality legislation, Secretary of State Hull argued that neutrality did not mean that the United States would not make a distinction between aggressors and their victims.[25] America's general support of the League of Nations meant acceptance of this principle. The weaknesses and failings of the League and the work of the Nye committee increased the demand for a nondiscriminatory neutrality. Villard himself had previously made moral distinctions: he referred to Great Britain and France as democracies and to Italy and Germany as "berserker nations."

The Ethiopian crisis was the acid test of Villard's willingness to take risks short of war. When the Senate Foreign Relations Committee deprived the President of any discriminatory power when invoking an arms embargo, Villard was delighted. In a letter to an official of the Foreign Policy Association, Villard conceded that sentimentally he would like to see the President allow the export of arms to Ethiopia, but in the long run he was sure that the country would be safer if it stuck "to keeping the power in the hands of Congress. . . . We may have to pay a heavy price for neutrality . . . but any price we may pay . . . is vastly cheaper than war."[26]

Villard's approval of the congressional action was a sharp contradiction to his previously expressed views on the role of the executive. Villard's fear of executive leadership and initiative in foreign affairs was increasing. He had long supported the idea that war should be declared only after a national referendum. As early as 1927 he encouraged former Ambassador Alanson B. Houghton's effort to gain acceptance of this idea. After World War I Villard developed the thesis that the President, by adopting policies that led to serious international commitments, usurped congressional prerogative and presented Congress with a *fait accompli*. Villard did not oppose the principle of representative government, but "the issue of declaring war and peace is one that stands on a different plane from all other power. It is the only power of all others which a self-governing people would logically reserve to itself." For this reason Villard became a strong supporter of the Ludlow Amendment calling for a national referendum before war could be declared. Until the referendum idea was accepted he believed every effort must be made to prevent "men in high places" from making decisions that might inevitably lead to war.[27]

Liberals were torn between the desire for collective security and the desire to avoid any involvement. Liberals of all persuasions were shocked by the challenge to peace and democracy but did not wish to have to discriminate between belligerents. *The New Republic,* under Bruce Bliven and George Soule, came to adopt the increasingly isolationist policy of Villard.[28] As for the limitation of presidential power, they felt Congress had a duty to lessen the terrible burdens on one man. By 1937 they were clamoring for mandatory neutrality.[29]

Villard's advocacy of mandatory neutrality without discrimination caused his first breach with the new editors of *The Nation.* The editors agreed with the administration that the restrictive legislation would hinder America in its obligation to lend support to the democratic nations of the world. They were for sanctions, arms embargoes, even extension of the neutrality ban to all materials that could be used for war purposes. But they felt the executive should hold the power to direct the embargo against the aggressors and not the victims. America's main objective, they argued, was not so much to keep America out of war as to keep war out of the world. The editors now wished the League well and supported American cooperation in any plan designed to thwart Mussolini or Hitler. They dismissed those who argued that to become involved with the League meant war. "If the United States and the League powers take a common stand [Mussolini] will have little choice against a war that may destroy all that is left of Western civilization." They placed great faith in collective security and frankly admitted that "acceptance of our responsibilities under such a system implies in turn a readiness to enforce economic and financial sanctions against aggressors."[30] These editorials seemed to Villard to mark a dangerous departure from the policy established during his tenure as editor.

Villard had considered the sale of *The Nation* ever since his retirement as active editor. His reasons were involved. His financial situation had suffered during the depression, but also his correspondence at the time indicates a growing resentment toward the editors. He had hoped that his sons, Hilgard and Oswald, Jr., would assume its management, but when they declined, he decided to sell on the condition that he would continue to write a weekly column with complete editorial freedom.[31] He finally sold the magazine to Maurice Wertheim, a wealthy New York stockbroker long associated with liberal causes. The sale took place on April 16, 1935, just a week after *The Nation's* first forceful editorial against mandatory neutrality.

Events on the international scene, as well as Villard's separation from editorial policy, seemed only to encourage the growing differences between himself and his former editors. The civil war in Spain brought their differences to a head. Actually the neutrality law did not apply to the situation in Spain since it was an internal struggle. It was a "time honored" right of neutrals to come to the aid of a recognized government fighting an insurrection. Roosevelt, who faced an election in 1936, decided to follow the nonintervention policy established by the British and French. On August 11, 1936, the government in Washington made its position public. The United States would act "in conformity with its well established policy of non-interference in the internal affairs of other nations and will scrupulously refrain from any interference whatsoever in the unfortunate Spanish situation." Although the government could not legally prohibit the export of arms by private individuals it discouraged companies from departing from the spirit of nonintervention.[32]

The war in Spain brought out fierce partisanship in America. Liberals and radicals viewed the Loyalists as fighting the battle against Fascism and denounced the noninterference policy. Russia, which sent soldiers and money to aid the Loyalists, became the hero nation to liberals everywhere, and the Spanish civil war provided the cement for the new Popular Front which had been announced at the Seventh World Congress of the Communist International held in Moscow in the summer of 1935. Instead of worldwide revolution, the Communists called for a united front of all democratic factions to defeat the Nazis and Fascists. Not only Communists and fellow travelers, but liberals, progressives, and Socialists stifled their bitter antagonisms and embraced Russia as the leader in the fight for democracy and freedom.

The Nation's support of collective security cannot be attributed to subservience to the Communist line. The editors fought nondiscriminatory neutrality legislation long before the proclamation of the World Congress. They were quick to recognize the motives behind the switch in Communist propaganda. Nevertheless they greeted the Communist olive branch with great hope and enthusiasm. It was interpreted as the inauguration of the long awaited progressive ecumenical movement. "The hope of the world may depend upon the reality behind the pronouncement of the Third International at Moscow."[33] Had not Stalin himself declared that the idea of world revolution had been a "tragic-comical misunderstanding"?[34]

The struggle of good and evil was being fought out in Spain. The editors did not hesitate to call for an end to the arms embargo and total revision of the neutrality legislation. Louis Fischer recalls that despite some gnawing doubts about internal conditions in the Soviet Union he was completely captured by their foreign policy: "Russia's help to the Loyalists was in sharp contrast with the stupid, scandalous pro-Franco behavior of the democracies—'Non-Intervention'—they called it."[35] The editors felt that "in a real sense the Spanish workers [and presumably their Russian allies] are battling for American liberties at the same time they struggle for their own."[36] Week after week they denounced American neutrality. "Neutrality," wrote Fischer, "followed to its logical conclusion has made America effectively pro-fascist."[37]

Villard for a time studiously avoided discussion of the Spanish question in *The Nation*. He was as confused as many of the Communists must have been at the sudden change in the Soviet line. For more than two decades he had admired the pacifistic proclamations of Russian leaders, and had accepted them as genuine. Now the old internationalism of their peace offensives was thrown overboard and they thirsted for a war in the name of democracy.

Villard's earlier sympathy for Russia had considerably diminished after the Moscow trials of 1934-35. While the editors of *The Nation* were following the schizophrenic policy that led to ill-conceived apologies for violation of political freedom in the name of the fight against Fascism, Villard stubbornly insisted that cold-blooded murder and tyranny, whether Fascist or Bolshevist, was still tyranny and bloodshed. He was, he admitted, "still old fashioned enough not to believe the ends justified the means." He did not fail to make the connection between conservatives who admired Mussolini because he was a man of action and liberals who ignored Russian tyranny because they too wanted effective action.[38] To Villard, Russia's domestic actions only undermined her allegedly democratic foreign policy and made moral judgments of any of the belligerents impossible.

The Communist-dominated organ of the Popular Front, *Soviet Russia Today*, portrayed people with scruples like Villard's as hopeless reactionaries. In one article entitled "Aid and Comfort for the Fascists" he was singled out for particular condemnation because of his statement that many liberals would not support Russia, in the event of an attack by Ger-

many and Japan, because of Stalin's "blood and treachery."
The editors found this kind of talk coming from "an old liberal, honored in the struggle for human freedom in America
incredible as the confessions of Piatakov and Radek."[39]

Villard replied that he was neither a Trotskyite nor a
Stalinist and only interested in "the social and human side of
the Russian experiment. When I see that checked if not
blasted . . . when I read of those judicial murders, I am going to
express my profound regret at these reactionary happenings
whomever it may encourage or discourage." He added that
since John Dewey, "possessor of one of the greatest minds in
America," had only recently been characterized by the Communists as "a tragic dupe of evil forces" he felt himself in
pretty good company. Dewey's crime was his leadership of the
American Committee for the Defense of Leon Trotsky, which,
after a detailed inquiry into the charges, had presented a verdict of "not guilty" and had exposed the more incredible
aspects of the Moscow trials.[40]

Villard's equilibrium was not unsettled by Communist
slander. He was, however, not immune to criticism from
former liberal associates now in the vanguard of the Popular
Front. *The Nation* blithely cast doubt on the objectivity of the
Dewey committee and concluded that the whole performance
was a "waste of time, effort and money." The editors of *The
Nation* were determined to suspend their Olympian judgment
—perhaps even for a century.[41] They were most incensed by
Villard's defiant stance on noninterference and strict neutrality legislation since his sympathy unquestionably lay with the
Spanish Loyalists and since he continued to attack the British
and the French for their policy of appeasement. On January 2,
1937, the editors criticized Villard's position and referred directly to his article in the same edition. They reminded their
readers that Villard had been a staunch foe of Hitler and yet he
was now supporting a policy that was to Hitler's advantage.[42]
Villard only adopted a more extreme position. Once again he
repeated his assertion that the proposal of the Secretary of
State to allow the President to decide "between aggressor and

aggrieved will only assure America's taking part in future wars." America might set itself up as judge in a war with which "we have no concern." He then made the astonishing statement that he found it difficult to discover who was the aggressor nation. Villard did not stop here. He came out frankly for a policy of complete disengagement from Europe:

> The American people want no risks of this kind taken. They want cast iron automatic mandatory laws that will say "a plague o' both your houses" we are going our own way. They will not be moved by the argument that wrong may triumph. They are thoroughly convinced that right and justice were not born of our participation in the World War and that they were deceived by lying propagandists, the entanglement of big businessmen with the English war machine and the false Wilson slogans. . . . They will not be moved this winter by arguments that this policy will wreck the League of Nations, for they wish to have nothing to do with the League. They will not be swayed by assertions that this would be an ignoble and selfish course and perhaps lead to the downfall of civilization. They will reply: We have had enough of that bunk from Woodrow Wilson, with his war to safeguard democracy and end war. We propose to be purely for ourselves this time.[43]

What had happened to Villard's earlier beliefs? Once he had felt that the democracies could not "sit silent until disaster comes; there will be no escape from the challenge of Hitler." Perhaps Villard was gripped by the same fear as Baldwin, Chamberlain, and Daladier, whom he had castigated so severely. He now believed that liberal Americans were again swallowing slogans and half truths that distorted their judgment and made them perfect victims of the professional propagandists. By the end of 1936, perhaps driven by some of the more sinister aspects of the Popular Front, he lost hope. He became obsessed with only one thing—keeping America out of war. This overriding fear and disillusionment caused him to repudiate and contradict his earlier firm convictions. His tone grew increasingly bitter and resentful. Despite the valid arguments of liberal colleagues that 1937 was not 1914, Villard re-

245

turned to the past and recalled the grim lessons of 1914-1917.

Villard found renewed comfort in the old conspiracy thesis, and wrote Senator Nye congratulating him on his wonderful "contribution to history," while he engaged himself in digging up material to "raise hell about the secret treaties." He listened with relish as Harry Elmer Barnes promised a new history which would place "the J. P. Morgan firm on a lower plane than Al Capone."[44] In 1937 he could ask, with apparent sincerity, of those who demanded a discriminatory neutrality: "How do they know that we ought to be on the side of the democracies, that the cause of the democracies will be any juster than that of the allies in 1914-1917? . . . What editor . . . can know whether the democracies may not be the aggressors for their own evil ends?"[45]

It is hard to believe that this statement is from the same man who had described Hitler's Germany as "rule by maniacal gangsters" bent upon "returning the world to a time when everybody carried a weapon and was clad in the skin of a wild beast."[46] But one must appreciate the surrealistic world of these years. Louis Fischer announced, in August of 1936, between reports of executions and exiles, that with the new Soviet constitution "the reign of law is now definitely established in the USSR" and that the constitution marked "the abdication of the dictatorship and the inauguration of a new era of civil liberties in the Soviet Union." Not long after Earl Browder announced to the world that the Communist party had found leadership in "the head of the most powerful capitalist nation, President Roosevelt."[47] It was a topsy-turvy world where utopian hope and soul-sickening despair distorted thought and reason. Villard was one of its countless victims. He turned to the past, from which he was never to return. He once again made strange alliances and alienated himself from former friends. He understood the consequences of his action, but openly admitted that he would accept the support and encourage the work of any group that would fight to keep America out of the war.

CHAPTER FIFTEEN

The Great Conspiracy

1935-1940

The Nation editors were solidly behind Roosevelt in the campaign of 1936. So were *The New Republic* and the vast majority of liberals, fellow travelers, and even many Communists. Despite this overwhelming endorsement, Villard, immediately before the election, came out for Norman Thomas: "Each of us has a paramount issue. Mine is the question of war and peace and the saving of civilization. I feel that Mr. Roosevelt, unwittingly if you please . . . has set us on the road to war and to the death of civilization."[1] Roosevelt's landslide victory confirmed Villard's fears. The people, he felt, were apathetic; they were willing to follow anywhere. Foreign policy outweighed all domestic issues in Villard's mind. From 1936 on he supported state and national candidates almost entirely on the basis of their neutrality records. He championed Senators Burton K. Wheeler, Gerald P. Nye, Robert LaFollette, Jr., Henrik Shipstead, Homer T. Bone, and Bennett Champ Clark. Although most had staunch progressive reputations, Villard supported them regardless of their position on domestic issues.

In order to thwart the President's growing internationalism, Villard and other liberal pacifists, joined by an ever growing number of isolationists, demanded that Roosevelt tend to the unfinished business of implementing the New Deal and steer clear of foreign adventures, calculated to turn attention away from failure and mismanagement at home.[2]

Villard was able to maintain his liberal standing for a while because his criticism of the administration was still from the Left. He was not immediately accused of hopeless conservatism, as was Walter Lippmann, who supported Landon in 1936.[3] But Villard had voted for Thomas and expressed discouragement that Roosevelt's New Deal had not gone far enough. Even after the election Villard still hoped that Roosevelt would not bargain with the "masters of America, the great Capitalists," but would "strike boldly toward the reorganization of our economic and social life and the further reorientation of the government to industry and labor."[4] Many liberals regretted his position on neutrality but they could not relegate him to the ranks of the reactionaries.

When the President presented a proposal for the "reorganization" of the Supreme Court, Villard, along with many *bona fide* liberals, found to their discomfort that their opposition to the President's plan was applauded by traditional Roosevelt haters and conservative opponents of the New Deal. It was this issue that caused a decisive break between Villard and his fellow liberals. Villard had long criticized the Court's failure to respect the economic needs of the country and to recognize the indispensability of New Deal regulatory programs. Long before this he had called for a convention to bring the Constitution up to date so that "the Government can subordinate wealth and business to the common welfare and give to labor the rights and privileges it deserves."[5] Three months before, Villard predicted that during Roosevelt's new administration the issue of the Court would be brought before the people. He scorned those who considered the Court "a magnificent, sterilized institution whose members divest themselves of all prejudice and economic beliefs . . . and then pass on legislation with sole reference to the basic law of the land."[6] When a minimum wage law was declared unconstitutional, he agreed with Irving Dillard's comment in the *St. Louis Post Dispatch* that "the Constitution is . . . what the judges who stay on the bench *longest* say it is . . . ." Villard believed that the important work of the Court was not to deal with economic and social legislation but to protect civil rights and personal liberties: "There is where we need a real bulwark, as the readiness of our legislatures to pass teachers' oath bills and anti-red and anti-syndicalism statutes clearly shows."[7]

Villard based his opposition to the President's Court proposal on its form rather than its content. He favored a constitutional amendment empowering Congress to pass social and economic legislation without judicial review. An amendment was the traditional and democratic means to effect a change in one of the governmental branches and the procedure should not be ignored no matter how urgent the measure was. This was a matter of principle, and Villard refused to submit to the arguments of expediency. The President, in turn, rejected the idea of a constitutional amendment as unrealistic. He proposed to guarantee a New Deal majority by either enlarging the Court or forcing the resignation of some Justices. He did not even attempt to deal with the principle of judicial review.

The concern of Villard and other liberals over the President's high-handed procedure illustrates the difference of opinion that would sharply divide liberals during Roosevelt's second administration. Many agreed with Thurmond Arnold that liberals were strong on principle but weak on "practical realization of actual situations."[8] Others like Villard were disheartened by the continual resort to political expediency. When *The New Republic*'s straw vote of progressives revealed a general consensus with Arnold's position, John Haynes Holmes wrote, "If we are looking for the bankruptcy of liberalism, of the collapse of contemporary middle class intellectualism here it is. . . . I find scarcely a trace of principle or idea. . . . I discover no clear cut philosophy of life."[9] Villard feared that Roosevelt might misuse his power: his election had been a remarkable victory and Congress was obedient. Opposition to Roosevelt's Court-packing plan was a way of pointing out the danger to the public: "to draft such a bill as this in secret without any public demand for it, and then to seek to jam it through by cracking the party whip, that is a procedure which if frequently or regularly repeated will lead directly to the downfall of Congress and again open the path to a dictator."[10]

Certainly Villard did not believe that Roosevelt had dictatorial aspirations. Nor could he really believe that the President's proposal had been the illegal monstrosity that he described. It was the tenor of the times that gave Villard cause for anxiety. He noted too much "hot impatience with democratic government."[11] He repeatedly alluded to the years 1915-1917, when hysteria gripped the country and presidential leadership ultimately led to war. Before the Senate Committee on the Judiciary he testified, "War may come. . . . If it does, the assault on our liberties is going to be greater than ever. . . . Let us not show any future President how to find a short cut to the alteration, in either war time or peace time, of our governmental system."[12] More than the suppression of civil liberties, Villard feared that the President might find ways of taking short-cuts on foreign policy decisions which would enable him to "put us into war." He was willing to delay the objectives of the New Deal if it insured diminishing the President's initiative and direction of foreign affairs.

New Dealers, even though skeptical of the President's methods, attacked "weakhearted" liberals for failing to see what the politics of the situation demanded. *The Nation* editors continued to support a constitutional amendment, but felt that for the moment the President's plan was necessary. They charged hesitant liberals with playing into the hands of the reactionaries. The suggestion that the President was illustrating Fascistic and dictatorial tendencies was the slander of "Roosevelt's old enemies, the Liberty Leaguers . . . public utility barons, the hirers of spies, and the big industrialists who own the newspapers."[13]

"What is *The Nation* Coming To?" was Villard's incredulous response. His answer was directed primarily at Heywood Broun, the "hottest and most terrifying of all the scribes [his] own editorial associate and next page neighbor in *The Na-*

tion," who had used the Supreme Court to berate liberals in general and Villard in particular for their association with every conservative and reactionary opponent of the measure he knew of.[14] In mock dismay Villard confessed his own inadequacy. He had not known that one made political decisions so simply. All you had to do was to see what the conservatives were saying and then say the opposite. For years he had wasted his time attempting to decide issues on the basis of their merits. He would now assume that, since Heywood Broun and William Green, inveterate enemies, stood shoulder to shoulder in opposition to Hitler, Broun would reverse his position and support the dictator. Lodge and Hearst had opposed the League of Nations. According to Broun's formula Villard should have supported it. But he would continue to make his decisions independently of the bandwagon.[15]

Villard received a storm of criticism, much of it from old friends and admirers.[16] Broun refused to cease the attack and was angered that Maurice Wertheim, the owner of the paper, felt their readers should be presented with both sides of the issue. "I am getting a little sick of *The Nation*'s policy of fair play, and everybody must be heard whether or not he has anything to say. This isn't an amateur tennis match."[17] After the bill was defeated in June, Broun took the opportunity to vent his disgust for all liberals who acted according to their conscience:

> Liberals, blown in the bottle liberals, are fond of saying that their every action is guided by high principle and that under no circumstances would they ever stoop to mere opportunism. . . . It is difficult to convert a liberal. . . . I merely ask those who have unconsciously aided in a great betrayal to look at the record. Liberalism will never be a force in America until the children of light have made up their minds that they must be at least half as smart as the children of darkness. Oswald Garrison Villard please note.[18]

The editors echoed the same charges as they came to demand a more aggressive foreign policy. Liberal opposition to revision of the neutrality laws was playing into the hands of the Fascists. Villard was on the receiving end in both cases.

On a cold and windy day in March, during the heat of the battle over the Court, John Haynes Holmes passed Villard on the street in New York. When Villard looked the other way he felt it was because Villard was not certain of Holmes's views on the Court issue and did not wish to face another embarrassing encounter. Holmes quickly wrote Villard a note of support for Villard's position on the Court and on neutrality. He deplored the collapse of the liberals' critical facilities under "the test applied by the President's fantastic proposal." He wondered if the world were not going "utterly to pieces morally and intellectually as well as politically and socially. You take the situation with commendable good humor, but I am wondering if you are not putting on a brave front and thus feeling within exactly as I do, a profound sense of depression and almost despair."[19]

Villard was putting up a brave front in his battle with his editors and liberal associates. He poured out his feeling of anguish and frustration to Holmes: "I do feel a sense of depression. To put it more accurately I feel that I have been left high and dry by a backwash, and I wonder if you and I and other steadfast liberals are not merely back numbers left stranded because of the alarming clash between radical and fascist forces." *The Nation*'s editorial policy was "heartbreaking" to him. He found particularly odious Max Lerner's "jesuitical defense of the Moscow Trials" and his demands for more armaments and "for keeping the country ready to help out the democracies if they should be attacked by despots." Again Villard talked of retiring to the farm to "live quietly and to dodge work of a philanthropic character that I would have welcomed ten years ago." He was sure this would not bother *The Nation*, for they "are getting many letters criticizing me as a reactionary and cancelling subscriptions. New times, new morals once more."[20]

In June 1937 Maurice Wertheim, also distraught over the course of *The Nation,* abandoned the cause and sold the magazine to Freda Kirchwey. Miss Kirchwey, like Villard, was a victim of the clash between the radical forces of the Right and the Left. James Wechsler recalled that she still "looked like an animated lovely college senior who seemed to be wavering between the two camps trying to keep everyone contented."[21] She had maintained the liberal, starry-eyed idealism that had brought her from the campus in 1921 to the offices of *The Nation.* As managing editor and now as editor and owner, she had wanted the best from all factions and sincerely felt that Communists, fellow travelers, Socialists, and liberals could all work together for a humane and reasonable world. She worked diligently to stop such intramural squabbling as had occurred between Broun and Villard.[22]

It was a pretty hopeless task. Lerner was in the front ranks of the Popular Front, supported ably by Maxwell Stewart, who was also a contributing editor of *Soviet Russia Today.* On the other side of the fence were Robert Bendiner, who became managing editor in 1938; Margaret Marshall, the literary editor; and Joseph Wood Krutch, the drama critic. Bendiner, who had been an editor of *The New Masses,* was a violent anti-Stalinist.[23] Miss Kirchwey had difficulty maintaining even an armed peace between the two factions, and Villard's column seemed only to encourage the strain. Editorials continued to openly refute Villard's position. She sent Villard a poll of *Nation* readers indicating antagonism toward his column. Villard replied that many of his old friends and supporters had dropped the paper and that the poll merely indicated that the quality of *The Nation*'s readership had changed. The new readers were unfamiliar with his work and "distinctly more radical." Villard was losing his confidence, however, and complained of writing under great strain. The rift seemed to make him "self conscious and probably less effective."[24]

Week by week the tension between Villard and the regular staff increased. At Miss Kirchwey's request, Villard tried to write on less controversial topics and to recall events of days gone by, but it was difficult for the crusader to play the role of the cozy philosopher. Heywood Broun's frequent gibes at his age and creeping senility infuriated him.[25] The feeling that friendly forces were betraying the liberal cause increased. Villard attended a party at Ben Huebsch's house in which a number of prominent liberals were present such as Harold Laski, Max Lerner, and the crusading liberal lawyers, Morris Ernst and Arthur Garfield Hayes, and "about twenty-five others." Villard wrote Holmes that "Of that group of old fighters only Ben Huebsch stood with me in opposition to all war."[26] As Villard's bitterness increased, he found a counterpart in the years 1915-1917 for every current event. He viewed himself as a martyr fighting a losing struggle against overwhelming odds though in fact the American people, by and large, agreed with the neutrality legislation and were not ready to engage in a policy that risked even the remote possibility of war. The President was required to repeat his pledge to keep America aloof from the conflicts in Europe and Asia. Public opinion polls, taken after the Japanese fired on an American gunboat in Chinese waters on December 12, 1937, showed that over 53 per cent felt that America should withdraw entirely from China and only 29 per cent said they felt that America should take steps to have our neutral rights respected. Perhaps the close vote in the House of Representatives, in January 1938, on the Ludlow Amendment, requiring a nationwide referendum on a declaration of war, is an even clearer indication of the pacifist strength. Villard correctly viewed the close vote as evidence that the American people and their representatives were intent on limiting the President's power on the international scene.[27]

The British betrayal of Czechoslovakia at Munich in September of 1938 marked the real break in the isolationist pacifist front in America. Villard was dismayed and utterly confused. He wondered what had become of "the English Conscience and common sense. At any rate this finishes the League of Nations and ends any collective security that would tie us up to a country capable of Chamberlain's monstrous wickedness."[28] Villard could not come out and say that Britain should have resorted to arms, so he mused over what might have happened if she had adopted economic sanctions before aggression had reached a stage where men could plausibly argue that only force would solve the problem. There was only one redeeming feature: "We have escaped war."[29]

While bitterly attacking Chamberlain, Villard sympathized with him for, at this point, he supposed there was nothing else he could have done.[30] The world would have been better off if Germany had won the battle of the Marne: "No Hitler, No Mussolini, No Stalin; a weak and stupid Kaiser . . . no such thing as Fascism or National Socialism."[31] He seemed to recognize briefly the contradictions in his attitude toward Chamberlain. He wrote in *The Nation* that he had never felt so badly about a "lost peace." But "now it has come back to me that like all other pacifists I have repeatedly said that those who believe that war must be avoided must be prepared to suffer . . . injustices and wrongs, and the same is true of nations . . . The Czechs have obeyed the Biblical injunction 'Resist not evil' and they are paying the price."[32]

On February 18, 1939, *The Nation* printed a letter from Albert Guerard, professor of French literature at Stanford, a frequent contributor to *The Nation*'s columns, and a staunch supporter of collective security. Guerard said that he had plagued Villard with the following question many times but never received a reply. In view of the recent events in Europe he hoped that Villard might meet the challenge: "If you adopt against an aggressor nation certain measures short of war; if these measures prove so effective that the aggressor nation will actually be hampered by them; if the aggressor nation sends you an ultimatum to withdraw these measures or fight, what will you do?" Villard replied "I should never fight under any circumstances. . . . I should not withdraw any non-intercourse or boycott measures to which any dictator country might ob-

ject." He told Guerard that his question was "an iffy and un-
called for question because neither Germany nor Japan nor
Italy the 'so-called' aggressor nations could make war upon us
whatever we did to them."[33]

Villard's answers were as confused and contradictory as they
had been at the time of the Spanish civil war. If Germany,
Italy, and Japan constituted no threat, why had Villard avoided
distinguishing between the aggressor and aggrieved? If the aggressor nations were only "so-called" aggressor nations, then
why had Villard repeatedly denounced Chamberlain and
Daladier for their cowardly appeasement policies? His argument for nonviolence under any circumstances was not compelling if it rested on the premise that America was under no
conceivable threat anyway. He further weakened the pacifist
position by implying that others nearer the conflict might
justifiably abandon nonresistance. In 1939, when Germany
was threatening to overrun Poland, Villard confirmed this
double standard by writing that the Poles were "an incalcula-
ble people full of idealism. They may decide to go down fighting in which case England would have to join in or be branded
as utterly treacherous."[34] Presumably the Poles were unlike the
Czechs, who had followed the biblical injunction.

Villard seemed willing to have other nations take up arms
in order to permit America to claim a pure pacifist position.
Until the Munich crisis, Villard frequently asserted that he
was not an isolationist except on the question of war and
peace, that he still advocated America's support of other
nations in all measures that would not lead to war. As in the
1920's, however, he saw almost every attempt at direct aid to
democracies as leading toward American involvement. He
made a particularly untimely attack on Roosevelt, shortly before Hitler's invasion of Poland, in an open letter to the President; the American people, he asserted, "wish you would turn
your eyes away from Europe, cease announcing that war is
just at hand over there and cease joining England and France
in their great power politics game of seeking to maintain
peace by overawing and bluffing the dictators."[35]

Villard was not alone in his inability to see the writing on the wall. In January 1938, when war with Japan seemed imminent, a well-known group of liberal and Leftist journalists, including Alfred M. Bingham, John Chamberlain, Louis Hacker, Dwight MacDonald, Bertram Wolfe, and Sidney Hook, attacked *The Nation*'s support of collective security. *The Nation*, they argued, has admitted that sanctions, military and economic, might lead to war: "We believe that the first result of another War to Make the World Safe for Democracy will be the establishment of virtual fascism in this country. Is it patriotism, under the guise of warding off the remote possibility of fascist invasion, to prepare the way for domestic despotism?" These writers also looked back to the days of the Red raids and Palmer and Burleson. They closed with a statement that could have been taken from Villard: "As readers, as contributors, as Friends of *The Nation* we protest against what seems to us a betrayal of its splendid liberal tradition."[36]

The nonaggression pact between Stalin and Hitler was announced in August 1939, at the height of a flurry of recriminations between disciples of the Popular Front and skeptical Leftists who were disillusioned with Stalin's Russia. The Committee for Cultural Freedom, under the leadership of Sidney Hook, John Dewey, and other opponents of the Popular Front, had circulated a statement, which Villard signed, denouncing those intellectuals who berated German totalitarianism while apologizing for the Russian variety. The statement closed with a call upon "all others to join us, on the basis of the least common denominator of a civilized culture—the defense of creative and intellectual freedom."[37] Freda Kirchwey questioned the motives of the signers. She correctly interpreted the circular as an attack on the Communists and fellow travelers, but lamented its encouragement of unnecessary and ill-timed factionalism. She conceded that the Communists were guilty of vituperation, slander, and "unscrupulous and callous" tactics, but then went on to review their gallant fight against Fascism.[38] Two of the editors, Maxwell Stewart and I. F. Stone, and former editor, Max Lerner (who had recently left *The Nation* to join the faculty of Williams College), along with 400 other intellectuals, signed a rebuttal, which accused the Committee for Cultural Freedom of deliberately "sowing suspicions between the Soviet Union and other nations interested in maintaining peace." After listing several points in defense of the Soviet Union, they concluded with the statement: "There exists a sound and permanent basis in mutual ideals for cooperation between the U.S.A. and the U.S.S.R. in behalf of world peace and the security and freedom of all nations."[39] The letter was published in the same issue as the announcement of the Soviet-German nonaggression pact. Miss Kirchwey wrote that in view of subsequent events further commentary seemed unnecessary. She added lamely: *"The Nation's* editorial board was opposed to the letter—despite the fact that two members of the staff signed it."[40]

The pact shattered the faith of those who believed in ideals and principles. The world was meaningless. James Wechsler wrote that a passage from Dr. Irwin Edman's *Candle in the Dark* summed up the feelings of many:

> Whatever be the causes, whatever the necessity, the fact that there could be such causes and such necessity has already eaten like a canker into the bloom of every value we enjoy and every ideal we cherish. It has seemed to make a mockery of all our hopes, and nonsense of all our knowledge. . . . It has made even private joys seem precarious and shamefaced. What do all these things avail, when they end in deliberate death and incalculable chaos? Men in the nineteenth century were sad that they could no longer believe in God. They are more deeply saddened now by the fact that they can no longer believe in man.[41]

Although many liberals like Max Lerner developed a new respect for the irrational and a deep-rooted distrust of ideology, they did not hark back the theme of the "futile brutality of war."[42] They had discovered the hard way that absolutes only cloud and distort the vision. The menace of totalitarian aggression still remained and these liberals continued their efforts to promote effective collective security.

The pact only increased Villard's bitterness and need for vindication. Since it proved that it was impossible to distinguish between aggressor and victim, all talk of collective security should end:

> America must keep out of the whole revolting European mess and free ourselves from the delusion that we have got to back England and France in order to save democracy. The kind of game that is being played over there is one that we cannot play, if we wish to preserve our integrity. . . . Not all my tremendous sympathy for the British people and the French estops my saying today, "America first." I do not speak in any selfish or holier-than-thou spirit: everyone who has followed my life's work knows that I have never been an isolationist except in the matter of war and peace.[43]

Such statements brought Villard's relations with *The Nation* to the breaking point. The editors had not abandoned their devotion to collective security, and the pact only increased the need to unite all the forces of resistance. Freda Kirchwey was infuriated, especially by Villard's charge that third term talk for Roosevelt meant potential Fascism for America, which echoed reactionary extremists opposed to the administration. Villard replied that it was not he but the editors who played into the hands of Fascists and reactionaries, since they supported "Roosevelt's abominable militarism" and refused to criticize his obvious failures.[44] Miss Kirchwey's charge was justified; Villard's criticisms reflected the traditional accusations of conservatives when he harped on the waste, extravagance, and inefficiency of the administration.[45] Freda Kirchwey returned to openly refuting Villard's columns in the editorial paragraphs of *The Nation*.[46]

Villard momentarily relieved the tension by sailing late in August to visit England and Germany. He left almost immediately after the declarations of war by France and Great Britain.

He spent three weeks in Germany, making side trips, under Nazi supervision, to Prague and Vienna. What he saw in Berlin sickened him. On his return to England he wrote that he was sure that Germany could not win the war: "Freedom, human decency, and dignity forbid it. . . . I am no churchman, but I believe profoundly that there are moral and ethical values and imponderables and that the side on which these are to be found will win in the long run."[47]

In his articles for *The Nation* and the English press Villard no longer saw the belligerents as morally equal. The Baldwin Government had made some horrible blunders but England was on the right side and the steadfastness of her people was magnificent: "To come back to the free, clean air of England after breathing the foul atmosphere of Germany, so poisoned by its murderous government's malignity, hate and vituperation . . . is to enter a new, a wholesome, a free world; is to experience an exaltation of the spirit."[48]

His last article in *The London Telegraph and Morning Post* was a stirring account of the English nation's determination to preserve the rights of its citizens. In doing so, England was guarding the right of free men everywhere. Germany might be planning to destroy London but he warned they had best pause because the "great city that looms so sombre and so vast is not England's alone. This is the heritage of all who say that men shall be free. For him who lays violent hands upon it there will be forgiveness never."

Villard ended with an eloquent farewell to England that was applauded widely in the English press:

Goodby, London! I take back to America . . . the unforgettable picture of the men and women who bring this city's streets to life. . . .

I shall behold, whenever I please, the faces of British youth in uniform, handsome, clear-eyed, cheery—wholesome, wholesome, wholesome. Too fine to lose, too fine to die. . . .

But more than that, as long as I live there will be with me the quiet faces of those without uniforms, without titles, the plain people who carry on; who have nothing yet if they have sons, everything—to lose; who must pay and pay and pay. For these are England—the England that must be made free of wars, free of fear, free of injustice. For them after the war must be built the England that is to come, better and finer than ever before.

Goodby, England! I go unafraid, for Justice, Humanity and the Right are standing on your right hand. And to them victory will come in time.[49]

Some readers of this glowing tribute, reprinted in *The Nation,* understandably thought that Villard had abandoned his position on neutrality and even his pacifism and would now come out in support of direct aid to the British. They were mistaken. He insisted that he had not changed his position. In spite of England's imperialistic past, her government, "perhaps unwittingly," found herself "defending everything that is decent in the life of nations." Nevertheless he would support, as he had in the past, only "all measures short of war, to help preserve the British people and nation,"[50] and for the next two years Villard opposed every practical measure to aid England. The arguments of 1915-1920 reappear: the American people were dedicated to peace at any price; a negotiated peace was desirable and very possible because the German people were overwhelmingly against the Nazi government and could be encouraged to revolt at the first setback of the Nazis, but even if Hitler should win, there was no threat to America; Roosevelt, like Woodrow Wilson, was deliberately conspiring to whip up hysteria along with other conspiratorial elements in an effort to put America into the war and thus to divert attention from the domestic failures of his administration.[51]

Freda Kirchwey now lost all patience with Villard and began to reject his manuscripts.[52] In May she told him that his contract with *The Nation* had expired, and considering the difficulties she would keep him only on a week-to-week basis and cut his fee from $50 a column to $30.[53] These disputes were compounded by *The Nation*'s weekly columns asserting that America's life line was England and that the country was evading its responsibilities and endangering its very existence. When Miss Kirchwey came out in June for a broad program of defense and aid to Britain which included universal military training as the "first program for a democratic defense," Villard found his connection with the magazine as intolerable as did the editors.[54] Freda Kirchwey must have been relieved when he wrote that his next column would be his "valedictory."

Villard's letter to Freda Kirchwey was bitter with recriminations over her editorial policy, which in his view represented an absolute break with all of the most hallowed traditions of *The Nation*. He hoped there would be an explanation some day of how "Freda Kirchwey, a pacifist in the last war, keen to see through shams and hypocrisy, militant for the rights of minorities and the downtrodden had now struck hands with all the forces of reaction against which *The Nation* had battled so strongly." Because Freda Kirchwey and her associates had "prostituted" *The Nation*, he hoped that it would "die very soon or fall into other hands."[55] Miss Kirchwey attempted to soothe Villard: "We are all suffering in our efforts to find a way through the desperate choices presented by the fascist challenge." But the policy he advocated was "exactly the policy for America that the Nazi propaganda in this country supports."[56]

Villard's last column of "Issues and Men" appeared in *The Nation* of June 29, 1940. It is the poignant document of a man who felt betrayed by those he loved most. He recalled his long association with *The Nation*, noting that his very first article had ironically been on military affairs. He had known for a long time that a break was inevitable. When *The Nation* abandoned its antimilitarism and embraced armaments and universal military service, there was nothing left for him to do but resign. He held hopes that the hysteria would pass and the editors and others who supported them would return to sanity. Villard's complaints were reminiscent of the soldier who insists that the rest of the regiment is out of step; his thinking was based on signposts of years gone by.[57] The principles he had held inviolable provided insufficient answers in a world changing so fast that assumptions made one day became obsolete the next. Even though he himself had once admitted (in 1935) that the "voice of reason" seemed ineffective in a world "pushed over the abyss by the deeds of a mad man," he still persisted in demanding those rules of reason that denied coercion and called for a return to the absolute principles of Christianity.[58]

Freda Kirchwey was frightened by this dream world created by many well-intentioned people who recognized the nature of the horror facing democracy but seemed to say that the terrible conditions "are our concern only if we choose to make them so." It was, she said in an editorial comment, "a retreat from the grimmest reality that has confronted our nation in many generations. . . ." Pacifism had become appeasement. It had accepted the fantastic idea that America could exist a free and independent country with Europe dominated by Hitler. The alternative that all rational men must see was "stouthearted resistance" to tyranny wherever it existed, not as an altruistic program to save the unfortunate victims of aggression but as a necessary protection of America's own security and future. In the same issue of *The Nation* Reinhold Niebuhr charged that a blind faith in the goodness of men and the power of morality were leading the world to self-destruction. His article was entitled "An End to Illusions."[59]

CHAPTER SIXTEEN

Valedictory

1940-1949

Villard's "Valedictory" was a farewell to *The Nation* but it was not a farewell to battle. He fought on in the face of increasing despair. He was now sixty-eight years old, but the buoyancy, optimism, and vigor of only a half dozen years earlier had deserted him. His speeches and writings became more and more intemperate and parochial and, in many instances, hardly distinguishable from the utterances of the most reactionary forces in America. Even his pacifism lost its lustre. In the face of such horrors as Dachau, Belsen, and Auschwitz, he took a position that denied the very Christian brotherhood it was supposed to proclaim. The pacifist argument of Villard and John Haynes Holmes, which had had meaning in 1917 and which was an integral part of liberal thought, now became a moral equivalent of the economic self-interest theories that pacifists had always denounced. It argued that in the long run the world community would benefit if the United States pursued its own interests by remaining aloof from the European controversy.

Villard continued his fight against American involvement in speeches and in articles for *The Christian Century, The Progressive,* and other magazines ranging from the extreme isolationist *Uncensored* and *Human Events* to the eminently respectable *Harper's* and *Atlantic Monthly. The Christian Century* became his home base for the years leading up to Pearl Harbor. Its editor, Charles Clayton Morrison, had been a leading liberal theologian of the social gospel movement. In

the early thirties, the magazine had called for social and economic reform of the capitalist economy, but after interminable
discussion, it joined the ranks of the Republicans when war
became imminent. By 1940 it was in the isolationist camp.

By this time Villard was cooperating openly with isolationist organizations. A prime example is his association with the
America First Committee, which had been founded specifically
to combat William Allen White's Committee to Aid America
by Defending the Allies.

In June 1940 Robert Sherwood, the playwright, presidential speech writer and ardent interventionist, published an
advertisement entitled "Stop Hitler Now." It was designed to
arouse the American people to the threat posed by a German
victory over England. Sherwood asked: "Will the Nazis con-
siderately wait until we are ready to fight them? Anyone that
urges that they will wait is either an imbecile or a traitor."
Villard indignantly wrote White that: "There are millions of
Americans who are not fifth columnists nor imbeciles or
traitors who do not agree that [if Hitler wins] we are going to
be 'alone in a barbarous world' and that we are in jeopardy.
We may be wrong but we are entitled to be treated as just as
loyal, just as sincere, and just as earnest Americans as Sherwood
or anyone else." White responded by writing Sherwood that
the phrase in question was unnecessary since he could find
"another phrase that would do just as well."[1]

On August 21, 1940, in response to an appeal by Douglas
Stuart, Jr., Villard joined the Emergency Committee to Defend America First, which later became known as the America
First Committee. The first statement in a list of principles was,
"The United States must build an impregnable defense for
America." The principles went on to state that no foreign
power could attack a prepared America, that America could
preserve democracy only by keeping out of the European war:
"Aid short of war weakens national defense at home and
threatens to involve America in war abroad."[2] When Villard
accepted a position on the national executive committee, he

reserved "the right to differ with the Committee as to what constitutes an impregnable defense for America."³ Nevertheless Villard's association with the America First Committee was a compromise of his lifelong position on preparedness and militarism. Freda Kirchwey was quick to call his attention to an advertisement listing Villard as one of the sponsors, which read: "For a prepared America we need an impregnable defense. Let us arm to the teeth for that defense. We need guns. We need planes. We need tanks. We need ships enough for a two ocean navy." How, she asked, could the Oswald Garrison Villard she knew possibly endorse such a position? She then pointed out that "many of the other persons on the board are extreme reactionaries."

Villard frankly admitted his compromise: "With me the supreme objective is to keep the United States out of war. You know it has always been my main purpose in life so far as I could bring it about. I am willing to be associated with any non-Communist group that is working sincerely for the same end." He remarked facetiously that he was gratified to see "the reactionaries, the daughter of Theodore Roosevelt and two generals, trying to keep America out of war, when similar groups are joining hands with you to put us in."⁴

The America First group was largely dominated by well known conservatives, disgruntled and disillusioned New Dealers, and some pacifists and isolationists. Its director was General Robert E. Wood, president of the National Association of Manufacturers and Chairman of the Board of Sears Roebuck and Company, one of the staunchest anti-union corporations in the country. Hanford MacNider, a leading sponsor, was an Iowa manufacturer and former national chairman of the American Legion. William R. Regnery, a businessman and book publisher was a backer of American Action Incorporated, organized to oppose the Congress of Industrial Organizations. General Thomas Hammond, the head of a business organization, was an outspoken defender of the American free enterprise system. Wayne S. Cole, the historian of the America First

Committee, points out that many liberals and socialist non-interventionists worked with the group, but "most executive and national committee members of the America First represented varied shades of conservatism on domestic and economic issues. The core of the America First Committee leadership and financial backing was provided by businessmen."[5] Villard had attacked such people for most of his journalistic career.

Villard's experience proved his own maxim that liberalism and preparedness cannot lie down together. His intellectual dilemma was even more involved. The sort of men who backed America First made it difficult to revive the old conspiracy thesis about the "masters of privilege" once again contriving to send America into war. Nor could he attack the clique of generals, since he constantly cited military men who supported his views.[6] Still, Villard could not abandon the idea of conspiracy, because he was certain that most Americans did not want war and yet the country was drifting toward war. He came to the conclusion that the Jews were behind much of the interventionist propaganda. He wrote an article on the subject that he said was approved in essence by Norman Thomas, John Flynn, and a rabbi; Freda Kirchwey refused to publish it.[7] He was fearful of the deep commitment of American Jews to intervention and he felt that they were using all the money and resources at their command to encourage it. Thus he was led to take a position which seemed to contradict all his previous efforts in defense of racial minorities.

The New York Evening Post, in March 1941, printed a cartoon portraying Hitler with his arm around Burton K. Wheeler, the leader of the isolationist filibuster against the administration's lend-lease bill. The caption read: "You're my boy." Villard, who had supported Wheeler, was furious with George Backer, the editor of the *Post* and a liberal Jew, for allowing such smear tactics. "I am all the more shocked by the action," he wrote, "because you are a Jew and if a reign of intolerance and smashing of one's opponents is to control

American life, you Jews will be the first to pay the price." When Villard accused the Jews of encouraging American intervention, Backer replied that Villard seemed to expect him to abandon his right of political action because of his Jewishness. Backer accused Villard of asking him to accept his status as a Jew within the community, "a concept that Hitler had introduced into the modern world."[8]

In the past, Villard had been the American journalist who had most vehemently denounced anti-Semitism. *The Nation,* throughout Villard's editorship, was aided by Jewish philanthropists. In 1932, when *The Nation's* finances were suffering, *The Jewish Daily Forward* lent the magazine $5,000. In 1936 Villard was honored by the influential Baltimore Zionist organization for his attack on Nazi treatment of the Jews and Father Coughlin's anti-Semitic outbursts. In the thirties he repeatedly devoted his column to denouncing the unbelievable bestiality of the Nazi persecution of the Jews.[9] Villard resigned from a number of respectable German-American organizations that were too timid to condemn the persecution publicly.[10]

Villard's defense of Charles A. Lindbergh in 1941 was a final personal tragedy for this man who had stood so long for the rights of minority groups. Lindbergh, whose anti-Semitic and pro-Nazi sentiments had been recognized for some time, announced in a speech representing America First that "the British, the Jewish [sic] and the Roosevelt Administration" were the most important pressure groups pushing America into war.[11]

Villard should not be criticized because he felt Lindbergh's statement was true—undeniably most American Jews desired Hitler's defeat—but his public defense of the statement at a time when racist organizations in the country were physically attacking Jews was an irresponsible act. Villard called Lindbergh's efforts for nonintervention "magnificent" and regretted only that his statement weakened "the only courageous and adventurous leadership" the anti-interventionist forces had.[12] This was a new Oswald Garrison Villard, who had completely abandoned his idea of principle over political expediency.

Villard, who had honestly earned his reputation as a respected liberal journalist, rapidly became an object of contempt and derision. Harold Ickes, an old friend, included Villard's name in a list of "Nazi Fellow Travelers" in a speech in April 1941. Villard saw this as another betrayal of the liberals.[13] His correspondence became largely a process of ticking off old friends who had abandoned the ship. He agreed with Harry Elmer Barnes that there had been a "stampede of the intellectuals before Hitler and Hitlerism." When the field editor of *The Christian Century*, Harold Fey, expressed his hope that 1941 would be another "fighting year," Villard told him there would probably be no more fighting years: "Almost everyone I meet has gone over to the war party" —Max Eastman, Lewis Gannett, Robert Morss Lovett, Bruce Bliven.[14]

The "betrayal" of his intimate friends and immediate family hurt Villard the most. He wrote John Palmer Gavit that both sons were engaged in the preparation for war. Hilgard had been called from his professorial duties at Amherst to a post in the Treasury Department. Villard felt that Oswald, Jr., who was working as a radio researcher at Stanford, was participating in the "killing business." Villard's wife still had little interest in his position or in his causes. His son Hilgard recalls that although the family's lack of support saddened him, "he loved the violent arguments that resulted so much that I am sure they went a long way to make up for his disappointment."[15] But Villard did not spare his friends the burden of his despair. He wrote John Haynes Holmes: "We have got to accept it, however overwhelming the disappointment. . . . We who are now in the loneliest of furrows ought to get together more. . . . I am deliberately beginning a *Life of Wendell Phillips* to go along with my *John Brown* to seek escape from what is happening and to refresh my soul with another study of the

finest and most successful group of Americans who ever lived."
Villard added that he did take "a certain sardonic pleasure in
sitting back and laughing at the Lilliputians, learning nothing,
seeing nothing and hearing nothing."[16]

Villard still dreamed of new ways to fight back. He looked
upon himself and his allies as fighting for the cause of the plain
people, the ones who paid the highest price in war. His language began to take on the anti-intellectualism of former dis-
affected groups in American life. Villard wrote Colcord that
he was trying to get together a group of journalists to start a
new magazine despite the fact that "the usual Jewish sources
have dried up." He hoped to reach "the disconnected anti-
war groups in New England and the Midwest." He did not
want "the sophisticated intellectual group to which *The Nation* and *The New Republic* now appeal," although for years
he had been proud of the predominance of this group among
Nation subscribers. In *The Christian Century* he defined the
sophisticated intellectuals as the college professors and the editors of liberal journals, "a small minority who would put their
own country into war . . . in opposition to the wishes of their
fellow citizens."[17] In May 1941 Villard submitted to *The
Christian Century* a bitter satire on the world situation: a
chapter from *Jeremiah Smith's Standard School History of the
Late Government of the Republic of Washington, Lincoln,
and Roosevelt,* published in 1971. It described how President
Roosevelt "together with the editors of the daily and weekly
press and the masters of the movies" conspiratorily set about
to whip up hysteria, hate, and fear. A Gallup poll reported
that 83 per cent of the people opposed the war, but they were
deluded and frightened by the "duplicity of certain political
leaders." The President worked the hardest of all to "strike
fear into the peoples' hearts."[18]

The attack on Pearl Harbor was the spiritual death of Oswald Garrison Villard. During the war he continued his association with reactionary elements. He wrote for the liberal but
isolationist *Progressive,* but when he became interested in

Taft's presidential candidacy, the editor, Morris Rubin, found the magazine could no longer use his services.[19] "I feel the need of communion with understanding people. . . . I feel terribly isolated," he wrote Dorothy Thompson from his country home. "Either the magazines don't want me or my hand is slipping."[20] This little band of people who had tried to save the world kept in touch and comforted one another with the reflection that the world was coming to an end—it was no longer worth living in.[21]

Villard could still take some pleasure in his prophecies. He wrote Robert L. O'Brien, the former editor of the isolationist *Boston Transcript*: "I will bet the few normal remaining teeth I have that when you and I have passed off the scene the country will be called upon by some cheap poor white like Harry Truman to save the world from bolshevism and preserve the Christian religion." Villard had the slogan for the next war against the Russians: "Save Jesus from Joseph."[22] By 1945 Franklin D. Roosevelt had replaced Woodrow Wilson in his rogues' gallery of conspirators. Villard pronounced him "the greatest falsifier and prevaricator in American History."[23]

Villard died on October 1, 1949, but he had chosen his epitaph as far back as 1941:

> He grew old in an age he condemned
> Felt the dissolving throes
> Of a Social order he loved
> And like the Theban seer
> Died in his enemies' day.[24]

*   *

From our perspective Villard's life has the aura of some past happy time when hope was possible. That vision has vanished and it is only the innocence of youth or the nostalgia of age that can entertain the hopes that absorbed Villard and his contemporaries. Despair has become almost popular. Students and laymen are attracted to the crisis theology of the neo-orthodox or the stoic acceptance of the existentialist. In either case the modern message is escape through recognition and acceptance of man's predicament in a world without God or principle.

It is strange that in a time when many intellectuals have conceded that God is dead we have had an almost religious conversion. After more than a century and a half of ignorance we have come to understand the meaning of original sin. We have, writes one of the more articulate of the new realists, "discovered a new dimension of existence—the dimension of anxiety, guilt and corruption."[25] This is not a new revelation but it is doubtful that it has ever received such widespread acceptance. We no longer underestimate the powers of darkness in the heart of every man. As a contemporary Harvard philosopher has noted: "These are the days in which Dewey's views are being replaced by Kierkegaard's in places where once Dewey was king."[26]

Villard's political views, his support of the liberal programs of his day, even his pacifism, reflected the vision of John Dewey. Villard himself was not a profound thinker. Nevertheless, instinctively he was on the side of the angels. He fought for human dignity, for political, social, and economic equality, and for as much freedom for the individual as was consistent with the demands of a modern industrial society. He understood earlier and with more intensity than most of his class or generation the degrading plight of minority groups, and he championed their cause without hesitation. Despite his blind spots, which led to occasional failures of insight and analysis, his integrity and the genuine measure of his achievements cannot be overlooked.

And yet there is still something about Villard that grates on us. What we cannot take is his style. He was capable of moral indignation; he was driven by it. This attitude appears to us most dated and ineffective. Moral indignation can be achieved only through an uncompromising commitment to an ideal or set of principles. But moderation and reasonable compromise have become the highest virtues of this age, which is distinguished from Villard's time by a lack of confidence and loss of certainty. This erosion of liberal confidence and optimism began as far back as the French Revolution; death took place during the days of the second World War.

It is, however, not only a failure of nerve that causes us to suspect Villard's zeal. The hard-boiled *Realpolitik* of the new realists has gained greater respect. We are daily reminded that this is an age that has witnessed the "End of Ideology"; we live in the period "After Utopia."[27] Villard's world was utopian despite its own repeated shocks. Even his critics firmly believed in the idea of progress and in man's ability to transform his world. During the heat of the debate over specific issues they constructed a straw man—unfortunately some historians have accepted their interpretation—which portrayed Villard as fundamentally out of step with his time. We now realize that the difference between them was at best a difference in kind, not in substance. When Freda Kirchwey accused Villard of building a dream world she was also describing the fantasy of her own political vision throughout the previous decade.

All sides during the struggles of the twenties and thirties adopted positions which defined the issues in terms of inviolable absolutes. Even the spokesmen of a pragmatic realism made an absolute out of their faith in flexibility. In any debate —the entrance of America into the first World War, the treaty and the League, the World Court and the Kellogg pact, the Supreme Court, the Spanish civil war, collective security, neutrality legislation—the alternatives were always absolute. This road leads to hell, that one to heaven. As Reinhold Niebuhr pointed out at the time of Villard's resignation from *The Nation*, the introduction of moral absolutes into a struggle for power leads only to despair. Villard and his kind would hitch their wagons to a star—there was so much to gain. They did not know how much there was to lose. In our new wisdom we hesitate to gamble.

Of course reform is not dead. Many men individually and in organizations devote their time and energy to fighting for

the same ends that Villard fought for. Some of his most strongly held positions have gained renewed prestige. Nonviolent
action has its roots in the ideals of Garrison and Gandhi, who
were the spiritual teachers of Villard, but one must concede
that in America at least the style is different. In those few
cases where it is similar, it is characteristic of youth. We are
not willing to go the whole way because we fear failure and
disillusionment. We are determined not to be burned again.

This circumspection has deeply affected our politics. Piecemeal reform and short-range goals are accepted by the modern
liberal as the only realistic approach. Moderation and compromise, not as means to achieving ends but as ends in
themselves, have become the cure for the intemperate and
unwarranted optimism of a previous age. Intellectuals have
begun to praise themselves for looking at politics through the
eyes of the politician. They have abandoned their role as independent critics. The alternative to despair is uncritical acceptance and there is relative security in membership in the
establishment.[28]

It would be absurd to expect that reformers today could or
should adopt the style that characterized Villard's time.
Nostalgia is tempting but dangerous. Rigid perfectionism is
justifiably passé. A too facile acceptance of an ideological
position can be irresponsible and dangerous. Maturity, not
youthful innocence, is an absolute prerequisite for effective
participation in world politics. A pacifism that cannot stand
the test of fire and counsels only self-protection cannot be revived without peril. A self-righteous moralism that fails to
recognize that all political action involves a degree of compromise and accommodation is destined to remain powerless
and ineffective. But can we blithely repudiate the gadfly temper
and the utopian imagination and succumb to the slow attrition
that undermines any desire to stand firm? To chant that the
road to hell is paved with good intentions is not an argument
for abandoning good intentions altogether. We cannot possibly
conclude, in the face of conditions around us, that there are no

important issues left to debate, and we cannot live in constant fear of making fools of ourselves without assuring thereby a far more horrible fate.

Max Lerner warned, after the disillusioning impact of the Stalin-Hitler pact, that a recognition of irrationality in the world need not demand a glorification of it. We are in danger of turning our acceptance of the "End of Ideology" into a slogan or, even worse, a new ideology of complacency. It provides an easy, superficial justification for acquiescence to the status quo. As Irving Howe has noted, the leap of many reformers and intellectuals from Marx to Machiavelli has been marked not so much by new realism as by a growing insensitivity to the harsh realities of our own times.[29]

We can ill afford to deprecate the "old fashioned" liberal tradition which at its best maintained a critical perspective and was always sensitive to the shortcomings of society and its institutions. Despite its occasional extravagance and overzealous dedication it provided the impetus and the inspiration that all lasting reform requires, and it serves as a yardstick with which to measure and judge the costs of compromise and accommodation. Villard's son, Henry Hilgard, has stated the case as well as any other. When I wrote to him, expressing an impatience with his father's inflexibility and refusal to entertain any compromise, he replied: "Just as Churchill argued for a square House of Commons so that people would know when they changed sides, I believe in the importance of those who have unchanging standards so that when we have to compromise we are not allowed to forget that we are compromising."[30] That a man's reach should exceed his grasp is as much a part of the human predicament as his realization of human frailty. Now, when even thoughts of survival seem visionary and utopian, one wonders if the world will be any freer and more humane without the prodding consciences of men like Oswald Garrison Villard.

275

NOTES

All references to Villard correspondence and manuscript material are from the Villard Papers, Houghton Library, Harvard University, unless otherwise indicated. Unsigned editorials and articles attributed to Villard or other writers have been verified by checking them against the Villard Papers scrapbooks or the annotated set of *The Nation* deposited by Villard in the New York Public Library.

1. Introduction

1. "Trumpet to the People: The Story of Oswald Garrison Villard," *The World Tomorrow*, XIII (November, 1930), 440.

2. Ellery Sedgwick to Villard, October 13, 1925; R. L. Duffus to Villard, January 31, 1935; Waldo Cook, statement made at tenth anniversary dinner of Villard's editorship, March 1928 (Pamphlet in Villard Papers); John Haynes Holmes to Miss Blanche Watson (n.d., presumably in the late twenties).

3. Quoted in Louis S. Gannett, "Villard's *Nation*," *The Nation*, CL (February 10, 1940), 158.

4. Villard, *Fighting Years: Memoirs of a Liberal Editor* (New York, 1939), p. 108.

2. A Mixed Heritage

1. Villard to James Blaine Hedges, November 7, 1933; Villard, *Fighting Years: Memoirs of a Liberal Editor* (New York, 1939), pp. 9-17; 77-79; Henry Villard, *Memoirs of Henry Villard: Journalist and Financier* (2 vols.; Boston, 1904).

2. Villard, *Fighting Years*, p. 12.

3. For the best study of Henry Villard see James Blaine Hedges, *Villard and Railways of the Northwest* (New Haven, 1930); Gustave Meyers, *History of Great American Fortunes* (New York, 1936), pp. 683-689.

4. Joseph Wood Krutch, *More Lives Than One* (New York, 1920), pp. 170-171.

5. Villard, *Fighting Years*, p. 21.

6. R. L. Duffus, "Grandson of the Liberator," *American Mercury*, XII (December, 1927), 449-451; Cameron Rogers, "Villard and *The Nation*," *Outlook*, CLI (March 6, 1929), 384; Duffus to Villard, September 13, 1927; Villard to Duffus, September 27, 1927; Cameron Rogers to Villard (n.d.); Villard to Cameron Rogers, March 14, 1929.

7. Matthew Josephson, *The Politicos* (New York, 1938), p. 489; Allan Nevins, *Cleveland: A Study in Courage* (New York, 1933), pp. 481, 510, 533; Allan Nevins, *A Century of the New York Post* (New York, 1922), pp. 440-441; John Chamberlain, *Farewell to Reform* (New York, 1933), p. 8.

8. *Selections from the Writings and Speeches of William Lloyd Garrison* (Boston, 1852), p. 63.

9. Quoted in Phillip Foner, *The History of the Labor Movement in the United States* (New York, 1947), p. 270; John L. Thomas, *The Liberator: William Lloyd Garrison* (Boston, 1963), pp. 297-299.

10. "Dr. Ely on the Labor Movement," *The Nation*, XLIII (October 7, 1886), 293-294.

11. Alan Pendleton Grimes, *The Political Liberalism of The New York* Nation: *1865-1932* (Chapel Hill, 1953), p. 40; Vernon L. Parrington, *The Beginnings of Political Realism in America* (New York, 1930), p. 163.

12. Villard Papers, Rogers Morse correspondence file; Villard *Diary*, 1889; Villard to parents, August 8, 1886; Villard *Diary* entry, June 27, 1889, for academic information; Villard, *Fighting Years*, pp. 35-36, 71-76; Villard, "Abraham Jacobi—The Last of the Forty-Eighters," *The Nation*, CIX (July 19, 1919), 74-75.

13. Villard to parents, 1889-1893; Norman Hapgood, *Changing Years* (New York, 1930), p. 146; Robert Morss Lovett, *All Our Years* (New York, 1948), chapter II; Frederick Howe, *The Confessions of a Reformer* (New York, 1925).

14. Villard, *Fighting Years*, pp. 81, 101, 103; W. E. B. Du Bois, "That Outer Whiter World of Harvard," in *The Harvard Book: Selections from Three Centuries*, ed. William Benlinck-Smith (Cambridge, Mass., 1953), p. 230.

15. Villard to parents, 1890-1893; see also Villard *Diary* for same years.

16. Villard to parents, May 25, 1891.

17. Villard to his son Henry Hilgard Villard about his younger brother Oswald, Jr., April 4, 1933.

18. Villard *Diary*, January 29-30, 1889; Villard to parents, January 11, 1891; Villard to parents, October 27, 1894.

19. Fanny Villard to Oswald Villard, November 7, 1892.

20. Villard to parents, July 5, 1894; Villard, "Army Reforms," *The New York Post*, October 6, 1893, (Villard Papers, clipping file). The paper, during most of the years in which Oswald Villard wrote for it, was entitled *The Evening Post*; in this study it will be referred to as *The Post*. Villard, *Fighting Years*, p. 100.

21. Villard to parents, April 14, 1893. All of these early articles and stories may be found in the Villard Papers scrapbooks; Villard, "Spaniards at Melilla," *The Nation*, LVIII (January 11, 1894), 27-28.

22. Villard Papers, scrapbook clippings, 1894-1895; Nevins, *Century of the Post*, p. 576.

23. Villard to parents, September 22, 1895; Henry Villard to Oswald Villard, September 30, 1895.

24. Villard to R. L. Duffus, September 27, 1927; Villard to Ernest Gruening, May 13, 1931.

25. Villard, *Fighting Years*, p. 97; Albert Bushnell Hart to Villard, July 12, 1894; Hart to Villard, April 13, 1939.

26. Villard to parents, May 5, 1895.

27. Villard to Henry Villard, March 11, 1896; letters of November, 1894.

28. Villard to parents, February 19, 1896; *Boston Advertiser*, January 15, 1896 (Villard Papers, clipping file); *The Nation*, XVIII (May 14, 1894), 312.

29. Villard to parents, February 7, 1896; Villard, *Fighting Years*, p. 100.

30. Villard, *Fighting Years*, p. 105; Henry Villard to Oswald Villard, June 7, 1896.

31. Villard to parents, November 17, 1896; Villard, *Fighting Years*, pp. 105-115.

32. Lincoln Steffens, *The Autobiography of Lincoln Steffens* (New York, 1931), pp. 272, 279, 311-314; Hapgood, *Changing Years*, pp. 127-129.

33. Villard to Henry Villard, April 28, 1897; Henry Villard to Oswald Villard, May 6, 1897; Villard, *Fighting Years*, p. 118.

34. A. J. P. Taylor, *The Troublemakers: Dissent Over Foreign*

Policy, 1792-1939 (London, 1957), pp. 57, 62 ff.; Lawrence Martin, *Peace Without Victory: Woodrow Wilson and the British Liberals* (New Haven, 1958), p. 2; Arno J. Mayer, *Political Origins of the New Diplomacy, 1917-1918* (New Haven, 1959), pp. 56-58.

35. Admiral Alfred T. Mahan, *The Problem of Asia and Its Effects Upon International Policies* (Boston, 1900), p. 187.

36. Villard to Henry Villard, March 11, 1896.

37. *The Post,* February 18, 1898 (Villard Papers, scrapbook clipping).

38. *The Post* articles reappeared in *The Nation,* October 27, November 10 and 19, 1898; Villard to Henry Villard, May 6, 1898. For Villard's later reference to McKinley, see Villard to Walter Millis, June 25, 1931, and his statement in *Fighting Years,* p. 137.

39. Villard to Henry Villard, May 6, May 13, May 24, June 10, June 21, June 28, 1898.

40. Fred Harrington, "The Anti-Imperialist Movement in the United States, 1898-1900," *Mississippi Valley Historical Review,* XXII (September, 1935), 227-228.

41. *Ibid.,* 211-212; Robert E. Osgood, *Ideals and Self-Interest in America's Foreign Relations* (Chicago, 1953), pp. 48-50; Villard to Henry Villard, August 14, 1900; Villard to R. J. Mock (undated letter to a Ph.D. candidate).

42. Villard to Henry Villard, July 22, 1898; Villard to parents, August 14, 1898.

43. *Ibid.;* T. M. Osborne to Villard, July 28, 1900.

44. Villard to William Lyon Phelps, July 21, 1916.

45. Villard to parents, July 5, 1898.

46. Garrison statement cited in Russel B. Nye, *William Lloyd Garrison and the Humanitarian Reformers* (New York, 1955), p. 200.

47. Villard to Stanwood Menken, April 21, 1926.

48. Villard, "Two Americans: Hillquit and Adler," *The Nation,* CXXXVII (October 25, 1933), 473-474.

49. Villard to Reverend Leavell, December 19, 1912.

50. Nye, *William Lloyd Garrison,* pp. 200-202.

3. Respectable Reform

1. Richard Hofstadter, *The Age of Reform* (New York, 1955), p. 142.

2. William Allen White to Villard, April 28, 1908; Villard to White, May 7, 1908.

3. Villard, *Fighting Years: Memoirs of a Liberal Editor* (New York, 1939), pp. 176-177; Villard to Thomas Mott Osborne, October 7, 1912.

4. Villard to Charles Evans Hughes, December 3, 1908.

5. Villard to Ray Stannard Baker, April 17, 1929; Villard, *Fighting Years*, p. 526.

6. Villard to Lillian Wald, September 7, 1907.

7. Villard to Paul Kellogg, December 7, 1910; Villard to Mary White Ovington, May 7, 1908 (Villard Papers, organizational file).

8. Villard, *Fighting Years*, p. 344; Villard to wife, March 19, 1918.

9. Villard to T. M. Osborne, October 7, 1912; Osborne to Villard, October 12, 1912.

10. Arthur S. Link, *Wilson: The Road to the White House* (Princeton, 1947), pp. 502-503.

11. See Villard memorandum of interview with Wilson, August 13, 1912; Villard to R. H. Leavell, August 15, December 12, 1918. Leavell, a professor of economics at Texas A & M, was the originator of the National Race Commission idea.

12. Villard to Wilson, August 22, 1913; Villard to Joseph Tumulty, August 15, November 23, 1913; Villard to Charles Eliot, September 28, 1913; John Palmer Gavit to Villard, September 26, 1913. Gavit was *The Post*'s Washington correspondent and was in close touch with the President's secretary.

13. Villard to Wilson, August 22, 1913; Villard to Moorfield Storey, September 10, 1913.

14. Arthur S. Link, *Woodrow Wilson and the Progressive Era* (New York, 1954), pp. 18-20; Hofstadter, *Age of Reform*, pp. 246-247; Eric F. Goldman, *Rendezvous with Destiny* (New York, 1953), pp. 216 ff. Allan F. Davis, "The Social Worker and the Progressive Party," *American Historical Review*, LXIX (April, 1964), 671-673; Norman Hapgood, *The Changing Years* (New York, 1930), pp. 215-220.

15. "Veblen's Business Enterprise," *The Nation*, LXXXI (July 13, 1905), 38; editorial paragraph, *The Nation*, CIV (April 5, 1917), 410; "In Status Quo," *The Nation*, XCV (September 5, 1912), 204.

16. In a letter to the author, June 5, 1960, Mrs. William English

Walling, a contemporary of Villard's and a thorough-going pacifist, disagrees with my implication that Villard in these years tended to cling to the past. She writes: "As a journalist, if nothing more, he was contemporaneous and aware of the movements and changes in society and I do not believe that he even rejected Socialism as wholeheartedly as my husband, for instance, took for granted that he did."

17. Mary White Ovington, *How the National Association for the Advancement of Colored People Began* (New York, 1914); Flint Kellogg, "Villard and the NAACP," *The Nation*, CLXXXI (February 14, 1959), 137-138; Jack Abramowitz, "Origins of the NAACP," *Social Education*, CV (January, 1951); Elliott M. Rudwick, "W. E. B. DuBois: In the Role of *Crisis* Editor," *The Journal of Negro History*, XLIII (July, 1958), 214-240.

18. H. G. Wells, "The Contemporary Novel," *The Atlantic Monthly*, CIX (January, 1912), 11. For material on the intellectual rebellion of the pre-war years I am indebted to Henry F. May's *The End of American Innocence: A Study of the First Years of Our Own Time, 1912-1917* (New York, 1959) and Richard Drinnon's *Rebel in Paradise: A Biography of Emma Goldman* (Chicago, 1961), pp. 145-154.

19. Cited by Drinnon, *Rebel in Paradise*, p. 147; Villard, *Fighting Years*, pp. 91-92.

20. Quoted in Drinnon, *Rebel in Paradise*, p. 143.

21. Mabel Dodge Luhan, *Movers and Shakers* (New York, 1936), pp. 39 ff.

22. Quoted in Floyd Dell, *Homecoming: An Autobiography* (New York, 1933), p. 218.

23. *Harvard College Class of 1893: Secretary's Report*, Nos. 2, 3, 4, 5, and 6.

24. Villard, *Fighting Years*, pp. 174-175.

25. Henry H. Villard to author, February 20, 1961.

26. This incident was told to the author by a friend and associate of Villard's in an interview in April 1962.

27. Henry Villard to author, October 13, 1964.

28. Villard to wife, September 14; September 18, 1920; Villard to Robert L. O'Brien (editor of the *Boston Herald*), February 26, 1945.

29. Villard, *Fighting Years*, p. 175.

30. Villard to wife, December 25, 1918.

31. Interviews with Henry Hilgard Villard, Roger Baldwin, Freda Kirchwey and Norman Thomas, April 1962.

32. Max Eastman, *Enjoyment of Living* (New York, 1948), pp. 301-303, 329-330, 441.

33. Villard, *Fighting Years*, pp. 199-200; Villard to George Mc-Aneney (n.d., 1913), Villard Papers, Diners' Club file; *Harvard Class Report*, No. 4 (1910).

34. Hutchins Hapgood, *A Victorian in the Modern World* (New York, 1939), pp. 260-261.

4. Neutrality: 1914-1915

1. Rollo Ogden to Villard, n.d., 1914.

2. Villard to Charles H. Strong, June 2, 1916.

3. *The Post*, August 3, 1914; Villard to Francis Jackson Garrison, August 3, 1914.

4. *The Post*, August 8, August 3, October 21, 1914.

5. Oswald Garrison Villard, *Germany Embattled* (New York, 1915).

6. C. F. Adams to Villard, March 13, 1915; *London Illustrated*, October 2, 1915; *London Morning Post*, n.d., 1915; *Manchester Guardian*, August 19, 1915; A. B. Hart to Villard, December 19, 1914; William L. Phelps to Villard, March 8, 1915. Hart's letter was in response to Villard's article "Germany Embattled," in *Scribner's Magazine*, LVI (December, 1914), 725-732. Newspaper citations are from Villard Papers, clipping file.

7. *The Post*, August 31, 1914.

8. Villard to Rollo Ogden, September 10, 1914.

9. Cited in Thomas A. Bailey, *A Diplomatic History of the American People* (New York, 1950), p. 612.

10. Stoddard Dewey to Villard, December 23, 1914; Villard to Dewey, January 8, 1915; September 14, 1914.

11. Gruening to author, April 19, 1960.

12. Villard to August Blum, September 19, 1921; Oswald Garrison Villard, *The Two Germanies* (New York, 1914).

13. Chadwick to Villard, January 4, 1915.

14. Villard to Chadwick, September 24, 1914; *The Post*, September 16, 1914.

15. Villard to Roy Martin, December 14, 1914; Villard to John Barran, November 28, 1914; Villard to Lady Barran, July 30, 1915.

16. James Loeb to Villard, December 31, 1914.

17. *The Gaelic American,* December 4 and 11, 1915 (Villard Papers, clipping file).

18. Villard to James Loeb, February 3, 1915; Villard to Professor Rudolph Leonhard, University of Breslau, October 21, 1914. Villard editorial in *The Post,* October 21, 1914.

19. This speech was reported in *The Springfield Republican,* September 5, 1915.

20. Hugo Munsterberg, "The Impeachment of German Americans," *The New York Times Magazine* (September 19, 1915), p. 4.

21. Charles Evans Hughes to Villard, April 22, 1909; *The New York Times,* November 9, 1915, p. 4.

22. Norman Angell, "The Errors of Pacifism," *McNaught's Monthly* (July, 1927). Tear sheets in Villard Papers, clipping file.

23. Villard to W. H. Short (Secretary of the New York Peace Society), April 26, 1909; January 8, 1915. Villard speech, "What is Wrong With our Pacifists?" (n.d.) in Villard Papers, speech file, presumably late 1916.

24. Villard, "What is Wrong With our Pacifists?"

25. Villard to parents, July 6, 1899, describes being taken for T. R.; Villard, *Fighting Years,* p. 154.

26. Villard to R. L. Duffus, September 23, 1927; Villard to William L. Garrison, Jr., May 10, 1919; Villard to wife, February 26, 1919.

27. Villard to Charles H. Strong, June 27, 1916; Villard, "Non Resistance," *The Post,* October 17, 1914; Villard, "Preparedness is Militarism," *The Annals of the Academy of Political and Social Science,* LXVI (July, 1916), 224; Villard, "In Time of Hesitation," speech before the National Federation of Religious Liberals, March 17, 1917 (Villard Papers, speech file).

28. Oswald Garrison Villard, *Preparedness* (Washington, D.C., 1915), a series of articles collected from *The Post.*

29. *The Post,* September 21, October 19, 1914. General Friedrich von Bernhardi was a famous German militarist and the author of *Deutschland und der nächste Krieg* (1912), which placed him in a class with Nietzsche and Treitschke as a worshipper of force.

30. Villard, unsigned editorial, *The Post,* November 18, 1914.

31. Villard, editorials, *The Post,* August 11, September 11, September 21, 1914.

32. Woodrow Wilson to Villard, August 24, 1914.

33. Villard to F. J. Garrison, December 2, December 4, 1914.

34. Ray Stannard Baker and William E. Dodd (eds.), *The Public Papers of Woodrow Wilson* (6 vols.; New York, 1925-1927), I, 223-227.

35. Villard to F. J. Garrison, December 2, 4, 1914.

36. Transcript of debate on "Preparedness" before the Economic Club of Buffalo between Villard and Henry Wise Wood, Chairman of the Finance Committee of the National Security League (Villard Papers, speech file).

37. *The Post*, November 18, September 2, September 21, 1914.

38. *The Post*, May 8, 1915; Elting E. Morison and Joseph Blum (eds.), *The Letters of Theodore Roosevelt* (8 vols.; Cambridge, 1954), VIII, 922.

39. Villard claimed credit for coining this phrase in a conversation with Joseph Tumulty: Villard, *Fighting Years: Memoirs of a Liberal Editor* (New York, 1939), pp. 256-257.

40. Baker and Dodd (eds.), *The Public Papers of Woodrow Wilson*, III, 321.

41. Quoted in Bailey, *A Diplomatic History of the American People*, p. 629.

42. *The Post*, May 10, 1915; Roosevelt to Henry Reuterdahl, November 30, 1915; Morison and Blum (eds.), *The Letters of Theodore Roosevelt*, VIII, 993.

43. Villard to Secretary Lansing, July 30, 1915; *The Post*, May 17, 1915.

44. Villard to James Oppenheim, May 23, 1917; Villard to W. R. Castle (editor of *The Harvard Bulletin*), February 16, 1917; Villard to Captain von Boyed, June 15, 1915.

45. *The Post*, May 15, August 24, 1915; Villard to G. F. Peabody, May 25, 1915.

46. Villard to Wilson, June 7, 1915; Wilson to Villard, May 10, 1915.

47. *The Post*, September 2, 1915.

48. *Ibid.*; Villard to Leroy Vernon, September 2, 1915.

49. Villard to Lansing, July 30, 1915; Lansing to Villard, August 10, 1915; Villard, *Fighting Years*, pp. 267-269; Ernest R. May, *The World War and American Isolation, 1914-1917* (Cambridge, 1959), p. 173.

50. *The New York Herald*, August 29, 1915; *The New York Times*, November 9, 1915 (Villard Papers, clipping file); George

Harvey, "Pacifist at Work," *North American Review*, 202 (July, 1915), 8-11.

51. Villard, *Fighting Years*, pp. 270-273; Villard to Gavit, June 2, 1915.

5. The Maelstrom of Militarism: 1915-1916

1. Villard to F. J. Garrison, December 11, 1914; Villard to Tumulty, April 28, 1915.

2. *The Post*, July 22, 1915.

3. Villard to George Foster Peabody, August 18, 1915; Villard to wife, October 6, 1915.

4. Villard to Wilson, September 3, 1915; Wilson to Villard, September 7, 1915; Villard, *Preparedness* (Washington, D.C., 1915).

5. Villard to wife, October 6, 1915; Wilson to Villard, September 2, 1915; Tumulty to Villard, September 2, 1915; House to Villard, September 2, 1915.

6. Villard to Congressman James Slayden of Texas, February 9, 1916; Villard to Tumulty, July 8, 1916; Villard to Leroy Vernon (Washington correspondent of *The Chicago Daily News*), October 25, 1915.

7. J. P. Gavit to Villard, November 17, 1920.

8. Villard to Joseph Sturge, October 29, 1915. The Sturges were brother and sister and were British liberals who had a long and honorable Abolitionist background.

9. Villard, unsigned editorial, *The Post*, October 18, 1915.

10. Villard to Wilson, October 30, 1915.

11. Wilson to Villard, November 2, 1915.

12. Villard, *Preparedness;* Ernest R. May, *The World War and American Isolation* (Cambridge, 1959), pp. 174-178.

13. Villard to Joseph and Sophia Sturge, January 19, 1916.

14. *The Post*, January 29, 1916.

15. F. J. Garrison to Villard, February 25, 1916; Villard to Garrison, March 1, 1916; Villard to Sturge, January 19, 1916.

16. Jane Addams, *Peace and Bread in Time of War* (New York, 1922), chapter II.

17. *Ibid.*, p. 16.

18. Balch to Villard, September 28, 1915.

19. Villard to Emily Balch, August 10, 1915.

20. Lawrence W. Martin, *Peace Without Victory: Woodrow Wilson and the British Liberals* (New Haven, 1958), pp. 79, 105;

Ernest R. May, *The World War and American Isolation, 1914-1917* (Cambridge, 1959), p. 348; Charles Seymour, *American Diplomacy During the War* (New York, 1934), pp. 182, 187.

21. Villard to Fanny Garrison Villard, February 11, 1916.

22. It seems to the author that by the winter of 1915-1916 Villard had become the butt of a good deal of humor on the part of fellow journalists in Washington. Ernest Gruening, his long time associate and fellow journalist, now senator from Alaska, has written that he does not feel that this was ever the case: "Villard was considered by his contemporaries as an excellent reporter." Gruening to author, April 19, 1960.

23. *The New York Herald*, November 25, 1915 (Villard Papers, clipping file).

24. Villard to Leroy Vernon, November 25, 1915; Villard to Theodore Delavigne (Ford's secretary) December 17, 1915; Dr. Samuel Marquis to Villard, July 18, 1916; Villard to S. Anderson (Ford's assistant secretary), August 8, 1916.

25. The two scoops were the prediction of a note from Lansing censuring the British (*The Post*, May 17, 1915), repudiated the following day, and Villard's statement the day before Bryan's resignation that the Secretary would not resign: see Villard, *Fighting Years: Memoirs of a Liberal Editor* (New York, 1939), pp. 263-264, 267. He later claimed that Wilson had lied to him. Villard to Morgenthau, April 10, 1916; Leroy Vernon to Villard, September 2, 1915.

26. Villard to Morgenthau, April 10, 1916; Villard to Peabody, February 7, 1916; Villard to Phelps, July 21, 1916; Villard to Lawrence, May 9, July 7, 1916.

27. *The Post*, June 14, 1916.

28. Arthur S. Link, *Woodrow Wilson and the Progressive Era* (New York, 1947), p. 239; Arno J. Mayer, *Political Origins of the New Diplomacy, 1917-1918* (New Haven, 1959), p. 347.

29. Villard to Charleton B. Thompson, July 7, 1916.

30. Villard to G. F. Peabody, September 19, 1916.

31. Villard to Tumulty, November 10, 1916.

32. Link, *Wilson and the Progressive Era*, p. 220; Charles Seymour (ed.), *The Intimate Papers of Colonel House* (4 vols.; Boston, 1926-1928), II, 307-308; Ray Stannard Baker, *Woodrow Wilson: Life and Letters* (8 vols.; New York, 1939), VI, 311-325.

33. May, *The World War and American Isolation*, pp. 362-363;

Seymour (ed.), *Intimate Papers of House*, II, 388-398; Baker, *Woodrow Wilson: Life and Letters*, VI, 372-373.

34. Baker, *Woodrow Wilson: Life and Letters*, VI, 392; Seymour, *American Diplomacy During the World War*, p. 188; Seymour (ed.), *Intimate Papers of House*, II, 388-389.

35. Wilson to Villard, March 26, 1915.

36. Villard to Tumulty, December 14, 1916.

37. Villard, *The Post*, December 18, 1916.

38. May, *The World War and American Isolation*, pp. 359-362, has the most detailed analysis of the pressures on Wilson. See also, Seymour (ed.), *Intimate Papers of House*, II, 390-406.

39. *Ibid.*, II, 200.

40. *Ibid.*, II, 403-404; Baker, *Woodrow Wilson: Life and Letters*, VI, pp. 387-396; May, *The World War and American Isolation*, pp. 365-367.

41. Baker, *Woodrow Wilson: Life and Letters*, VI, 396.

42. Walter Millis, *Road to War: America, 1914-1917* (New York, 1935), pp. 367-369.

43. Villard to Tumulty, December 20, 1916.

44. Villard, *Fighting Years*, p. 230.

45. Seymour (ed.), *Intimate Papers of House*, II, 413. Charles Callan Tansill, *America Goes to War* (Boston, 1938), p. 631.

46. *The Post*, February 22, 1917.

47. Villard speech, February 18, 1917, quoted by *The Public* (a single tax paper) in Villard Papers, clipping file.

48. Baker, *Woodrow Wilson: Life and Letters*, VI, 462.

49. *The Post*, March 6, 1917.

50. Villard to James Oppenheim, March 23, 1917; Villard to W. R. Castle (editor of *The Harvard Bulletin*), February 16, 1917.

51. *The New York Times*, March 14, 1917; Villard speech, "What's Wrong With Our Pacifists?" February, 1917; Reinhold Niebuhr, "The Nation's Crime Against the Individual," *The Atlantic Monthly*, CXVIII (November, 1916), 609-614; *The New York Sun*, February 19, 1917; *The Evening Telegram*, February 20, 1917; *The Outlook*, CXV (March 14, 1917), 450-451; *The Literary Digest*, LIV (March 3, 1917), 538.

52. Villard to Fanny Villard, February 20, 1917.

53. Baker, *Woodrow Wilson: Life and Letters*, VI, 489-491; Seymour, *Intimate Papers of House*, II, 471; John L. Heaton, *Cobb of The World* (New York, 1924), pp. 267-270.

54. *The Post*, April 4, 1917.

55. John M. Blum, *Woodrow Wilson and the Politics of Morality* (Boston, 1956), p. 111; George F. Kennan, *American Diplomacy: 1900-1950* (Chicago, 1951), pp. 95 ff.; other representative works of the "realist" school are Hans J. Morgenthau, *In Defense of The National Interest* (New York, 1951); Louis J. Halle, *Dream and Reality: Aspects of American Foreign Policy* (New York, 1958); Robert E. Osgood, *Ideals and Self-Interest in America's Foreign Relations* (Chicago, 1953).

56. Osgood, *Ideals and Self-Interest*, pp. 290-291.

57. *Ibid.*, pp. 121-122.

58. In the following brief discussion I have relied heavily upon Charles B. Forcey's *The Crossroads of Liberalism: Croly, Weyl, and Lippmann and the Progressive Era, 1900-1925* (New York, 1961), chapters VII and VIII, Book III, which deal with the development of editorial policy.

59. Cited in Forcey, *The Crossroads of Liberalism*, p. 247.

60. "The Great Decision," *The New Republic*, X (April 7, 1917), 280.

61. Randolph Bourne, "Twilight of Idols," in *The History of a Literary Radical and Other Papers*, ed. Van Wyck Brooks (New York, 1956), pp. 254-255.

62. David Lawrence to Villard, April 12, 1917.

63. Villard to Joseph Tumulty, April 13, 1917.

6. The New Diplomacy: 1916-1917

1. Hutchins Hapgood, *A Victorian in the Modern World* (New York, 1939), p. 260.

2. Hapgood to Villard, May 15, 1919; Villard to Hapgood, May 19, 1919.

3. Charles Seymour (ed.), *The Intimate Papers of Colonel House* (4 vols.; Boston, 1926-1928), III, 427; Ray Stannard Baker and William E. Dodd (eds.), *The Public Papers of Woodrow Wilson* (6 vols.; New York, 1925-1927), V, 67.

4. George Creel, *The War, The World, and Wilson* (New York, 1920), pp. 145-146.

5. *American Socialist*, April 21, 1917, pp. 1-2.

6. James H. Callender to Villard, February 20, 1917. Callender, a New York businessman, threatened a campaign to have *The Post* removed from all New York clubs, libraries, and reading rooms.

7. Villard, *Fighting Years: Memoirs of a Liberal Editor* (New York, 1939), pp. 329-331; "The Gerard Slanders," *The Post*, April 12, 1917; Gerard statement in unidentified April, 1917, clipping (Villard Papers, clipping file).

8. Villard to Mrs. William Jay, a member of the board of the Philharmonic Society, March 13, 1917; Villard to the Board of Directors, January 2, 1918; *The New York Times*, January 5, 1918, p. 7; *The New York Sun*, January 5, 1918 (Villard Papers, clipping file).

9. Henry F. May, *The End of American Innocence: A Study of the First Years of Our Own Time, 1912-1917* (New York, 1959), pp. 42, 363-366, *passim*. May presents a comprehensive account of the ideals and traditions of the "custodians of American culture" upon which I have relied heavily for an understanding of Villard's contemporaries.

10. Randolph Bourne, "The War and the Intellectuals," *The History of a Literary Radical and Other Papers*, ed. Van Wyck Brooks (New York, 1956), p. 207.

11. Villard, *Fighting Years*, pp. 331-332.

12. Villard, *Fighting Years*, p. 323; Joseph Freeman, *An American Testament: A Narrative of Rebels and Romantics* (New York, 1936), pp. 92-93; May, *The End of American Innocence*, p. 368.

13. *Fellowship of Reconciliation*, Pamphlet in Villard files.

14. Printed statement of the Fellowship of Reconciliation, published April 23, 1917, Villard files.

15. Villard to Norman Thomas, September 11, 1917; John Nevin Sayre to author, April, 1960.

16. Villard, *Fighting Years*, p. 326; Jane Addams, *Peace and Bread in Time of War* (New York, 1922), p. 141.

17. Villard to H. B. Brougham, April 4, 1917.

18. Villard to David Lawrence, October 9, 1917.

19. *The Post*, April 21, 1917; "Bryce on the Real Prussian Menace," *The Nation*, CIV (April 26, 1917), 481.

20. Villard to Tumulty, September 26, 1917; Tumulty to Villard, September 29, 1917.

21. Villard, *Fighting Years*, p. 335; Villard to Tumulty, July 27, 1917.

22. *The Post*, April 9, 1917; "Censorship and Suppression," *The Nation*, CIV (April 12, 1917), 424.

23. *The Post*, August 8, December 3, 1914; April 25, 1915.

24. Robert Osgood, *Ideals and Self-Interest In America's Foreign Relations,* (Chicago, 1953), pp. 17-19, 49, 257, 262, 303, *passim.*

25. I am indebted in part for this criticism of American historians to Arno J. Mayer's *Political Origins of the New Diplomacy, 1917-1918* (New Haven, 1959).

26. Lawrence W. Martin, *Peace Without Victory: Woodrow Wilson and the British Liberals* (New Haven, 1958), p. 50. This study of the close relationship between Wilson and the British liberals provides convincing evidence that the idealism culminating in the Fourteen Points was hardly unique to America. See also, Henry R. Winkler, *The League of Nations Movement in Great Britain: 1914-1917* (New Brunswick, 1952). Mayer, *Political Origins of the New Diplomacy,* p. 163; Philip Viscount Snowden, *An Autobiography* (2 vols.; London, 1934), I, 360.

27. Helen M. Swanwick, *Builders of Peace* (London, 1924), pp. 30-34; Martin, *Peace Without Victory,* p. 62.

28. *Ibid.,* p. 13.

29. *The Post,* March 10, April 21, 1915.

30. Joseph Sturge to Villard, September 7, 1914; Villard to Joseph Sturge, May 1, 1917.

31. Villard to the Sturges, December 12, 1914.

32. Snowden, *An Autobiography,* I, 350-357; Charles Trevelyan, *From Liberalism to Labor* (London, 1921), p. 25; Martin, *Peace Without Victory,* pp. 12, 48-49.

33. David Lawrence to Villard, October 6, 1917. Enclosed is a copy of Wilson's letter to Lawrence; Villard to Wilson, October 9, 1917.

34. Villard to Lawrence, December 7, 1917; Martin, *Peace Without Victory,* pp. 138-140; letter of Ramsay MacDonald to William H. Buckler, August 17, 1917, quoted in Allan Nevins, *Henry White: Thirty Years of American Diplomacy* (New York, 1930), pp. 342-345.

35. Baker and Dodd (eds.), *The Public Papers of Woodrow Wilson,* V, 120; Seymour (ed.), *Intimate Papers of House,* III, 274; Ray Stannard Baker, *Woodrow Wilson: Life and Letters* (8 vols.; New York, 1939), VII, 396-397.

36. Mayer, *Political Origins of the New Diplomacy,* p. 290; Christopher Lasch, *The American Liberals and the Russian Revolution* (New York, 1962), p. 65.

37. George Kennan, *Russia Leaves the War,* Vol. I of *Soviet*

American Relations, 1917-1920 (Princeton, 1956), 141-144; Martin, *Peace Without Victory*, p. 154; Mayer, *Political Origins of the New Diplomacy*, pp. 279-280; Seymour (ed.), *Intimate Papers of House*, III, 318.

38. Villard, *Fighting Years*, pp. 341-343; Villard to Ray Stannard Baker, March 6, 1922.

39. Villard to Baker, February 28, 1922.

40. *The New York Times*, November 25, 1917, Section II, p. 2.

41. Villard to Ray Stannard Baker, February 28, March 6, 1922.

42. Seymour (ed.), *Intimate Papers of House*, III, 40-41, 60-61; Charles Seymour, *American Diplomacy During the World War* (New York, 1934), pp. 266-267; Samuel Flagg Bemis, *A Diplomatic History of the United States* (New York, 1936), pp. 619-620.

43. Kennan, *Russia Leaves the War*, pp. 92-93, 141-143; Mayer, *Political Origins of the New Diplomacy*, pp. 276-277.

44. Martin, *Peace Without Victory*, p. 154.

45. Victor S. Mamatey, *The United States and East Central Europe, 1914-1918: A Study in Wilsonian Diplomacy and Propaganda* (Princeton, 1957), pp. 168-169.

46. Charles B. Forcey "Intellectuals in Crisis: Croly, Weyl, and Lippmann" (Ph. D. thesis, University of Wisconsin, 1954), p. 123; see also published version, *The Crossroads of Liberalism: Croly Weyl, Lippmann and the Progressive Era, 1900-1925* (New York, 1961), pp. 288, 296.

47. *The Nation*, CV (November 29, 1917), 581.

48. Villard to R. L. Duffus, November 29, 1927.

49. Villard to Francis W. Garrison, February 13, 1918.

50. Villard to Garrison, February 13, 1918.

51. Villard to William Lloyd Garrison, Jr., May 2, 1918.

52. Villard to Simeon Strunsky, September 21, 1938.

53. Villard, *Fighting Years*, p. 344.

54. *The Fourth Estate* (trade journal) August 3, 1918 (Villard Papers, clipping file); Villard to William Lloyd Garrison, Jr., March 2, 1918.

55. William MacDonald to Villard, August 30, 1919.

56. Villard to Upton Sinclair, August 19, 1919.

57. Villard to Thomas Lamont, June 19, 1939.

58. Allan Nevins, "Rollo Ogden," in *The Dictionary of American Biography*, XXII, Supplement II (New York, 1958), pp. 498-499; Nevins to Villard, October 31, 1922.

59. Villard to Nevins, January 22, 1929.

60. Villard to David F. Swenson, December 31, 1919. Swenson was a member of the department of philosophy at the University of Minnesota and interested in Villard's active editorship of *The Nation.*

61. Quoted in Arthur Hazard Dakin, *Paul Elmer More* (Princeton, 1960), pp. 145, 179; see also May, *The End of American Innocence,* pp. 296, 354, 368-369 on *The Nation* under More and Fuller.

62. H. C. Peterson and Gilbert C. Fite, *The Opponents of War* (Madison, 1957), p. 103.

63. *The Fourth Estate,* August 3, 1918 (Villard Papers, clipping file), noted how, in a matter of a month or so, *The Nation* had changed its character.

7. The New *Nation:* 1918

1. Passage from Draper letter quoted by Villard in a letter to David Lawrence, December 7, 1917.

2. Ray Stannard Baker and William E. Dodd (eds.), *The Public Papers of Woodrow Wilson* (6 vols.; New York, 1925-1927), V, 93-96.

3. Lawrence W. Martin, *Peace Without Victory: Woodrow Wilson and the British Liberals* (New Haven, 1958), pp. 146-150. Christopher Lasch, *The American Liberals and the Russian Revolution* (New York, 1962), pp. 100-101.

4. Villard to David Lawrence, December 7, 1917.

5. Villard to Frank W. Garrison, August 3, September 4, 1918.

6. Villard, "Some Reconstruction Proposals," *The Nation,* CVI (January 3, 1918), 8-10.

7. "The Press and International Relations," March 20, 1918 (Villard Papers, speech file).

8. Baker and Dodd (eds.), *The Public Papers of Woodrow Wilson,* V, 202; Rollo Ogden, "Has Germany Lost Her Reason?" *The Nation,* CVI (April 11, 1918), 439.

9. William MacDonald, "The President at Mount Vernon," *The Nation,* CVII (July 13, 1918), 31.

10. Villard to Colonel House, February 14, 1918.

11. Quoted in Charles Forcey, *The Crossroads of Liberalism: Croly, Weyl, Lippmann and the Progressive Era, 1900-1925* (New York, 1961), pp. 284-286.

12. Forcey, *Crossroads of Liberalism,* p. 286.

13. Quoted in Arthur A. Ekirch, Jr., *The Decline of American Liberalism* (New York, 1955), p. 230.

14. Lincoln Steffens, *The Autobiography of Lincoln Steffens* (New York, 1931), pp. 774-775.

15. "The Republican Plight," *The Nation,* CVII (July 6, 1918), 6-7.

16. "The Proper Attitude Toward Socialism," *The Nation,* CV (December 27, 1917), 711-712; Editorial paragraph, *The Nation,* CVI (June 22, 1918), 727.

17. Charles Seymour (ed.), *The Intimate Papers of Colonel House* (4 vols.; Boston, 1926-1928), III, 401-403; Lasch, *American Liberals and the Russian Revolution,* pp. 108-126; Robert K. Murray, *Red Scare: A Study in National Hysteria, 1919-1920* (Minneapolis, 1955), pp. 41-45; George F. Kennan, *Russia Leaves the War,* Vol. I of *Soviet American Relations, 1917-1920* (Princeton, 1956), pp. 441 ff.

18. Editorial paragraph, *The Nation,* CVII (August 10, 1918), 135; *The Nation,* CVII (August 17, 1918), 159.

19. Arno J. Mayer, *Political Origins of the New Diplomacy, 1917-1918* (New Haven, 1959), p. 95; Kennan, *Russia Leaves the War,* pp. 20-22; Lasch, *American Liberals and the Russian Revolution,* pp. 41-44; *The Nation,* CVII (August 17, 1918), 159.

20. Henry Pelling, *America and the British Left: From Bright to Bevan* (London, 1956), pp. 112-128; Granville Hicks, *John Reed: The Making of a Revolutionary* (New York, 1936), p. 244; Joseph Freeman, *An American Testament* (New York, 1936), p. 362; Lasch, *American Liberals and the Russian Revolution,* p. 39.

21. "Civil Liberty is Dead," *The Nation,* CVII (September 14, 1918), 282; "The One Thing Needful," *The Nation,* CVII (September 14, 1918), 283.

22. Villard to William Lloyd Garrison, Jr., September 12, 1918; Villard to Francis W. Garrison, September 4, 1918.

23. Villard, *Fighting Years: Memoirs of a Liberal Editor* (New York, 1939), pp. 354-355.

24. Harvey's comments were in the *War Weekly* of *The North American Review,* October 5, 1918 (Villard Papers, clipping file).

25. Villard to Judge Lamar, September 23, 1918.

26. Charles T. Hallinan to Villard, September 23, 1918; Villard, *Fighting Years,* p. 357.

27. Ray Stannard Baker, *American Chronicle* (New York, 1945), pp. 352-353; Baker, *Woodrow Wilson: Life and Letters* (8 vols.; New York, 1939), VIII, 518, 253.

28. Baker and Dodd (eds.), *The Public Papers of Woodrow Wilson*, V, 253-261.

29. Villard, "Clearing Skies and a Triumphant Call," *The Nation*, CVII (October 5, 1918), 360; Editorial paragraph, *The Nation*, CVII (October 5, 1918), 357.

30. *The New York Times*, October 24, 1918 (Villard Papers, clipping file).

31. Elting E. Morison and Joseph Blum (eds.), *The Letters of Theodore Roosevelt* (8 vols.; Cambridge, 1954), VIII, 1380-1381; *The New York Times*, October 24, 1918.

32. Villard, "The German Collapse," *The Nation*, CVII (November 2, 1918), 502.

33. William MacDonald, "Woodrow Wilson, Politician," *The Nation*, CVII (November 2, 1918), 503.

34. Villard to David Lawrence, November 15, 1918.

35. Villard, "Peace At Last," *The Nation*, CVII (November 16, 1918), 572.

36. Villard, "Choose Ye This Day," *The Nation*, CVII (November 16, 1918), 573.

37. *Ibid.*

38. Selig Adler, *The Isolationist Impulse* (New York, 1957), pp. 56-57; Robert Osgood, *Ideals and Self-Interest in America's Foreign Relations* (Chicago, 1953), pp. 302-304.

39. Martin, *Peace Without Victory*, p. 206; A. J. P. Taylor, *The Troublemakers: Dissent Over Foreign Policy, 1792-1939* (London, 1957), pp. 157-158.

8. Victory Without Peace: 1918

1. Villard to William MacDonald, January 4, 1919.

2. Editorial paragraph, *The Nation*, CVII (November 23, 1918), 611.

3. Villard to George Edmonds, July 13, 1922; Villard to Tumulty, June 29, 1930. Edmonds was a member of the House from Pennsylvania.

4. Villard, "Hands Off in Europe," *The Nation*, CVII (November 23, 1918).

5. Villard to David Lawrence, November 12, 1918.

6. Villard, "Hands Off in Europe," 614.

7. Villard to wife, December 18, 1918. Noel Buxton and Charles Roden Buxton were prominently associated with the U.D.C. and leading British pacifists. Noel was in constant communication with Colonel House on the state of pacifist opinion in England: see Lawrence Martin, *Peace Without Victory: Woodrow Wilson and the British Liberals* (New Haven, 1958), pp. 116-117, 121-123.

8. Villard, *Fighting Years: Memoirs of a Liberal Editor* (New York, 1939), p. 376.

9. Charles Forcey, *The Crossroads of Liberalism: Croly, Weyl, Lippmann and The Progressive Era, 1900-1925* (New York, 1961), p. 231.

10. Villard to wife, December 18, 1918.

11. Villard to Fanny G. Villard, December 23, 1918.

12. Villard to wife, December 25, 1918.

13. *Ibid.*

14. Villard to children, December 24, 1918.

15. Villard to his son, Hilgard, January 1, 1919.

16. Villard to wife, January 1, 1919.

17. *Ibid.*

18. *Ibid.*

19. Villard to Henry R. Mussey, January 21, 1919.

20. Villard to Mrs. Henry G. Leach (a patron of *The Nation*), January 29, 1919.

21. "Peace Maneuvers," *The Nation*, CVIII (January 11, 1919), 51.

22. *The New York Times*, January 17, 1919, p. 1.

23. Elting E. Morison and Joseph Blum (eds.), *The Letters of Theodore Roosevelt* (8 vols.; Cambridge, 1954), VIII, 1422. This was a letter to Richard M. Hurd (January 3, 1919), who was president of the American Defense Society, and it was to be read before an All-American benefit concert sponsored by the society.

24. Villard to wife, January 8, 1919.

25. Villard to William MacDonald, January 4, 1919.

26. Villard to wife, January 8, 1919.

27. Villard *Diary*, January, 1919.

28. Villard to wife, January 20, 1919.

29. Norman Angell, *After All* (New York, 1951), pp. 210-211; William Allen White, *The Autobiography of William Allen White*

(New York, 1956), p. 550; Villard, *Fighting Years*, p. 398; Villard to wife, January 20, 1919.

30. *The Brooklyn Eagle,* February 9, 1919 (Villard Papers, clipping file).

31. Villard, *Fighting Years,* p. 386.

32. Villard *Diary,* January 18, 1919; Villard to wife, January 20, 1919.

33. Villard to Henry Mussey, January 21, 1919; "Secrecy at Versailles," *The Nation,* CVIII (January 25, 1919), 122; Thomas A. Bailey, *Woodrow Wilson and the Lost Peace* (New York, 1944), pp. 128-129; Ray Stannard Baker, *Woodrow Wilson and the World Settlement* (3 vols.; New York, 1923), I, 145-160.

34. Villard to Henry Mussey, January 21, 1919.

35. Villard, "On the Eve of the Conference," *The Nation,* CVIII (February 8, 1919), 193-194.

36. Villard to wife, February 5, 1919.

37. Walter Lippmann, "The Peace Conference," *The Yale Review,* VIII (July, 1919), 710-712.

38. Villard to William MacDonald, January 4, 1919.

39. A. J. P. Taylor, *The Troublemakers: Dissent Over Foreign Policy, 1792-1939* (London, 1957), p. 158.

40. Villard, "Personalities at Berne," *The Nation,* CVIII (March 8, 1919), 351-352. This cable was written February 7.

41. Villard, *Fighting Years,* pp. 404-405; Heinrich Stroble, *The German Revolution and After,* trans. H. J. Stenning (London, 1923), pp. 137-141; Rudolf Coper, *Failure of A Revolution: Germany in 1918-1919* (Cambridge, 1955), pp. 256-258.

42. Villard to General Smuts, February 28, 1939.

43. Villard, *Fighting Years,* pp. 409-411; Raymond Leslie Buell, *Europe: A History of Ten Years* (New York, 1929), pp. 160-168.

44. Villard to wife, February 26, 1919; Villard to Herbert Horwill, March 20, 1919; Villard to William Lloyd Garrison, Jr., May 10, 1919. Chapters 21 and 22 of Villard's *Fighting Years* deal with these experiences and were obviously based on letters that he wrote at the time.

45. Villard, *Fighting Years,* pp. 422-423.

46. Villard, "Who Shall Inherit the Power?" *The Nation,* CVIII (April 12, 1919), 544-545; cabled articles dated Munich, February 28, March, 1919; Villard, *Fighting Years,* p. 423.

47. Villard, *Fighting Years,* p. 433.

48. Villard to wife, February 26, 1919; Villard to Herbert Horwill, March 20, 1919; Villard, *Fighting Years*, p. 420.

49. Villard to wife, February 26, 1919; Villard, *Fighting Years*, p. 413.

50. Villard, *Fighting Years*, pp. 428-429; Villard, *The German Phoenix* (New York, 1933), pp. 22-25.

51. "Food or Chaos," *The Nation*, CVIII (March 29, 1919), 464.

52. Villard to wife, March 16, 1919.

53. Villard to wife, March 30, 1919.

54. Villard to Herbert Horwill, March 20, 1919; Villard to wife, March 30, 1919; Villard to William Lloyd Garrison, Jr., May 10, 1919.

55. Villard to Herbert Horwill, March 20, 1919; "The Grave Situation at the Peace Conference," *The Nation*, CVIII (April 5, 1919), 496.

56. "The Grave Situation at the Peace Conference," 496; Villard to wife, March 30, 1919; Villard to William Lloyd Garrison, Jr., May 10, 1919.

57. Villard to Herbert Horwill, March 20, 1919; Villard to wife, March 30, 1919.

58. Charles Seymour (ed.), *The Intimate Papers of Colonel House* (4 vols.; Boston, 1926-1928), IV, 362; Bailey, *Woodrow Wilson and the Lost Peace*, pp. 216-217; Baker, *Woodrow Wilson and the World Settlement*, I, 308.

59. Baker, *Woodrow Wilson and the World Settlement*, I, 307 ff.

60. *Ibid.*, 1.

61. Villard to Herbert Horwill, March 20, 1919.

62. *Ibid.*; "The Grave Situation at the Peace Conference," 469; John Dos Passos, *1919*, Vol. II of *U.S.A.* (New York, 1930), p. 248.

63. Villard to Herbert Horwill, March 20, 1919; Villard to wife, March 30, 1919.

64. Walter Johnson, *William Allen White's America* (New York, 1947), p. 300.

65. Villard to wife, February 15, 1919.

66. William Allen White, *The Autobiography of William Allen White*, p. 558; see also, White to Villard, July 20, 1937.

67. Villard, "The Crisis at Paris," *The Nation*, CVIII (April 12, 1919), 553; Editorial paragraph, *The Nation*, CVIII (April 26, 1919), 643; "The Latest Allied Dealing with Russia," *The Nation*, CIX (July 12, 1919), 34; Villard, *Fighting Years*, pp. 448-449.

68. Villard to wife, March 30, 1919.

9. The Little Band of People Who Saved
the Country: 1919-1920

1. "The Net Result," *The Nation*, CVIII (February 22, 1919), 268.

2. "The End and the Means," *The Nation*, CVIII (March 22, 1919), 416-417.

3. Villard, "The Truth About the Peace Conference," *The Nation*, CVIII (April 26, 1919), 646-647.

4. Editorial paragraph, *The Nation*, CVIII (May 17, 1919), 775.

5. Robert Osgood, *Ideals and Self-Interest in America's Foreign Relations*, (Chicago, 1953), p. 299.

6. Villard, *Fighting Years: Memoirs of a Liberal Editor* (New York, 1939), pp. 458-459.

7. William MacDonald, "The Madness at Versailles," *The Nation*, CVIII (March 17, 1919), 778-780.

8. Villard to William MacDonald, May 22, 1919.

9. *The New Republic*, XIX (May 24, 1919), cover; Villard to William MacDonald, May 22, 1919.

10. Henry Mussey to Villard, March 5, 1919.

11. Villard to wife, January 28, 1919.

12. Figures are taken from "A Strictly Confidential Report of the Problems of *The Nation*," printed October 20, 1919. This was a prospectus for potential patrons (Villard Papers, *The Nation* file). These figures are misleading. *The Nation* had been a weekly supplement of *The Post*. When it became an independent journal of opinion, it added readers.

13. Selig Adler, *The Isolationist Impulse* (New York, 1957), p. 67.

14. Villard to Ramsay MacDonald, February 2, 1927. Villard said that it was the first time in seventy years that *The Nation* had broken even. Villard to R. L. Duffus, November 29, 1927, wrote "we are now only nearly breaking even." Freda Kirchwey to Villard, June 6, 1937, in an argument over the history of *The Nation*'s finances, remarked that the first solvent year was 1928. Villard to Cameron Rogers, March 14, 1929, announced that *The Nation* "has been making a profit for nearly a year." All reference to finances point to a touch and go situation for *The Nation* throughout Villard's career as editor; the magazine showed a deficit more often than a profit.

15. Erick W. Allen's praise is quoted in a letter from Allen Eaton to Villard, April 20, 1919. Villard had defended Eaton, a professor at the university, when he was attacked for his membership in the Peoples Council of America for Peace and Democracy, a radical pacifist group.

16. *The New York Times,* December 7, 1918, p. 2.

17. Robert K. Murray, *Red Scare: A Study in National Hysteria, 1919-1920* (Minneapolis, 1955), p. 41; *The New York Times,* January 25, 1919, p. 4.

18. These quotations are taken from "Extracts from the Testimony of Archibald E. Stevenson before the Overman Committee on January 21 and January 22, 1919, compiled by Ernest L. Meyer with the Compliments of the Season, such as it is, from the American Civil Liberties Union" (Villard Papers). For the official transcript, see U.S. Congress, Senate Subcommittee on the Judiciary *Reports and Hearings, Investigation of The Brewing and Liquor Interests and German and Bolshevik Propaganda,* Senate Document 62, 66th Congress, 1st session, II, 2716 *passim.*

19. Villard address before the American Academy of Political and Social Science, May 3, 1919; address before the Church of the Messiah Forum, April 27, 1919.

20. Villard to New York State Senator Clayton R. Lusk (Chairman, Joint Legislative Committee on Investigation of Seditious Activities), June 10, 1919.

21. Christopher Lasch, *The American Liberals and the Russian Revolution* (New York, 1962), pp. 134-142.

22. Villard, "Crime Against Russia," *The Nation,* CIX (August 2, 1919), 136.

23. Speech reported in *The New York Herald,* April 29, 1919 (Villard Papers, clipping file).

24. *The New York Tribune,* May 14, 1919; see also, *Brooklyn Citizen,* May 14, 1919; *Lyon's Republican* (Maryland), May 23, 1919. See also *New York Globe,* May 14, 1919; *Kansas City Times,* May 16, 1919; *Portland Oregonian,* June 1, 1919 (Villard Papers, clipping file).

25. Villard to *The New York Tribune,* May 14, 1919; Villard to Clayton R. Lusk, June 10, 1919; Villard to A. R. Strother, April 30, 1919. Strother, a Kansas attorney, cancelled his subscription because of the radical tendencies of *The Nation.*

26. Villard to Frank Cobb, June 4, 1919; Cobb to Villard, June 10, 1919.

27. Mussey, "Reason and Revolution," *The Nation,* CVIII (June 14, 1919), 932; MacDonald, "Take Every Empty House," *The Nation,* CXI (August 28, 1920), 232; see also, *Fighting Years,* p. 467.

28. R. L. Duffus, "Grandson of The Liberator," *American Mercury,* XII (December, 1927), 449-457.

29. Villard to Emily Balch, November 14, 1919.

30. E. H. Carr, *The New Society* (New York, 1951), p. 84. For the analysis of the failures of the Versailles treaty I am indebted to the other provocative works of E. H. Carr: *The Twenty Years' Crisis, 1919-1939* (New York, 1939) and *The Conditions of Peace* (New York, 1942). They all have the advantage of viewing the Versailles treaty and the philosophy behind it in the perspective of recent world events. William Appleman Williams in *The Tragedy of American Foreign Policy* (New York, 1959), especially chapter III, gives a provocative interpretation of the conservative, if not reactionary, aspects of Wilsonian foreign policy. I have turned to such classic accounts as John Maynard Keynes, *The Economic Consequences of the Peace* (New York, 1920) and Etienne Mantoux's articulate if unconvincing rebuttal, *The Carthaginian Peace or the Economic Consequences of Mr. Keynes* (New York, 1946).

31. Walter Lippmann, "The Peace Conference," *The Yale Review,* VIII (July, 1919), 715-716; see also Lasch, *The American Liberals and the Russian Revolution,* pp. 198-199; Charles Forcey, *The Crossroads of Liberalism: Croly, Weyl, Lippmann and The Progressive Era, 1900-1925* (New York, 1961), pp. 289-291.

32. Villard, "The Truth About the Peace Conference," *The Nation,* CVIII (April 26, 1919), 647.

33. Julian Huxley, *The New York Times,* November 20, 1959, p. 33; Keynes, *The Economic Consequences of the Peace,* p. 134.

34. Villard to Ramsay MacDonald, March 31, 1920.

35. Villard to Clayton Lusk, June 10, 1919. See The Lusk Committee, 4 Vol. report: *Revolutionary Radicalism: Its History, Purpose and Tactics with an Exposition and Discussion of the Steps Being Taken and Required to Curb It* (New York, 1920), II, 1310, 1421-1427, and index.

36. *The Nation Supplement,* CVIII (May 24, 1919).

37. Villard to William MacDonald, May 22, 1919.

38. William MacDonald to Villard, June 9, 1919.

39. Villard to William MacDonald, June 25, 1919.

40. "The Peace That is No Peace," *The Nation,* CVIII (June 28, 1919), 998.

41. Adler, *The Isolationist Impulse,* p. 66.

42. Charles T. Hallinan to Villard, August 1, 1919; Villard to Hallinan, August 4, 1919.

43. Hallinan to Villard, August 6, 1919; Villard to Hallinan, August 9, 1919; Villard to William Allen White, August 9, 1919.

44. "Defeat the Treaty!", *The Nation,* CVIII (June 21, 1919), 972; *The Nation,* CVIX (July 26, 1919), 114.

45. Lincoln Colcord, "The Opening of Congress," *The Nation,* CVIII (May 31, 1919), 860.

46. "An Exhausted Virtue," *The Nation,* CVIII (June 14, 1919), 929; Lincoln Colcord, "A Receivership for Civilization," *The Nation,* CVIII (June 28, 1919), 1009-1010; Editorial paragraph, *The Nation,* CIX (July 5, 1919), 3.

47. Editorial paragraph, *The Nation,* CIX (November 15, 1919), 627.

48. Villard to Ramsay MacDonald, September 27, 1919.

49. Villard to Senator Borah, May 26, 1919.

50. Senator Borah to Villard, November 28, 1919.

51. Villard to William MacDonald, June 7, June 25, 1919.

52. Charles Seymour (ed.), *The Intimate Papers of Colonel House* (4 vols.; Boston, 1926-1928), IV, 410-411. Thomas A. Bailey, *Woodrow Wilson and the Lost Peace* (New York, 1944), p. 215.

53. Lord Robert Cecil to Villard, July 12, 1919.

54. Villard to Cecil, August 15, 1919.

55. "General Smuts on the Peace," *The Nation,* CIX (July 5, 1919), 10-11; Villard to General Jan Christian Smuts, October 15, 1919; General Smuts to Villard, January 20, 1920; Fridtjof Nansen to Villard, November 23, 1919; Villard to Nansen, December 29, 1919.

56. Villard to Robert LaFollette, August 5, 1919.

57. Villard to Ramsay MacDonald, September 27, 1919: Villard to Herbert Horwill, September 27, 1919.

58. "President Wilson as Evangelist," *The Nation,* CIX (September 13, 1919), 360.

59. Villard to Ramsay MacDonald, September 27, 1919; Villard to Herbert Horwill, September 27, 1919; Villard to Fridtjof Nansen and Jan Christian Smuts, October 15, 1919.

60. Editorial paragraph, *The Nation,* CIX (October 4, 1919), 449; Lincoln Colcord, "Black Is White," *The Nation,* CIX (September 13, 1919), 364.

61. Editorial paragraph, *The Nation,* CIX (November 22, 1919), 652.

62. "A Covenant with Death," *The Nation,* CIX (November 1, 1919), 557. I am not certain that this unsigned article was written by Villard but he repeatedly used the phrase "Covenant with Death."

63. Editorial paragraph, *The Nation,* CIX (November 22, 1919), 652.

64. *Ibid.*

65. Editorial paragraph, *The Nation,* CIX (September 6, 1919), 323.

66. "Constructive Steps After The Treaty," *The Nation,* CX (March, 1920), 388.

67. Lincoln Colcord to Villard, December 16, 1919; Villard to Ramsay MacDonald, December 31, 1920; Villard to Howard S. Whitehouse, January 19, 1920. Whitehouse was a liberal member of Parliament and a close friend of Villard's.

68. William Hard to Villard, March 3, 1925.

10. Reaction, Revision, Reform: 1920-1924

1. Villard, "The Triumph of Reaction," *The Nation,* CX (November 17, 1920), 842.

2. "Our Foreign Policy," Villard Papers, speech file (n.d.); Villard to Ralph B. Strassburger, April 4, 1921; Villard to Paul Warburg, April 21, 1921. These letters were to patrons of *The Nation.*

3. *The New York Times,* January 8, 1921, p. 2.

4. *Boston Herald,* November 29, 1920; Villard to Robert L. O'Brien.

5. *The American Commission on Conditions in Ireland: Interim Report* (Washington, D.C., 1921), Villard Papers, organizational file.

6. Villard to Jane Addams, February 19, 1921; Hollingsworth Wood to Villard, January 21, 1921; Villard to Wood, January 26,

1921; Norman Thomas to Villard, March, n.d., 1921; Villard to Norman Thomas, March 29, 1921.

7. *Cincinnati Enquirer*, February 7, 1921; see Cincinnati Riot file (Villard Papers, clipping file).

8. Villard to Mrs. Frederick N. Robinson (n.d.).

9. Villard to Ann Hard, February 19, 1921.

10. Mussey to Villard, August 11, 1918.

11. Villard, *Fighting Years: Memoirs of a Liberal Editor* (New York, 1939), pp. 461-462.

12. Villard to A. R. Strother, April 30, 1919.

13. "The Press and the World Crisis," n.p., n.d. (Villard Papers, speech file).

14. G. E. Plumb, "Labor's Solution to the Railroad Problem," *The Nation*, CIX (August 16, 1919), 200-201.

15. Mussey to Villard, January 27, 1919.

16. Villard to Mussey, January 21, 1919.

17. Mussey to Villard, August 3, 1919.

18. Villard to William MacDonald, August 2, 1919.

19. Mussey to Villard, August 3, 1919.

20. Francis Neilson to Villard, July 22, 1919; Francis Neilson, *My Life in Two Worlds* (Appleton, Wisconsin, 1953), pp. 40-41.

21. Daniel Kiefer to Villard, December 13, 1919. Kiefer, chairman of the Joseph Fels Fund, was a single taxer with money to spend.

22. Villard to Neilson, July 23, 1919; Villard to Frank W. Garrison, August 1, 1919.

23. Villard, Editorial paragraphs, *The Nation*, CX (March 13, 1920), 319; *The Nation*, CX (March 20, 1920), 353; Nock to Villard, March 16, 1920; Nock to Villard, undated memorandum of March 1920.

24. Villard to William MacDonald, July 27, August 2, September 27, 1919.

25. Speech to the staff of *The Nation*, late fall, 1919 (Villard Papers, speech file).

26. Harold E. Stearns (ed.), *Civilization in the United States* (New York, 1922), p. vii.

27. Mark Van Doren, "First Glance," *The Nation*, CXX (March 11, 1925), 268.

28. Joseph Wood Krutch, *More Lives Than One* (New York, 1962), pp. 173-174.

29. *Ibid.*, p. 171.

30. Villard to wife, May 27, 1926. Villard describes a jaunt to a Village night club to see the Greenwich Village follies which had "the usual number of stark naked women [that] seems to be inseparable from such shows."

31. Krutch, *More Lives Than One*, p. 170.

32. Interview with Freda Kirchwey, April 19, 1962; Mark Van Doren, *Autobiography of Mark Van Doren* (New York, 1958), p. 156.

33. Villard to Van Doren, September 15, 1924.

34. Kirchwey interview, April 19, 1962.

35. Upton Sinclair to Villard, January 5, 1928.

36. Villard to Dorothy Van Doren, December 25, 1929; Krutch, *More Lives Than One*, p. 171.

37. Villard to Frank W. Garrison, April 8, 1946.

38. Ludwig Lewisohn, *Mid-Channel: An American Chronicle* (New York, 1929), pp. 51-54.

39. Krutch, *More Lives Than One*, p. 172.

40. *Ibid.*

41. Freda Kirchwey to Villard, September 19, 1925; Villard to Kirchwey, September 21, 1925; Villard to Lewis Gannett, September 25, 1925.

42. Krutch, *More Lives Than One*, p. 171.

43. Villard to Jane Addams, October 11, 1919; "A Strictly Confidential Report of The Problems of *The Nation*," October 20, 1919 (Villard Papers, *The Nation* file); Villard to Rudolph Spreckles, July 12, 1920; Villard to Agnes Leach (Mrs. Henry Goddard Leach), December 31, 1919; January 15, March 9, 1920.

44. *Prospectus of* The Nation *Preferred Stock Issue of April 1920*, (Villard Papers, *The Nation* file).

45. Quoted in Hutchins Hapgood, *A Victorian in the Modern World* (New York, 1939), p. 415.

46. Editorial paragraph, *The Nation*, CXII (April 13, 1921), 528; Editorial paragraph, *The Nation*, CXIII (August 17, 1921), 164.

47. Villard to Joseph Sturge, January 26, 1922.

48. Villard to M. L. H. Moore, February 23, 1922.

49. Villard to Ray Stannard Baker, August 17, 1929; Villard to wife, September 23, 1920.

50. Selig Adler, "The War-Guilt Question and American Disil-

lusionment, 1918-1928," *The Journal of Modern History*, XXIII (March, 1951), 10.

51. Villard to Joseph Tumulty, January 31, 1917; "Woodrow Wilson: A Supreme Tragedy," *The Nation*, CXVIII (February 13, 1924), 157.

52. Selig Adler, *The Isolationist Impulse* (New York, 1957), pp. 71-73. A. J. P. Taylor, *The Troublemakers: Dissent Over Foreign Policy, 1792-1939* (London, 1957), pp. 177-186.

53. E. D. Morel, *Truth and The War* (London, 1916), p. 51.

54. Francis Neilson to Villard, October 3, 1919.

55. Villard to Ray Stannard Baker, February 28, 1922.

56. Villard, unsigned editorial, *The Post*, November 18, 1914; Villard speech, quoted by *The Public*, a New York Socialist paper (Villard Papers, speech file).

57. The first article appeared in the July issue of *The American Historical Review*.

58. Albert J. Nock, *The Myth of a Guilty Nation* (New York, 1922), p. 5.

59. Villard to J. A. Hobson, October 6, 1921.

60. J. A. Hobson, "Germany's 'Moral Offensive'," *The Nation*, CXIII (December 7, 1921), 661-662.

61. Villard, "Germany 1922, II, The Price the People are Paying," *The Nation*, CXV (July 26, 1922), 88. See also, "Germany 1922, I, The Political Situation," *The Nation*, CXV (July 19, 1922), 61ff.; "Germany 1922, III, In the Occupied Territory," *The Nation*, CXV (August 2, 1922), 116 ff.; "Germany 1922, IV, Some Hopeful Signs," *The Nation*, CXV (August 9, 1922), 144 ff); Villard to wife, May 10, 1922.

62. Alanson B. Houghton to Villard, August 11, December 22, 1922; Villard to Houghton, December 12, 1922.

63. Ernest Gruening, "Is Democracy Recoverable?" *The Nation*, CXV (December 13, 1922), 667-668.

64. Frederick Bausman to Villard, July 31, 1922.

65. "Treachery to War," *The Nation*, CXV (September 20, 1922), 270.

66. Adler, "The War-Guilt Question," 8; Norman Angell, *After All* (New York, 1951), p. 173.

67. Lewis Gannett, "They All Lied," *The Nation*, CXV (October 11, 1922), 353-357.

68. "Utterly Brutal and Insane," *The Nation*, CXVI (January

24, 1923), 84; "Blood Money," *The Nation*, CXVI (January 31, 1923), 111.

69. Borah to Villard, February 9, 1923.

70. Quoted by Gannett, "Set The War Truths Free," *The Nation*, CXVIII (March 5, 1924), 247.

71. *United States Congressional Record*, LXV, 355-399.

72. Barnes to Villard, March 23, 1928.

73. "History and International Good Will," *The Nation*, CXIV (March 1, 1922), 253.

74. "Seven Books of History Against The Germans," *The New Republic*, XXXVIII (March 19, 1924), Part II, 10-15; Adler, "The War-Guilt Question," 16-17. Robert Osgood, *Ideals and Self-Interest in America's Foreign Relations* (Chicago, 1953), pp. 317-318.

75. "Historians and The Truth," *The Nation*, CXVIII (May 21, 1924), 576; Barnes to Freda Kirchwey, May 17, 1924; Villard to Barnes, May 21, 1924.

76. Barnes to Villard, January 4, 1927.

77. Villard to Strunsky, May 15, 1918; Strunsky to Villard, May 16, 1923; Villard to H. L. Mencken, April 10, 1923.

78. Osgood, *Ideals and Self-Interest,* p. 318.

79. "Success to Robert LaFollette!", *The Nation*, CXV (August 16, 1922), 160.

80. "Treachery To The War," *The Nation*, CXV (September 20, 1922), 270.

81. *Ibid.*

82. Albert Jay Nock, "Myth of a Guilty Nation," *LaFollette's Magazine* (April, 1922), pp. 63 ff.

83. Villard to Snowden, December 12, 1922.

84. "Election by Disgust Again," *The Nation*, CXV (November 22, 1922), 540.

85. Audit Bureau of Circulation Report (Villard Papers, *The Nation* files).

86. Villard to Nagel, July 16, 1919; Nagel to Villard, August 20, 1919.

87. Richard Hofstadter, *The Age of Reform* (New York, 1955), p. 281.

88. Villard to Ramsay MacDonald, May 23, 1921; August 4, 1922; Villard to Hobson, December, 1921; Villard to Borah, November 16, 1922; Borah to Villard, November 17, 1922; "The

Duty to Revolt," *The Nation,* CXV (August 9, 1922), 140; Hamilton Owens' remark quoted by Gerald W. Johnson, "Gentleman from Idaho," *The New Republic* (June 12, 1961), 12-19.

89. Villard to William Allen White, July 25, 1922; White to Villard, July 29, 1922; Borah to Villard, August 8, 1922.

90. *The Brooklyn Eagle,* June 3, 1924 (Villard Papers, clipping file); Ernest Gruening (unsigned article), "Trumpet to the People: The Story of Oswald Garrison Villard," *The World Tomorrow,* XIII (November, 1930), 422.

91. "Government Ownership of the Railroads," *The Nation,* CXVI (February 21, 1923), 204-205.

92. "Toward An Economic Program for America," *The Nation,* CXVI (January 17, 1923), 55; "The Call for Borah and LaFollette," *The Nation,* CXVIII (February 20, 1924), 194; "The LaFollette Revolution," *The Nation,* CXVIII (April 23, 1924), 469; "How Dangerous is LaFollette?" *The Nation,* CXIX (September 3, 1924), 229; "LaFollette the Wrecker," *The Nation,* CXIX (July 9, 1924), 32.

93. "LaFollette to the Front," *The Nation,* CXVIII (June 11, 1924), 118; Editorial paragraph, *The Nation,* CXIX (October 1, 1924), 321. See also an unsigned article, not by Villard, "Fooling the Farmers," *The Nation,* CXVIII (May 14, 1924), 549-550.

94. Villard, "An Honest Convention," *The Nation,* CXIX (July 16, 1924), 64; Editorial paragraph, *The Nation,* CXIX (October 1, 1924), 321.

95. "Aftermath," *The Nation,* CXIX (November 5, 1924), 485.

96. Russel B. Nye, *Midwestern Progressive Politics* (Lansing, 1959), p. 317; Arthur Link, "What Happened to the Progressive Movement in the 1920's," *The American Historical Review,* LXIV (July, 1959), 841-842.

97. Villard to LaFollette, September 13, 25, 1924.

98. "LaFollette's Foreign Policy," *The Nation International Relations Supplement,* CXIX (October 29, 1924), 476-480.

99. "The Parties and Our Foreign Policy," *The Nation,* CXIX (September 17, 1924), 276.

100. Villard to wife, August 20, 1924; Villard to J. A. Hobson, August 4, 1924; "The Prairies Catching Fire," *The Nation,* CXIX (October 15, 1924), 412-415; "The Chances of the Election," *The Nation,* CXIX (September 10, 1924), 250.

101. "Business Wins," *The Nation*, CXIX (November 12, 1924), 510.

102. *Ibid.*

103. Villard to Mrs. Gordon Norrie, November 30, 1925. Mrs. Norrie was chairman of the Womens' Committee for Political Action, a part of the National Federation of Progressive Women.

104. "Senator Borah's Opportunity," *The Nation*, CXIX (December 3, 1924), 592.

11. The Search for Peace: 1921-1928

1. Villard to J. A. Hobson, November 13, 1925; Villard to Sophia Sturge, January 26, 1922.

2. "A Constructive World League Program," *The Nation*, CXI (November 17, 1920), 549-550.

3. "Politics and Patriotism," Villard speech before Old South Forum, Boston, January 31, 1926 (Villard Papers, speech file).

4. "Our Foreign Policy," 1920 (Villard papers, speech file).

5. *Literary Digest*, LIX (June 4, 1921), 34; *The New York Times*, May 15, 1921, p. 10.

6. Editorial paragraph, *The Nation*, CXIII (August 3, 1921), 109; "The Conference, Second Phase," *The Nation*, CXIII (August 3, 1921), 618-619.

7. Villard to wife, July 7, 1921; Villard to Fanny Villard, July 8, 1921; Villard to Senator Borah, July 8, 1921.

8. Editorial paragraph, *The Nation*, CXIII (July 20, 1921), 56; Villard to Borah, December 26, 1922.

9. Nock to Villard, July 21, 1921; Villard to Nock, July 23, 1921; Nock to Villard, July 27, 1921.

10. Villard to Joseph Sturge, August 21, 1921; see also Villard, editorial paragraph, *The Nation*, CXIII (August 24, 1921), 188; (September 21, 1921), 307.

11. Villard to J. A. Hobson, October 6, 1921.

12. Villard, editorial paragraph, *The Nation*, CXIII (October 5, 1921), 361; Villard, "The Way to Disarm," *The Nation*, CXIII (November 9, 1921), 520.

13. "A Great Beginning," *The Nation*, CXIII (November 23, 1921), 589-591.

14. *Ibid.*, 590.

15. Villard, "The Conference: The Second Phase," *The Nation*,

CXIII (November 30, 1921), 618. Harold and Margaret Sprout, *Toward a New Order of Sea Power* (Princeton, 1940), 156.

16. William E. Borah, "The Ghost of Versailles at the Conference," *The Nation*, CXIII (November 9, 1921), 525-526. Villard to Borah, January 6, 1922; Borah to Villard, January 9, 1921.

17. Villard, "Briand's Failure," *The Nation*, CXIII (December 7, 1921), 641-642.

18. "The Conference and Its Experts," *The Nation*, CXIV (January 4, 1922), 11. "What is Lacking in Washington," *The Nation*, CXIII (December 7, 1921), 638; Villard to MacDonald, January 6, 1922; Villard to J. A. Hobson, December 29, 1921.

19. Denna F. Fleming, *The United States and World Organization* (New York, 1928), p. 96; Raymond Leslie Buell, *The Washington Conference* (New York, 1922), pp. 372 ff.

20. Fleming, *The United States and World Organization*, pp. 95-97.

21. "The Four Power Treaty," *The Nation*, CXIII (December 21, 1921), 720. This editorial was written by Villard and Norman Thomas. Thomas became an associate editor in October 1921.

22. *United States Congressional Record*, 67th Congress, Second Session, p. 3552. Editorial paragraph, *The Nation*, CXIV (March 8, 1922), 275.

23. S. O. Levinson, *Outlawry of War* (Chicago, December 25, 1921), issued by the American Committee for the Outlawry of War (Pamphlet in Villard Papers).

24. *Ibid.*

25. Villard to Levinson, April 15, 1920.

26. Villard, "Some Reconstruction Proposals," *The Nation*, CVI (January 3, 1918), 9; "Mr. Root's World Court," *The Nation*, CXI (September 25, 1920), 341. S. O. Levinson to Villard, October 4, 1920.

27. "Outlawing War," *The Nation*, CXIV (January 11, 1922), 32.

28. Levinson to Villard, January 21, 1922; Villard to Levinson, January 24, 1922.

29. John E. Stoner, *S. O. Levinson and the Pact of Paris* (New York, 1942), p. 146.

30. Editorial paragraph, *The Nation*, CXIV (February 15, 1922), 183.

31. Villard to Levinson, February 7, 1923; Levinson to Villard, February 19, 1923.

32. "Let Us Join The World Court of Justice," *The Nation*, CXVI (March 7, 1923), 258-259.

33. Levinson to Villard, March 6, 1923. Villard to Levinson, March 8, 1932.

34. "Let Us Join the World Court," 258.

35. Villard to Levinson, May 11, 1923.

36. Editorial paragraph, *The Nation*, CXXI (December 9, 1925), 691.

37. Borchard to Villard, October 31, 1924.

38. Borchard to Villard, January 14, 1926.

39. Villard to Borchard, January 21, 1926; Borchard to Villard, January 21, 1926.

40. "Is The World Court An Agency for Peace?", *The Nation*, CXXII (February 3, 1926), 104.

41. Villard to Hard, January 21, 1926.

42. Denna F. Fleming, *The United States and the World Court* (New York, 1945), pp. 64, 69.

43. *Ibid.*, p. 81.

44. Editorial paragraph, *The Nation*, CXXII (March 10, 1926), 243.

45. Editorial paragraph, *The Nation*, CXXII (March 3, 1926), 218; "The League Unveiled," *The Nation*, CXXII (March 31, 1926), 332.

46. "Politics and Patriotism," speech before Old South Forum, January 31, 1926 (Villard Papers, speech file).

47. Speech on pacifism and foreign policy before the Torch Club in Utica, New York, December 13, 1926, and the Emanuel Congregation in Chicago, February 6, 1927 (Villard Papers, speech file).

48. Samuel Flagg Bemis, "The Shifting Strategy of American Defense and Diplomacy," in *Essays in History and International Relations in Honor of George Hubbard Blakeslee*, ed. Dwight E. Lee and George E. McReynolds (Worcester, Mass., 1949), p. 8.

49. This was the delightful label of Senator Reed of Missouri, who fought the Kellogg-Briand Pact down to the last day in the Senate and then voted for it because he did not desire "to be hung in effigy out in Missouri" so relentless was popular pressure. *United States Congressional Record*, 70th Congress, Second Session, pp. 1187-1188; Robert H. Ferrell, *Peace in Their Time; The Origins of the Kellogg-Briand Pact* (New Haven, 1952), p. 252.

50. "Outlawing War," *The Nation*, CXIV (January 11, 1922), 33.

51. Editorial paragraph, *The Nation*, CXXXIII (July 22, 1931), 79; "What is Lacking at the Peace Conference," *The Nation*, CXIII (December 7, 1921), 638; "A Conference Cursed by Nationality," *The Nation*, CXIII (December 14, 1921), 696.

52. "Three Soldiers," *The Nation*, CXXIII (October 26, 1926), 481; Frederick J. Hoffmann, *The Twenties: American Writing in The Post War Decade* (New York, 1955), pp. 51-57.

53. "Briand's Failure," *The Nation*, CXIII (December 7, 1921), 642.

54. Ferrell, *Peace in Their Time*, pp. 71-74. Shotwell and Butler, professor and president, respectively, of Columbia, were early members of the outlawry movement and played an unofficial but important role in the development of the Kellogg peace pacts.

55. Nicholas Murray Butler, *Across The Busy Years* (2 vols.; New York, 1940), II, 208. See also, Ferrell, *Peace in Their Time*, p. 81.

56. Ferrell, *Peace in Their Time*, p. 101.

57. *Ibid.*, pp. 139-140, 144-145.

58. Editorial paragraph, *The Nation*, CXXII (April 25, 1926), 474.

59. Alanson B. Houghton to Villard, June 9, 1828; Villard to Houghton, June 30, 1928.

60. "Mass Opinion at Work," *The Nation*, CXXI (December 30, 1925), 750-751.

61. Villard to Senator Norris, April 13, 1926.

62. Villard to A. B. Houghton, August 22, 1927.

63. Levinson to Kellogg, June 27, 1927, quoted in Stoner, *S. O. Levinson*, p. 239.

64. "What is This Kellogg Talk About Peace?", *The Nation*, CXXVII (July 25, 1928), 76-77; Villard to Borchard, July 27, 1928.

65. Charles Buxton to Villard, December 22, 1927; Villard to Buxton, January 9, 1928; Editorial paragraph, *The Nation*, CXXVII (August 22, 1928), 165-166.

66. Editorial paragraph, *The Nation*, CXXVII (December 19, 1928), 671.

67. Charles G. Dawes, *Notes as Vice President: 1928-1929* (Boston, 1935), pp. 231-232.

68. Editorial paragraph, *The Nation*, CXXVIII (January 29, 1929), 91; see also, Editorial paragraph, *The Nation*, CXXVII (November 28, 1928), 561. Villard to Mr. Thomas Foxall (pastor

of the Hope Congregational Church, Worcester, Massachusetts), October 24, 1928.

69. Editorial paragraph, *The Nation*, CXXVIII (February 20, 1929), 215; Borchard to Villard, July 25, 1928, January 12, 1929.

70. Ferrell, *Peace in Their Time*, pp. 13-30.

71. Ray Stannard Baker, *Woodrow Wilson: Life and Letters* (8 vols.; New York, 1939), VI, 208.

72. Villard to J. P. Gavit, April 8, 1927.

73. Nevins to Villard, December 3, 1929; Villard to Nevins, January 24, 1929.

12. New Directions: 1928-1932

1. Louis Hartz, *The Liberal Tradition in America* (New York, 1922), p. 237.

2. Villard to Robert L. O'Brien, December 3, 1920.

3. "Fit to Rule," *The Nation*, CXXIX (December 11, 1929), 704.

4. Arthur A. Ekirch, Jr., *The Decline of American Liberalism* (New York, 1955), pp. 296-297; James Burnham, *The Managerial Revolution* (New York, 1941), pp. 256-257; Christopher Lasch, *The American Liberals and the Russian Revolution* (New York, 1962), pp. 138-139.

5. Villard, "If I Were Dictator," *The Nation*, CXXXIV (January 20, 1932), 67.

6. Henry Mencken, "Americans All," *The Nation*, CXXVII (July 25, 1928), 90.

7. R. L. Duffus, "Grandson of The Liberator," *American Mercury*, XII (December, 1927), 454.

8. Heywood Broun, "It Seems To Me," *The Nation*, CXXVIII (January 2, 1929), 7.

9. Belle C. and Fola LaFollette, *Robert M. LaFollette* (2 vols.; New York, 1953), II, 1117.

10. "The Real Issues of the Campaign," *The Nation*, CXXVII (October 24, 1928), 414.

11. Villard, "Presidential Possibilities, IV—Herbert Hoover," *The Nation*, CXXVI (February 28, 1928), 234-236; "Presidential Possibilities, II—Alfred E. Smith," *The Nation*, CXXV (November 30, 1927), 595-598; "Should Liberals Vote for Smith?", *The Nation*, CXXVII (September 26, 1928), 284-285.

12. Villard to William Taylor (a subscriber), July 7, 1924.

13. Villard to Joseph Sturge, November. 16, 1927; Villard to F. D. Roosevelt, September 11, 1928; Villard to Raymond Mussey, December 3, 1930.

14. Richard Hofstadter, *The Age of Reform* (New York, 1955), pp. 286-291.

15. Villard to Ramsay MacDonald, December 6, 1928; Villard, "Should Liberals Vote for Smith?", 284.

16. Villard, "Should Liberals Vote for Smith?", 284.

17. "Why Progressives Should Vote For Smith," *The New Republic*, LVI (September 5, 1928), 58-60.

18. Villard to Herbert Croly, September 25, 1928; Croly to Villard, September 26, 1928.

19. Norman Thomas to Villard, September 29, 1928; Villard to Thomas, October 2, 1928.

20. Norman Thomas to Villard, October 8, 1928; Villard to Thomas, October 8, 1928.

21. Villard to Ida Crouch, January 5, 1928.

22. Speech in New York, February 12, 1928 (Villard Papers, speech file).

23. "The Real Issues of the Campaign," 414.

24. Paul Douglas, "Why I Am For Norman Thomas," *The New Republic*, LVI (October 24, 1928), 268; Arthur M. Schlesinger, Jr., *The Crisis of the Old Order,* Vol. I of *The Age of Roosevelt* (New York, 1957), chapters 23-24.

25. "The Real Issues of the Campaign," 414.

26. Freda Kirchwey recalled that most of *The Nation* staff supported Thomas and were angered by Villard's refusal to endorse the Socialist candidate: Kirchwey to author, March 10, 1960.

27. Villard to Hilgard Villard, October 2, 1928; Villard to Ramsay MacDonald, December 6, 1928.

28. Galley proof in Scrapbook 9, Villard Papers.

29. Villard to Professor Wager, February 1, 1929.

30. "The League of Nations," *The Nation*, CXXX (January 15, 1930), 60; Editorial paragraph, *The Nation*, CXXXI (December 10, 1930), 635; Villard to J. P. Gavit, April 8, 1927.

31. "Mr. Hoover Moves Toward Peace," *The Nation*, CXXVIII (June 12, 1929), 687; "America Acts At Last," *The Nation*, CXXVIII (May 29, 1929), 637.

32. Villard to Ramsay MacDonald, June 5, 1929; "A Glorious Victory for Labor," *The Nation*, CXXVIII (June 12, 1929), 688.

33. "A New Liberal Party," *The Nation*, CXXVII (December 26, 1928), 702; David Shannon, *The Socialist Party of America* (New York, 1955), p. 208; Daniel Bell, "Marxian Socialism in the United States," in *Socialism in American Life*, ed. Donald Drew Egbert and Stow Persons (Princeton, 1952), p. 369.

34. Editorial paragraph, *The Nation*, CXXVII (December 26, 1928), 699; Villard to Mussey, April 19, 1919; Villard to Cameron Rogers, March 14, 1929; Villard to Simeon Strunsky, November 1, 1928.

35. Villard to Mussey, October 26, 1928; January 4, 1929; Mussey to Villard, January 30, 1929.

36. Villard to Mussey, August 3, 1928; Villard to John Palmer Gavit, January 13, 1922; Villard, "Herbert Croly," in *The Dictionary of American Biography*, XXI, Supplement I, p. 210.

37. Villard to Mussey, May 6, 1929.

38. Mussey to Villard, November 7, 1928; Villard to Mussey, November 12, 1928.

39. Villard to J. A. Hobson, June 20, 1928; Villard to Gannett, October 17, 1927; August 2, 1928; July 1, 1930.

40. Villard to Mussey, August 3, 1928; Mussey to Villard, August 6, 1928; September 24, 1928; Editorial paragraph, *The Nation*, CXXVIII (June 26, 1929), 753.

41. Editorial paragraph, *The Nation*, CXIX (November 26, 1924), 555; Harry F. Ward, "Civil Liberties in Russia," *The Nation*, CXX (March 4, 1925), 234-236; Maurice Hindus, "At a Peasant Soviet," *The Nation*, CXXI (November 11, 1925), 533; William Reswick, "An Experiment in Freedom," *The Nation*, CXXI (November 11, 1925), 535; Albert Rhys Williams, "The Real Situation in Russia," *The Nation*, CXXVII (November 14, 1928), 516-517.

42. Editorial paragraph, *The Nation*, CXXV (November 9, 1927), 494.

43. Louis Fischer, "Political Prisoners Under the Bolshevists," *The Nation*, CXXI (March 4, 1925), 237-239.

44. Phrase used by Professor Wager of Oberlin in a letter to Villard, February 1, 1929.

45. Editorial paragraph, *The Nation*, CXXIX (November 13, 1929), 536; see additional editorial paragraphs by Villard, *The Nation*, CXXII (April 21, 1926), 438; CXXVII (October 10, 1928), 333.

46. Villard to I. I. A. Kitten, October 20, 1927.

47. "Russia Leads The World," *The Nation*, CXXV (December 14, 1927), 670.

48. Villard address to the Association of Foreign Press Correspondents, March 31, 1927 (Villard Papers, speech file).

49. Villard, "Russia Through A Car Window: The Observer's Problem," *The Nation*, CXXIX (November 6, 1929), 516-517; *ibid.* "The Industrial Vision," (November 13, 1929), 542-544; *ibid.*, "The Spirit of the Government," (November 20, 1929), 576-578; *ibid.* "The Unfolding of a Great Drama," (November 27, 1929), 619-621; *ibid.* "The Soviets and the Human Being," (December 4, 1929), 654-656; *ibid.*, "The Soviets and the Future," (December 11, 1929), 712-714. The series of articles by Stuart Chase, "Prosperity, Believe It Or Not," ran from October 23, 1929, to January 8, 1930.

50. Villard to Ernest Gruening, September 30, 1929.

51. Villard, "Russia Through A Car Window: The Observer's Problem," 517.

52. Villard, "The Industrial Vision," 544.

53. Villard, "The Observer's Problem," 516.

54. Villard, "The Soviets and the Future," 714.

55. Villard to Sophia Sturge, October 14, 1929.

56. John Dewey, *Impressions of Russia and the Revolutionary World* (New York, 1929), pp. 14, 28, 38-39, 106-108, 116. The book first appeared as a series of articles in *The New Republic*.

57. Lasch, *The American Liberals and The Russian Revolution*, pp. 138-140; Max Lerner, "The Liberalism of Oswald Garrison Villard," *The New Republic*, XCVII (April 26, 1939), 342-344.

58. Quoted in Eugene Lyons, *The Red Decade* (New York, 1941), pp. 355-356. For a penetrating portrait of Roger Baldwin, see Dwight MacDonald, "In Defense of Everybody," *The New Yorker*, XXIX (July 11, 1953) and *ibid.* (July 18, 1953).

59. Lyons, *The Red Decade,* p. 182; Granville Hicks, *Where We Came Out,* (New York, 1954), pp. 56-58; Benjamin Stolberg, "Liberal Journalism," *Vanity Fair*, XLI (September, 1933), pp. 22-23, 58.

60. Villard, "Our Attitude Toward Russia," p. 173.

61. *Ibid.*

62. Robert Paul Browder, *The Origins of Soviet American Diplomacy* (Princeton, 1953), chapter II.

63. Villard, "Recognize Russia," *The Nation*, CXXXIV (May 18, 1932), 558.

64. Paul F. Boller, Jr., "The Great Conspiracy of 1933—A Study in Short Memories," *Southwest Review*, XXXIX (Winter, 1954), 97-112.

65. Browder, *The Origins of Soviet American Diplomacy*, p. 29.

66. "Our Attitude Toward Russia," *The Nation*, CXXXI (August 13, 1930), 173; "Recognize Russia," 558. Quotation from Paul Cravath is from Boller, "The Great Conspiracy," 102.

67. Cordell Hull, *Memoirs* (2 vols.; New York, 1948), I, 293. Bullitt to F.D.R. (n.d.), cited in Browder, *The Origins of Soviet American Diplomacy*, p. 111.

68. William C. Bullitt to Villard, November 23, 1933.

69. Villard, "Issues and Men," *The Nation*, CXXXVII (November 15, 1933), 558.

70. Boller, "The Great Conspiracy," 104-106; Browder, *The Origins of Soviet American Diplomacy*, p. 171.

71. "Russia: Caviar to Litvinoff," *Time*, XXII (December 4, 1933), 19.

72. Editorial paragraph, *The Nation*, CXXXVII (December 6, 1933), 637.

73. Villard to Lillian Wald, December 20, 1933.

74. "Mr. Hoover and the London Conference," *The Nation*, CXXIX (November 13, 1929), 538; Editorial paragraph, *The Nation*, CXXIX (December 4, 1929), 647.

75. "Parity, The Enemy," *The Nation*, CXXX (March 19, 1930), 314.

76. Villard to Lady Barlow, May 28, 1930; "The Crumbs of London," *The Nation*, CXXX (April 30, 1930), 506.

77. Editorial paragraph, *The Nation*, CXXX (May 21, 1930), 585; "Government by Abstention," *The Nation*, CXXX (June 4, 1930), 640.

78. Villard, "France Against the World," *The Nation*, CXXXIII (August 12, 1931), 149-151; Villard to Houghton, October 16, 1931; Villard to James C. MacDonald, July 14, 1931; Villard to Thomas Lamont, August 21, 1931.

79. Oswald Garrison Villard, *The German Phoenix* (New York, 1933).

80. Villard, "Germany Nears the Crisis," *The Nation*, CXXXI (December 3, 1930), 603-604; "On the German Front," *The Nation*, CXXXII (January 14, 1931), 37-38; "Can Germany Pay?",

The Nation, CXXXII (January 28, 1931), 91-93; "Europe's Darkest Hour," *The Nation*, CXXIII (May 20, 1931), 549-550.

81. "Hoover Denies Europe," *The Nation*, CXXIII (June 10, 1931), 624.

82. Villard to wife, July 26, 1931; "Hoover's Great Action," *The Nation*, CXXXIII (July 1, 1931), 4; "The Triumph of Hoover's Plan," *The Nation*, CXXXIII (July 15, 1931), 54.

83. Villard, "Congress, Debts and Bankers: An Appeal to Reason," *The Nation*, CXXXIII (December 30, 1931), 717-718.

84. "The Tariff Crime Complete," *The Nation*, CXXX (June 25, 1930), 720.

85. "Government and Business," *The Nation*, CXXXI (September 3, 1931), 239; "Headless Washington," *The Nation*, CXXX (March 5, 1930), 265.

13. A New Deal: 1932-1935

1. James Burnham, *The Managerial Revolution* (New York, 1941), pp. 256-259; Max Lerner, "The Liberalism of Oswald Garrison Villard," *The New Republic*, XCVIII (April 26, 1939), 343-344.

2. William Leuchtenburg, "Reform Was His Business," *The New York Times Book Review*, January 1, 1961, p. 6; Leuchtenburg to author, January 17, 1961.

3. Villard, "If I Were Dictator," *The Nation*, CXXXIV (January 20, 1932), 67; "The Failure of Big Business," *The Nation*, CXXXIV (May 25, 1932), 586; Editorial paragraph, *The Nation*, CXXXII (June 10, 1931), 621.

4. Villard to Harold L. Ickes, October 11, 1931.

5. "Headless Washington," *The Nation*, CXXX (March 5, 1930), 265; Burton K. Wheeler to Villard, March 1, 1930; Villard to Wheeler, March 10, 1930.

6. Editorial paragraph, *The Nation*, CXXX (July 30, 1930), 110.

7. "A Four Year Program," *The Nation*, CXXXIV (February 17, 1932), 185-186.

8. "The Challenge of 1932," *The Nation*, CXXIV (January 6, 1932), 4.

9. Villard, "If I Were Dictator," 67-70.

10. *Ibid.*; Villard to Henry Mussey, January 21, 1919.

11. Arthur M. Schlesinger, Jr., *The Crisis of the Old Order*, Vol. I of *The Age of Roosevelt* (New York, 1957), chapter 23.

12. "Mr. Hoover Wobbles on the Dole," *The Nation*, CXXXIII (August 26, 1931), 199; Editorial paragraph, *The Nation*, CXXXIII (September 9, 1931), 242; "That Terrible British Dole," *The Nation*, CXXXIII (September 9, 1931), 244; Editorial paragraph, *The Nation*, CXXXIV (June 15, 1932), 663; "Pity Herbert Hoover," *The Nation*, CXXXIV (June 15, 1932), 669.

13. "Mr. Hoover Call Congress," *The Nation*, CXXXIII (August 12, 1931), 146; "Free Trade, Its Moral Advantages," *The Nation*, CXXXIII (September 30, 1931), 327.

14. "That Terrible British Dole," 242; *The Cincinnati Post*, May 23, 1931 (Villard Papers, clipping file).

15. "The Way Out," *The Nation*, CXXXIV (June 8, 1932), 638; *Knickerbocker Press*, Albany, New York, April 10, 1932 (Villard Papers, clipping file).

16. "Roosevelt, Ritchie and Pinchot," *The Nation*, CXXXII (June 17, 1931), 650.

17. Editorial paragraph, *The Nation*, CXXXIV (January 20, 1932), 57-58.

18. Walter Lippmann in his *New York Herald Tribune* column, "Today and Tomorrow," January 8, 1932; Walter Lippmann, *Interpretations: 1931-1932*, ed. Allan Nevins (New York, 1932), p. 262.

19. "An Open Letter to Governor Roosevelt," *The Nation*, CXXXIV (May 11, 1932), 532-533.

20. Villard to Roosevelt, May 3, 1932.

21. Roosevelt to Villard, June 8, 1932; Frank Freidel, *Franklin D. Roosevelt: The Ordeal* (Boston, 1954), 267.

22. Roosevelt to Villard, June 8, 1932.

23. Villard to Roosevelt, June 17, 1932; Villard to Ratcliffe, June 15, 1932.

24. Thomas to Villard, April 11, 1932.

25. Villard to Henry Mussey, April 20, 1932.

26. Villard to J. A. Hobson, May 5, 1932.

27. David A. Shannon, *The Socialist Party of America* (New York, 1955), p. 218.

28. Dos Passos's quip cited from a questionnaire on "Whither the American Writer," *Modern Quarterly*, VI (Summer, 1932), 11.

29. Granville Hicks, *Where We Came Out* (New York, 1954), pp. 36-37.

30. Quoted in Hicks, *Where We Came Out*, pp. 34-35; see also, Schlesinger, Jr., *Crisis of the Old Order*, pp. 436-437.

31. Daniel Bell, "Marxian Socialism in the United States," in *Socialism in American Life*, ed. Donald Drew Egbert and Stow Persons (Princeton, 1952), p. 350. Bell attributes the omelet metaphor to Earl Browder.

32. Editorial paragraph, *The Nation*, CXXXIV (June 1, 1932), 610.

33. "The Tragedy of Chicago," *The Nation*, CXXXIV (June 29, 1932), 712; Villard to Ratcliffe, June 15, 1932; "The Democratic Trough at Chicago," *The Nation*, CXXXV (July 13, 1932), 26-27.

34. "The Pot and The Kettle: Our Invisible Government and Wasted Votes," *The Nation*, CXXXV (September 14, 1932), 229-230; "On Throwing Your Vote Away," *The Nation*, CXXXV (October 5, 1932), 299.

35. "The End of Herbert Hoover," *The Nation*, CXXXV (November 16, 1932), 470-471; Editorial paragraph, *The New Republic*, LXXIII (November 16, 1932), 1.

36. "The Victory," *The Nation*, CXXXV (November 23, 1932), 490.

37. "The Centenary of Godkin," *The Nation*, CXXXIII (October 7, 1931), 354.

38. W. Page to Villard, November 5, 1932; Villard to Page, December 19, 1932.

39. Villard to Page, December 19, 1932.

40. Theodore Peterson, *Magazines in the Twentieth Century* (Urbana, Illinois, 1956), pp. 362-363.

41. Villard, *Fighting Years: Memoirs of a Liberal Editor* (New York, 1939), 123.

42. Charles Angoff, *H. L. Mencken: A Portrait From Memory* (New York, 1956), pp. 36-37.

43. Quoted in George C. Kirstein, "The Myths of the Small Magazine," *The Progressive*, XXVII (June, 1963), 23-27.

44. Villard to R. L. Duffus, November 29, 1927.

45. Villard to Ernest Gruening, May 13, 1931; Villard to David Lawrence, February 13, 1929.

46. Villard to wife, May 15, 1931; Villard to Freda Kirchwey, October 14, 1931; Villard to Mussey, October 23, 1931; Mark Shorer, *Sinclair Lewis: An American Life* (New York, 1961), p. 577.

47. Villard to G. W. Page (subscriber), December 19, 1932.

48. Villard to wife (from London), February 3, 1931; Villard to wife, June 10, 1931.

49. See letters in Villard Papers, Kirchwey and *Nation* file, summer of 1932, for details of negotiation; Villard's first column of "Issues and Men," *The Nation*, CXXXVI (January 11, 1933), 34.

50. Villard to Felix Frankfurter, February 14, 1933.

51. Ernest Gruening (unsigned), "Trumpet to the People: The Story of Oswald Garrison Villard," *The World Tomorrow*, XIII (November, 1930), 443.

52. Villard to White, August 12, 1931; Villard to Mencken, December 30, 1932; Villard to Kerney, September 19, 1933.

53. Villard to Henry Mussey, February 20, 1928.

54. Villard to Maud Kimberly, September 4, 1923 and October 27, 1930; Villard to family (traveling in Europe), June 29, 1931; Villard to family, June 30, 1933.

55. Hilgard Villard to author, October 13, 1964.

56. Villard to Isadore Singer, June 28, 1923.

57. Hilgard Villard to author, October 13, 1964.

58. R. L. Duffus, "Grandson of The Liberator," *American Mercury*, XII (December, 1927), 452-453; see also, Gruening, "Trumpet to the People," 441.

59. Villard to Mussey, April 10, 1932; Villard to Ramsay Mac-Donald, May 27, 1932; Villard to Hilgard Villard, April 4, 1933; Villard to W. D. Howe, November 23, 1934.

60. Villard to wife, September 27, 1929, and June 29, 1931; Villard to Hilgard Villard, November 4, 1926, and September 26, 1928.

61. R. L. Duffus, "Grandson of The Liberator," 455-456.

62. Villard to Ernest Gruening, May 13, 1931; see Villard to R. L. Duffus, November 9, 1927.

63. Villard to Hilgard Villard, March 14, 1933.

64. Will Rogers, *Autobiography*, ed. Donald Day (Boston, 1949), pp. 312-313; Walter Lippmann, editorial, *Review of Reviews*, LXXXVII (May, 1933), 45; Villard, "Mr. Roosevelt's Two Months," *New Statesman and Nation*, 116 (May 13, 1933), 593. Villard wrote this article while in England.

65. "The Roosevelt Revolution," *The Nation*, CXXXVII (July 26, 1933), 91. Most of Villard's writings in *The Nation* from 1933 on were in his column entitled "Issues and Men." When these articles have a subtitle, as above, the subtitle shall be cited.

66. All students of American political history are familiar with

the limitations and confusions of the terms "Right" and "Left." However, these terms were meaningful in this period. The author uses Left in the way Villard would have understood it, Left meaning policies and programs "attractive to and favoring lower income groups, industrial workers, consumers . . . and also the increased use of government for wider distribution of income and social welfare." By Right is meant "policies more acceptable, and in the short run more favorable to, businessmen, professional groups, and upper income groups in general." James MacGregor Burns, *The Lion and The Fox* (New York, 1956), p. 513; Clinton Rossiter, *Conservatism in America* (New York, 1955), p. 15.

67. "Shall the Real Liberals Coalesce?", *The Nation*, CXXXVII (July 26, 1933), 147.

68. "The Idealist Comes to the Front," *The Nation*, CXXXVII (July 26, 1933), 371.

69. "The Gifts of the New Deal," *The Nation*, CXXXVIII (January 3, 1934), 8.

70. "A Statement to the President," *The Nation*, CXXXVIII (May 30, 1934), 617-618.

71. Villard to Stanwood Menken, April 21, 1926.

72. "Do We Need A Dictator?", *The Nation*, CXXXVI (March 1, 1933), 220; "Six Months of Franklin D. Roosevelt," *The Nation*, CXXXVII (September 13, 1933), 287.

73. "Congress Votes A Bill," *The Nation*, CXXXVI (March 22, 1933), 308.

74. Speech, November 20, 1933 (Villard Papers, speech file).

14. A Surrealistic World: 1933-1936

1. William L. Shirer, *Berlin Diary* (New York, 1941), p. 35.

2. Villard, "Mr. Stimson on Peace," *The Nation*, CXXXV (August 24, 1935), 159.

3. Villard, "Again A Challenge to Humanity," *The Nation*, CXXXVI (January 18, 1933), 52.

4. Quoted in Thomas A. Bailey, *A Diplomatic History of the American People* (New York, 1950), p. 727.

5. Villard to Salvemini, January 17, 1927.

6. Transcript of January 23, 1926, speech in Villard Papers, Thomas Lamont file.

7. Quoted in W. A. Swanberg, *Citizen Hearst: A Biography of William Randolph Hearst* (New York, 1961), p. 430.

8. Lincoln Steffens, *The Autobiography of Lincoln Steffens* (New York, 1931), p. 818.

9. George Soule, "Hard Boiled Radicalism," *The New Republic*, LXV (January 21, 1931), 261-265.

10. Lawrence Durrell and Henry Miller, *A Private Correspondence* (New York, 1963), pp. 107-108.

11. Upton Sinclair, *My Life Time in Letters* (Columbia, Missouri, 1960), pp. 372-373.

12. William Harlan Hale, "From the Ashes," review of Villard's *The German Phoenix*, in *Saturday Review of Literature*, IX (February 18, 1933), 435.

13. Villard to Hilgard Villard, April 4, 1933.

14. Villard to Hilgard, September 7, 1933.

15. *St. Louis Post Dispatch*, March 19, 1934 (Villard Papers, clipping file).

16. "War or Peace?", *The Nation*, CXXXVII (October 4, 1933), 368-369.

17. "Terrifying and Unchartered Paths," *The Nation*, CXLI (September 25, 1935), 343.

18. "Issues and Men," *The Nation*, CXLII (April 1, 1936), 416.

19. Villard, *The German Phoenix* (New York, 1933), p. 120.

20. "An Open Letter to Colonel House," *The Nation*, CXXXVI (April 5, 1933), 364-365; "The War Anniversary," *The Nation*, CXXXIX (August 22, 1934), 203; "Lansing Self Revealed," *The Nation*, CXLI (Ocotober 16, 1935), 427; "The War and the Pacifists," *The Nation*, CXLI (October 23, 1935), 455; "Elucidation and Correction," *The Nation*, CXLI (November 27, 1935), 613.

21. Gerald P. Nye to Villard, January 13, 1927; Editorial paragraph, *The Nation*, CXXXVIII (April 25, 1934), 455.

22. Villard to G. P. Nye, January 4, 1935; "Propaganda and the Movies," *The Nation*, CXXXIX (December 12, 1934), 665; "Mr. Lamont Defends the Morgans," *The Nation*, CXLI (November 6, 1935), 655; "Neutrality and The House of Morgan," *The Nation*, CXLI (November 13, 1935), 527; Thomas Lamont to Villard, November 14, 1935; Villard to Lamont, October 18, 1935.

23. Quoted in Robert Osgood, *Ideals and Self-Interest in America's Foreign Relations* (Chicago, 1953), p. 368; Robert A. Divine, *The Illusion of Neutrality* (Chicago, 1962), pp. 76-77.

24. Villard, "War and the Pacifists," 455.

25. Cordell Hull, *Memoirs* (2 vols.; New York, 1948), I, 406-408.

26. Villard to Miss Pratt of the Foreign Policy Association, October 31, 1935.

27. "Who Makes War in America," Villard speech, n.d., n.p., 1928 (Villard Papers, speech file); Villard to Alanson B. Houghton, August 22, 1927.

28. George Soule, "Will We Stay Out of the Next War?", *The New Republic*, LXXXIV (August 21, 1935), 38-41; "Neutrality or Shadow Boxing," *The New Republic*, LXXXIV (October 2, 1935), 202-203; Bruce Bliven, "Pacifism, Its Rise and Fall," *The New Republic*, LXXXIX (February 3, 1937), 37-38.

29. Unsigned editorial, "The President and Peace," *The New Republic*, LXXXVIII (August 26, 1936), 61; editorial paragraph, *The New Republic*, LXXXVIII (January 6, 1937), 284.

30. Editorial paragraph, *The Nation*, CXL (April 10, 1935), 404; unsigned editorial, "Must We Fight The Next War?", *The Nation*, CXLI (August 28, 1935), 228; "Sanctions or War," *The Nation*, CXLI (September 4, 1935), 256-257; "Can America Keep Unentangled?", *The Nation*, CXLI (October 16, 1935), 425.

31. Villard Papers, *The Nation* sale file, 1935. Villard to Hilgard, February 2, 1935; Hilgard Villard to author, February 20, 1961; Editorial paragraph, *The Nation*, CXL (May 8, 1935), 524.

32. Hull, *Memoirs*, I, 476-478.

33. "Moscow Offers an Olive Branch," *The Nation*, CXLI (August 7, 1935), 145.

34. Stalin's comment quoted in Franz Borkenau, *World Communism: A History of The Communist International* (Ann Arbor, Michigan, 1962), p. 395.

35. Louis Fischer in *The God That Failed*, ed. Richard Crossman (New York, 1950), pp. 199-200.

36. "Civil War and Intervention," *The Nation*, CXLIII (August 29, 1936), 229.

37. Louis Fischer, "Keeping America Out of War," *The Nation*, CXLIV (March 27, 1937), 347-348.

38. "The Russian Purging," *The Nation*, CXXXIX (December 26, 1934), 729; "Russia Murders Again," *The Nation*, CXL (January 23, 1935), 91; R. L. Duffus to Villard, January 31, 1935.

39. "Aid and Comfort to the Fascists," *Soviet Russia Today*, VI (March, 1937), 7.

40. "Issues and Men," *The Nation*, CXLIV (May 15, 1937), 564; Eugene Lyons, *The Red Decade* (New York, 1941), p. 251.

41. "The Trotsky Commission," *The Nation*, CXLIV (May 1, 1937), 496-497; Editorial paragraph, *The Nation*, CXLV (December 25, 1937), 703; "Behind the Soviet Trials," *The Nation*, CXLIV (February 6, 1937), 143-145.

42. Editorial paragraph, *The Nation*, CXLIV (January 2, 1937), 2.

43. "Issues and Men," *The Nation*, CXLIV (January 2, 1937), 19.

44. "A Measure of America's Betrayal," *The Nation*, CXLII (January 29, 1936), 119; Villard to Nye, January 29, 1936; Harry Elmer Barnes to Villard, November 27, 1935.

45. "Another Word on Neutrality," *The Nation*, CXLIV (May 1, 1937), 508.

46. "Hitler and the Youth of Germany," *The Nation*, CXXXVIII (March 7, 1937), 265; "Government by Gangsters," *The Nation*, CXLI (August 7, 1935), 147.

47. Louis Fischer, "Soviet Democracy: Second View," *The Nation*, CXLIII (August 22, 1936), 206-207; " 'Old Bolsheviks' on Trial," *The Nation*, CXLIII (August 22, 1936), 201; Earl Browder, *The People's Front* (New York, 1938), p. 338.

15. The Great Conspiracy: 1935-1940

1. "Issues and Men," *The Nation*, CXLIII (October 10, 1936), 420.

2. Villard to Dorothy Detzer (Executive Secretary of the Woman's International League for Peace and Freedom), October 30, 1934; Villard to Freda Kirchwey, September 24, 1936; Villard to Walter Van Kirk (Director of the National Peace Conference), September 2, 1936; "The Roosevelt Strategy Fails," *The Nation*, CXLI (December 25, 1935), 731.

3. Walter Lippmann, "Today and Tomorrow," *New York Herald Tribune*, November 5, 1936; Bruce Bliven, "Mr. Lippmann and a National Government," *The New Republic*, LXXXVIII (September 23, 1936), 180-181; John T. Flynn, "Other People's Money," *The Nation*, LXXXVIII (September 23, 1936), 183-184; Heywood Broun, "Broun's Page," *The Nation*, CXLIII (September 19, 1936), 336.

4. "The Great Extermination," *The Nation*, CXLIII (November 14, 1936), 576.

5. "The Supreme Court Bombshell," *The Nation*, CXL (June 12, 1935), 675. This was written after the Supreme Court's attack on the NRA; see also, "The Presidential Dilemma," *The Nation*, CXLII (January 22, 1936), 91.

6. "Issues and Men," *The Nation*, CXLIII (November 7, 1936), 547.

7. *Ibid.*

8. "How They Are Voting," *The New Republic*, LXXXVIII (September 30, 1936), 223.

9. "Correspondence," *The Nation*, LXXXIX (November 4, 1936), 19.

10. "Issues and Men," *The Nation*, CXLV (August 7, 1937), 152.

11. *Ibid.*

12. Transcript of hearings of the Committee on the Judiciary, April 5-15, 1937 (Villard Papers, Roosevelt file).

13. "Purging the Supreme Court," *The Nation*, CXLIV (February 2, 1937), 173.

14. "What is *The Nation* Coming to?", *The Nation*, CXLIV (March 27, 1933), 352; "Those Liberals Again," *The Nation*, CXLIV (March 6, 1937), 269.

15. "What is *The Nation* Coming to?", 352.

16. Richard Neuberger to Villard, July 26, 1937; see also William T. Evjue (editor of the Madison, Wisconsin, *Capitol Times*) to Villard, July 26, 1937; James F. Rabbitt to Villard, August 28, 1937; Edgar B. Byars to Villard, August 9, 1937.

17. "Is There a *Nation*?", *The Nation*, CXLIV (April 17, 1937), 437.

18. "Some Sleeping Beauties," *The Nation*, CXLIV (June 26, 1937), 730. See also Heywood Broun, "God and the Liberals," *The Nation*, CXLV (August 14, 1937), 173.

19. Interview with John Haynes Holmes, April 19, 1962; Holmes to Villard, March 25, 1937.

20. Villard to Holmes, March 26, 1937.

21. James A. Wechsler, *The Age of Suspicion* (New York, 1953), p. 138.

22. Freda Kirchwey, " 'Red Totalitarianism'," *The Nation*, CXLVIII (May 27, 1939), 605-606.

23. Wechsler, *The Age of Suspicion*, pp. 138-139; Benjamin

Stolberg, "Liberal Journalism: A House Divided," *Vanity Fair* (September, 1933), 22-23, 58-60; Benjamin Stolberg, "Muddled Millions: Capitalist Angels of Left Wing Propaganda," *The Saturday Evening Post* (February 15, 1941), 9-10, 88-92.

24. "Neutrality Makes War," *The Nation*, CXLIV (February 20, 1937), 200; "The Pack in Full Cry," *The Nation*, CXLV (July 31, 1937), 115-116; Freda Kirchwey to Villard, June 29, 1938; Villard to Kirchwey, July 5, 1938.

25. Freda Kirchwey to Villard, July 27, 1937; "Issues and Men," *The Nation*, CXLV (October 9, 1937), 379.

26. Villard to Holmes, April 15, 1937.

27. Thomas A. Bailey, *A Diplomatic History of the American People* (New York, 1950), p. 746.

28. Villard to Dorothy Thompson, September 22, 1938.

29. "The Disaster in Europe," *The Nation*, CXLVII (September 24, 1938), 299.

30. "More Parallel Action," *The Nation*, CXLVII (October 1, 1938), 325; "The Price of Peace," *The Nation*, CXLVII (October 8, 1938), 353; "Issues and Men," *The Nation*, CXLVII (October 15, 1938), 381; "Open Letter to Winston Churchill," *The Nation*, CXLVII (November 5, 1938), 480. See also Villard to Franklin Roosevelt, October 5, 1938; Villard to James M. Speyer, n.d., 1938; Villard to Jan C. Smuts, February 28, 1939.

31. "Issues and Men," *The Nation*, CXLVII (December 3, 1938), 594; *ibid.* (October 22, 1938), 411.

32. "Issues and Men," *The Nation*, CXLVII (October 15, 1938), 381.

33. "Letters to the Editors," *The Nation*, CXLVIII (February 18, 1939), 216.

34. "Issues and Men," *The Nation*, CXLIX (July 8, 1939), 45.

35. "Don't You Know Mr. President?", *The Nation*, CXLIX (August 5, 1939), 149.

36. "Letters to the Editors," *The Nation*, CXLVI (January 22, 1938), 111.

37. "Letters to the Editors," *The Nation*, CXLVIII (May 27, 1939), 626.

38. Freda Kirchwey, " 'Red Totalitarianism'," 605-606.

39. "To All Active Supporters of Democracy and Peace," (Letter to the Editors), *The Nation*, CXLIX (August 26, 1939), 228; unsigned editorial, "Red Star Swastika," *The Nation*, CXLIX (August 26, 1939), 211-212.

40. Editorial paragraph, *The Nation*, CXLIX (September 2, 1939), 231.

41. Quoted in Wechsler, *The Age of Suspicion*, p. 152.

42. For a good example of respect for the irrational, see Max Lerner, "Revolution in Ideas," *The Nation*, CXLIX (October 21, 1939), 435.

43. "Issues and Men," *The Nation*, CXLIX (August 5, 1939), 149.

44. Freda Kirchwey to Villard, July 31, 1939; Villard to Kirchwey, August 2, 1939.

45. "Issues and Men," *The Nation*, CXLVII (December 10, 1938), 621; *ibid.*, CXLVIII (February 4, 1939), 151; "No Third Term for Roosevelt," *The Nation*, CXLVIII (June 17, 1939), 702.

46. "Appeasement or War," *The Nation*, CXLIX (July 8, 1939), 33; unsigned article, "New Deal Crisis," *The Nation*, CXLIX (August 5, 1939), 135.

47. Oswald Garrison Villard, *Within Germany: With An Epilogue, England At War* (New York, 1940), p. 5. This is a compilation of articles written for *The Nation* and for *The London Telegraph and Morning Post*.

48. Villard, *Within Germany*, p. 81.

49. Villard, "The English People in War Time: A Study and A Tribute, Impressions of an Impartial American Observer," *The London Telegraph and Morning Post*, December 2, 1939.

50. "If This Be Treason," *The Nation*, CL (February 3, 1940), 130.

51. "Issues and Men," *The Nation*, CL (April 6, 1940), 450; *ibid.* (January 27, 1940), 101; *ibid.* (January 13, 1940), 47; *ibid.* (June 8, 1940), 710. Citations in order of assertions listed above.

52. Freda Kirchwey to Villard, n.d., 1940.

53. Kirchwey to Villard, May 7, 1940; Villard to Kirchwey, May 8, 1940.

54. Freda Kirchwey, "Saving the Front Line," *The Nation*, CL (June 8, 1940), 695; "A Democratic Program of Defense," *The Nation*, CL (June 15, 1940), 723.

55. Villard to Freda Kirchwey, June 13, 1940.

56. Kirchwey to Villard, June 19, 1940.

57. "Valedictory," *The Nation*, CL (June 29, 1940), 782.

58. Henry Hilgard Villard to author, February 20, 1961; "Ter-

rifying and Unchartered Paths," *The Nation*, CXLI (September 25, 1935), 343.

59. Editorial paragraph, *The Nation*, CL (June 29, 1940), 773-774; Reinhold Niebuhr, "An End to Illusions," *The Nation*, CL (June 29, 1940), 778-780.

16. Valedictory: 1940-1949

1. The Sherwood advertisement is reproduced in Walter Johnson's *Battle Against Isolation* (Chicago, 1944), p. 86; Villard to W. A. White, June 12, 1940; White to Villard, June 14, 1940.

2. Douglas Stuart to Villard, August 16, 1941. Stuart was the executive director of the committee.

3. Villard to Douglas Stuart, August 21, 1940.

4. Kirchwey to Villard, October 4, 1940; Villard to Kirchwey, October 5, 1940.

5. Wayne S. Cole, *America First* (Madison, 1953), pp. 69-73.

6. Oswald Garrison Villard, *Our Military Chaos* (New York, 1939).

7. Kirchwey to Villard, June 5, 1940; Villard to Kirchwey, June 19, 1940.

8. Villard to George Backer, March 15, 1941; Backer to Villard, March 17, 1941; see also Mrs. B. K. Wheeler to Villard, April 12, 1941.

9. Jacob Billikoff (Executive Director of the Federation of Jewish Charities of Philadelphia), November 27, 1928; June 30, 1932. Interview with William Resnick of *The Jewish Morning Journal*, n.d., (Villard Papers, press file). Villard to Hobson, August 22, 1932. Baltimore Zionist Organization to Villard, September 3, 1936. See Villard Papers, *Nation* Booster file, for letters praising Villard for his attack on Coughlin, published in *The Baltimore Sun*, August 30, 1936. See Villard Papers, *Nation* patron file, for significant Jewish financial supporters. Villard, "Nazi Barbarism," *The Nation*, CXLVII (November 26, 1938), 567.

10. Villard resigned his membership in the Germanistic Society in 1933. See Villard to F. W. LaFrentz, April 4, 1933; Villard to Franz Boas, June 30, 1933; Villard to Germanistic Society, November 27, 1933. He also resigned from the Carl Schurz Memorial Foundation: Villard to Wilbur K. Thomas, July 1, 1933.

11. Kenneth S. Davis, *The Hero: Charles A. Lindbergh and the American Dream* (New York, 1959), p. 411.

12. Villard to Lincoln Colcord, February 6, 1941; Villard to Lindbergh, May 27, 1940; Villard to George Gordon Battle (Chairman of the Council), September 23, 1941; Villard to Mark Shaw (Secretary of the National Peace Council), September 19, 1941

13. Villard to Harold Ickes, April 14, 1941.

14. Villard to Barnes, July 10, 1940; Villard to Lincoln Colcord, February 28, 1941; Colcord to Villard, March 3, 1941; Villard to Harold Fey, December 30, 1940.

15. Villard to John Haynes Holmes, April 1, 1941; Villard to Robert L. O'Brien, February 21, 1945; Hilgard Villard to author, February 20, 1961.

16. Villard to Holmes, June 27, 1940.

17. Villard to Lincoln Colcord, February 28, 1941.

18. This manuscript is in the Villard Papers, *The Christian Century* files.

19. Villard to Robert Taft, February 11, 1942; see Rubin to Villard, June 7, 1947.

20. Villard to Dorothy Thompson, August 7, 1945; see also, Thompson to Villard, November 12, 1945.

21. Charles Beard to Villard, October 19, 1944; Harry Elmer Barnes to Villard, October 28, November 4, June 23, 1948. Villard to Barnes, October 22, 1948.

22. Villard to R. L. O'Brien; Villard to Paul K. Hutchinson, January 9, 1946.

23. Villard to Morris Rubin, August 14, 1946; see also, "The Great Deception," *The Christian Century*, LXI (June 21, 1944), 745-746.

24. Villard to William L. Garrison, Jr., November 6, 1941.

25. Arthur Schlesinger, Jr., *The Vital Center: The Politics of Freedom* (Boston, 1949), p. ix.

26. Morton White, *Social Thought in America: The Revolt Against Formalism* (Boston, 1957), p. 3.

27. Daniel Bell, *The End of Ideology: On the Exhaustion of Political Ideas in the Fifties* (New York, 1961); Judith Shklar, *After Utopia: The Decline of Political Faith* (Princeton, 1957).

28. Irving Howe, "This Age of Conformity," *Partisan Review*, XXI (January, 1954), 7-33.

29. *Ibid.*, 18.

30. Henry Hilgard Villard to author, February 20, 1962.

BIBLIOGRAPHICAL NOTE

Villard Papers

This study rests primarily upon the source material in the Villard Papers, Houghton Library, Harvard University, Cambridge, Massachusetts. It is an enormous collection of fundamental importance for the history of America in the first half of the twentieth century. The personal correspondence file alone contains well over 4,500 addressees and many of the individual folders contain hundreds of letters. Villard kept carbon copies of practically every letter he wrote from the beginning of his professional career, so that it is possible to trace his correspondence from day to day with a good deal of accuracy. His letters written as a child are available in the papers of his father and mother, also housed in the Houghton Library. In addition to his personal and business correspondence, there are diaries, ledgers, and scrapbooks of his writings both anonymous and acknowledged, and a monumental speech file which contains nearly every address he ever gave. Throughout a great part of his career Villard also maintained a clipping file which, although in poor condition, was extremely helpful in locating critical press commentary on his activities. The Villard Collection contains an organizational file with the records of his membership in organizations and associations. In this file there are hundreds of additional letters which do not appear in the index to the papers. The records of *The Post* and *The Nation* throughout the Villard ownership, scattered throughout various files, include Audit Bureau of Circulation figures, minutes of business meetings, and a detailed account of the sale of both enterprises. There are also dozens of boxes marked "miscellaneous" containing additional correspondence and personal memorabilia. Throughout the Villard Papers there are innumerable published and unpublished manuscripts of articles for journals other than *The Nation,* pamphlets, and a complete file of the syndicated columns he wrote for twelve newspapers in the 1930's.

Bibliographical Note

Published Writings of Villard

Second in importance to Villard's personal papers are his published editorials and articles in *The Post* and *The Nation*. All unsigned editorials and articles attributed to Villard in this study have been verified either by the extensive scrapbooks in the Houghton Collection or by the annotated copies of *The Nation* deposited by Villard in the New York Public Library. Villard was also a regular contributor, toward the end of his life, to *The Christian Century* and *The Progressive,* and a frequent contributor to *The Atlantic, Harper's, The American Mercury, The North American Review, The New Statesman and Nation,* and various other periodicals. Aside from *The Christian Century* and *The Progressive,* the articles published outside of *The Nation* have not been of much use to me since most of them are little more than compilations of material appearing in *The Nation.*

Villard published several books. Few of them, unfortunately, have contributed much to this study. His autobiography, *Fighting Years,* is disappointing and does not do him justice. It was written at a time when he was under great emotional strain and suffering from an overriding bitterness and despair. Consequently it harks back to the good old days, is shrill in tone, and is devoted to recalling past victories and defeats; of 500 pages, less than 100 are devoted to his life after 1920. Despite these shortcomings, it did fill in early details of his life and career for me, and its general tone of failure and frustration provided insight into his feelings in the thirties. Villard's biography of John Brown is his one scholarly work and it remains the definitive study. His great respect for John Brown and his own personal abolitionist heritage made him sympathetic toward his subject. At the same time his acceptance of strict pacifism forced him to denounce the man's violent actions. The book points up at an early date what was to become the major dilemma of Villard's own life.

The remainder of Villard's works are journalistic and polemical. His study of the Weimar Republic, published in 1933, started out to be an ambitious history but ended as an attack on the Versailles treaty. It contains much sensible commentary but the tone of vindication destroys the book as a serious contribution to historical scholarship. Villard wrote two studies of the press which contain lively portraits of well-known editors and astute critical analyses of the more important newspapers across the country. Both works emphasize the rapid decline of independent liberal journalism and the rise of the newspaper chains, which he saw as being controlled by powerful business interests. Villard particularly lamented the loss of the personal journalism characterized by men like Godkin. Throughout his career on *The Nation* Villard wrote biographical portraits of the potential contenders during each presidential campaign, which were compiled in his volume, *Prophets True and False.* The sketches emphasize the weaknesses of politicians and statesmen and their tendency to sacrifice principle to expediency. Despite their didacticism and self-righteous air, these portraits are often brilliant criticism and reveal a mocking sense of humor that is not characteristic of most of Villard's writing. Other works of lesser importance are included in the list below.

The Disappearing Daily. New York, 1928.

The Duty of the Press in Wartime. New York, 1915.

The Early History of Wall Street. New York, 1897.

Fighting Years: Memoirs of a Liberal Editor. New York, 1939.

Free Trade, Free World. New York, 1949.

Germany Embattled. New York, 1915.

The German Phoenix. New York, 1933.

John Brown: A Biography Fifty Years After. Boston, 1910.

A Letter From Berlin. New York, 1915.

Lincoln on the Eve of '61 (in collaboration with Harold Villard). New York, 1941.

Our Military Chaos. New York, 1939.

Preparedness. Washington, D.C., 1915.

Prophets True and False. New York, 1928.

Russia from a Car Window. New York, 1929.

Shall We Rule Germany? New York, 1943.

Some Newspapers and Newspapermen. New York, 1923.

The Two Germanies. New York, 1914.

"Tribute to Henry Villard," *What I Owe My Father*, ed. Sydney Strong. New York, 1931.

"William Lloyd Garrison as seen by A Grandson," in *William Lloyd Garrison on Non-Resistance,* ed. Fanny Garrison Villard. New York, 1924.

Within Germany. New York, 1940.

Bibliographical Note

References to manuscript materials and to secondary sources consulted will be found in the Notes. I have not duplicated the bibliographical information that appears in the Notes or furnished an inclusive list of the sources that have been used in the preparation of this work, since in most cases this would be repetitive.

Index

Index

Index

Prinkipo conference, 120
Progressive, The, 264, 270-71
progressives, 11, 24, 25, 207, 242; and 1912 election, 29-30; on Negro equality, 31; and war, 53, 68, 76; and Wilsonianism, 131; and revisionist history, 155-56; German-Americans relation to, 163-64; and LaFollette campaign of 1924, 164-67; and Convention for Progressive Political Action, 167-68; and foreign affairs, 168; and prohibition, 190; and League for Independent Political Action, 195-96, 210, 212, 215
Prohibition party, 26, 63

revisionist history, 153-56; initiated in Europe, 156; and war guilt, 156-58; and conspiracy thesis, 156, 159, 161-62; and French guilt, 159-60, 161
Rockledge Farm, 224-25
Rogers, Will, 227
Root, Elihu, 97
Roosevelt, Franklin D., 246, 256, 259, 261, 268, 271; and Villard, 213-15; in 1932 election, 215, 218, 219; and New Deal, 227-30; and neutrality, 239, 254; and Spanish civil war, 241-42; in 1936 election, 247; and Supreme Court, 248-50; *see also* Villard, Oswald Garrison
Roosevelt, Theodore, 21, 26, 46, 47, 48, 73, 145, 231; and New Nationalism, 29; on American neutrality, 50; and Villard, 51; on Wilson's peace plan, 100, 101; on Soviet Russia, 110
Rubin, Morris, 271
Russia, Soviet: and peace offensive in World War I, 83-84, 92; U.S. recognition of, 94, 203-205; and Spanish civil war, 242-43; and nonaggression pact with Germany, 257, 258; *see also Nation, The;* Villard, Oswald Garrison

Schurz, Carl, 12, 21, 25, 38, 42
Sedgwick, Ellery, 2, 169
Seymour, George, 19
Sherwood, Robert, 265
Shotwell, James T., 182

Simonds, Frank, 111, 119, 120
Smith, Alfred E., 190, 191, 192, 194
Smuts, Jan Christiaan, 110, 137
Snowden, Philip, 81, 163
Social Darwinism, 19-20
Socialist party, in America, 63, 77; in 1928 election, 191, 192, 193; in 1932 election, 215-16, 217, 219
Socialist Second International conference, 113-14, 130
Socialists, in Germany, 105, 106, 109, 113, 114, 115, 116, 117
Soule, George, 240
Soviet Russia Today, see Popular Front
Spanish-American war, 19-21
Spanish civil war, 241-43
Spartacists, in Germany, 115, 116
Stearns, Harold, 148-49
Steffens, Lincoln, 18, 19, 95, 120; on Versailles conference, 154; on Mussolini, 233-34
Stevenson, Archibald E., 127
Stevenson, R. H., 143
Stewart, Maxwell, 253, 257-58
Stimson, Henry L., 205
Stone, I. F., 257-58
Strunsky, Simeon, 161
Stuart, Douglas, Jr., 265
Sturge, Sophia, 57, 81

Taylor, A. J. P., 113
Thayer, William Roscoe, 41
Thomas, Norman, 127, 142, 210; in Fellowship of Reconciliation, 77-78; in 1928 election, 190, 191, 192, 193, 194; in 1936 election, 247
Thomas and Maurer Committee of One Hundred Thousand, 215-16
Thompson, Dorothy, 222
Thorwood, 9, 33
Tumulty, Joseph, 56, 57, 73, 98
Turner, John K., 159, 160
Turner, Raymond, 161
Union for Democratic Control, 81-82, 114, 156

Van Doren, Carl, 148
Van Doren, Mark, as literary editor of *The Nation,* 148, 149, 150-51, 196-97

218, 219; and New Deal, 208, 227-30; and Court-packing plan, 248-50; and executive leadership in foreign affairs, 230-31, 239-40, 247, 249-50, 254, 256, 259

—and Soviet Russia, 75, 93, 97, 105-106, 128-30, 198, 199-201, 202, 203, 205; on peace offensive, 92, 199; on negotiations at Versailles conference, 110, 120-21; accused of Bolshevistic sympathy, 126-27, 129, 132; denounces violent methods, 128, 198, 201, 243-44; on recognition by America, 199, 203, 204-205; 1929 tour of Russia, 200-201

—and third-party movement, 186, 189; in 1924 Progressive campaign, 162-63, 164-67; considers runing for office as Progressive, 164-65; and Convention for Progressive Political Action, 167-68; concern over Socialist party name, 192-93, 218-19; and League for Independent Political Action, 195-96, 210; and Socialist party in 1932 election, 214, 215, 216, 217, 218, 219; and Socialist party in 1936, 247

—and Versailles treaty, 113, 123, 130, 131, 133-40 *passim,* 158, 206, 237; favors statement of racial equality, 131

—and Wilson (Woodrow), 68, 60-71, 73, 102, 104, 186, 231; in 1912 election, 28; as advisor on race relations, 28-29; role in administration's policy of neutrality, 49, 50, 51-53, 54, 55; and Wilson's policy toward Britain, 51, 63, 64, 69; on decision to prepare, 56, 57, 58, 59, 68; works to effect negotiated peace, 59, 60, 66-67; in 1916 election, 61-63; on Wilson's suppression of civil liberties during war, 78-80, 94-95, 96, 97-98, 100-101; on Wilson's belligerence during the war, 83; criticizes Wilson's ignorance of Russian secret treaties, 85; on Fourteen Points, 93, 102, 119; and Versailles conference, 110, 112, 118, 119, 120-21; and the League, 135, 138

—and World War I, 4-5, 38-39, 44, 45,

59, 60, 67, 68, 70, 75; German heritage influences position, 12, 38-45 *passim,* 49, 76-77; condemns British violations of American neutrality rights, 42-43, 51, 63-64, 69; and reform, 67, 68, 70; opposes American entrance, 69, 70, 71; calls for new diplomacy, 80, 81, 82; publishes Russian secret treaties, 84-86; views on the peace, 92-93, 100-101, 102, 103, 109

—and World War II: and Japan's expansion, 232; and Mussolini, 233; and Nazi Germany, 235-36, 260; urges economic sanctions, 236-37; desire to keep America out of conflict, 237, 255, 256, 259, 261; on neutrality legislation, 239, 240, 244-45, 246, 247; and Spanish civil war, 243; and America First, 265-66, 267, 268-69; and Jewish conspiracy thesis, 267-69

Villard, Oswald Garrison, Jr., 224, 225, 241, 269

Walling, Mrs. William English, 280-81

Walsh, Frank P., 221

Washington disarmament conference, 170-75

Wechsler, James, 253, 258

Wells, H. G., 31, 81

Wertheim, Maurice, 241, 251, 253

Weyl, Walter, 72-73, 86, 95

Wheeler, Burton K., 165, 166, 247, 267

White, Horace, editor of *Post,* 22, 25

White, William Allen, 25, 164, 265; at Versailles conference, 111, 112, 120

Williams, Talcott, 18

Wilson, Woodrow; in 1912 election, 28; on Negro equality, 28-29; in 1916 election, 62; and New Freedom, 29, 63; and foreign policy before American entrance in World War I, 39-40, 49-55 *passim,* 56, 57, 58-59, 63-67, 68, 69; and peace without victory, 67, 74, 76, 82, 83, 93; and World War I, 70, 72-73, 76, 82-83, 84, 85, 93-94, 98-99, 100; and civil liberties during the war, 79-80, 94-96, 97-98, 101; and European liberals, 80-81, 98, 99, 108, 112; and Russian peace